AMERICAN ECONOMIC POLICY

AMERICAN ECONOMIC POLICY

PROBLEMS AND PROSPECTS

Edited by
Gar Alperovitz and Roger Skurski

UNIVERSITY OF NOTRE DAME PRESS
NOTRE DAME, INDIANA

Library of Congress Cataloging in Publication Data

Main entry under title:

American economic policy.

Proceedings of the 1982-83 Graduate Public Policy
Workshop held at the University of Notre Dame and
sponsored by its Dept. of Economics.
Bibliography: p.
1. United States—Economic policy—1981-   —
Congresses. I. Alperovitz, Gar. II. Skurski, Roger.
III. Graduate Public Policy Workshop (1982 : Univer-
sity of Notre Dame) IV. University of Notre Dame.
Dept. of Economics.
HC106.8.A44 1984   338.973   83-40592
ISBN 0-268-00612-1
ISBN 0-268-00613-X (pbk.)

Contents

Contributors

GAR ALPEROVITZ is co-director of the National Center for Economic Alternatives, a Washington-based research organization. During 1982–83 he was guest professor of economics at the University of Notre Dame. He has a Ph.D. in political economy from Cambridge University, an M.A. from Berkeley and a B.S. from the University of Wisconsin. A Marshall Scholar, he has also been a fellow of King's College at the University of Cambridge, a guest scholar at the Brookings Institution, and a fellow at the John F. Kennedy Institute of Politics at Harvard University. Dr. Alperovitz testifies frequently before U.S. House and Senate committees, including the Joint Economic Committee, the Senate Subcommittee on Economic Stabilization, and the House Committee on the Budget. He has authored several books and a variety of professional and other articles. Dr. Alperovitz's latest book is *Rebuilding America*, co-authored with center co-director Geoffrey Faux.

RICHARD D. BARTEL has been the executive editor of *Challenge, The Magazine of Economic Affairs* since 1980. Before that he served as a staff economist for the Joint Economic Committee of Congress, and from 1969–1978 he held several research positions with the Federal Reserve Bank of New York, including a year with the Bank for International Settlements in Basel, Switzerland. Dr. Bartel was born in Wisconsin where he attended Ripon College, graduating with a B.A. in mathematics and economics. Later, he earned an M.A. and a Ph.D. in economics at Columbia University. A specialist in international and monetary economics, Bartel has published articles in journals, magazines, and government publications.

JOSEPH BLASI is director of the Project for Kibbutz Studies, Center for Jewish Studies and lecturer in social studies at Harvard University. Dr. Blasi began his higher education in a Jesuit seminary and continued it at the University of Pittsburgh where he completed a B.S. in psychology. He then earned both a master's and doctorate in education from the School of Education, Harvard University. Along the way, Blasi worked with the Pittsburgh YMCA as an organizational consultant and coordinator of a drug abuse program; as an intern teacher at the Cambridge Pilot School; as an intern therapist at the Boston State Hospital; as an instructor in anthropology at Massachusetts Bay Community College; as an instructor in sociology at Brandeis; and as a research associate, Project on the Kibbutz and Collective Education, School of Education at Harvard. Dr. Blasi has authored or co-authored several books, including *The Communal Future: The Kibbutz and the Utopian Dilemma*, and numerous articles in a variety of publications on the kibbutz, cooperatives, and worker participation.

MARTIN CARNOY is professor of education and economics at Stanford University, where he has taught for the last 14 years. He received his B.S. degree in electrical engineering from the California Institute of Technology, and his M.A. and Ph.D. from the University of Chicago economics department. Before his present tenure at Stanford, he worked at the Brookings Institution in Washington, D.C. in the foreign policy division. He is a specialist in Latin America and Africa, as well as the economics of education, labor economics, and the U.S. economy. Carnoy has published extensively in economics journals, *The Nation*, *The New Republic*, and *In These Times*. His books include *Industrialization in a Latin American Common Market*, *Education and Employment*, *Education as Cultural Imperialism*, *Segmented Labor Markets*, *Economic Democracy* (with Derek Shearer), and *A New Social Contract* (with Derek Shearer and Russell Rumberger). He has just completed *Theories of the State in Modern Marxism*, to be published by Princeton University Press in 1984 and *The Dialectics of Education and Work* (with Henry Levin), to be published by Stanford University Press in 1984.

JAMES K. GALBRAITH is executive director of the Joint Economic Committee, United States Congress. Earlier he served as an economist with the House Committe on Banking, Finance, and Urban Affairs, research assistant at the Joint Economic Committee, and visiting lecturer in economics at the University of Maryland. Dr. Galbraith received his A.B. in social studies from Harvard University and his Ph.D. in economics from Yale University. In between, he was a Marshall Scholar at King's College, Cambridge University. His fields include: economic policy, industrial organization, history of economic thought, and the economics of poverty and discrimination. Galbraith has authored several articles which have appeared in such publications as *Working Papers for a New Society*.

LEONARD A. RAPPING, professor of economics at the University of Massachusetts at Amherst and director of the Project on Economic Restructuring, graduated from the University of California, Los Angeles and received his Ph.D. from the University of Chicago. He was trained in the fields of economic theory and econometrics. He then turned his attention to the study of social and political institutions as they related to economic theory. Professor Rapping has been a consultant to numerous federal and private agencies including the RAND Corporation, Budget Bureau, Department of Defense, Maritime Administration, Center for Naval Analysis, Department of Transportation, and the Labor Department. He was a member of the economic advisory board of the Progressive Alliance and a past member of the editorial board of the *American Economic Review*. He has published extensively in the areas of labor economics, transportation economics, political economy, and the economics of inflation and unemployment. Presently his special interest is in problems of national and international banking as they relate to industrial policy.

COREY ROSEN is executive director of the National Center for Employee Ownership (NCEO), a private, non-profit clearinghouse and research organization. He was formerly a professional staff member in the U.S. Senate, where he worked on employee ownership legislation prior to founding the center in 1981. He received his B.A. from Wesleyan University and his Ph.D. from Cornell University. Dr. Rosen has authored many papers and books available through the NCEO, including: *Employee Ownership: A Handbook* (1982), *Employee Ownership: A Reader* (1983) and *Employee Buyouts: A Handbook* (1983).

A. ALLAN SCHMID is professor, Department of Agricultural Economics and Department of Resource Development, Michigan State University, where he specializes in land economics, rural development, public finance, and public choice. He has spent leaves from Michigan State with the Systems Analysis Group (Civil Works), U.S. Department of the Army, and with the Economic and Social Research Institute, Dublin, Ireland. His undergraduate degree in agricultural economics was earned at the University of Nebraska while his M.S. and Ph.D. in the same field were received from the University of Wisconsin. Dr. Schmid has served on the editorial boards of *Land Economics, The Journal of Economic Issues*, and *The American Journal of Agricultural Economics*, and has written many articles for a wide variety of journals, including the *American Economic Review*. He is the author of *Converting Land from Rural to Urban Uses* (1968) and *Property, Power and Public Choice* (1978), as well as the co-author (with Warren Samuels) of *Law and Economics: An Institutionalist Perspective* (1981).

x

x CONTRIBUTORS

GAIL GARFIELD SCHWARTZ is president of Garfield Schwartz Associates, Inc., an economic and development consulting firm in Washington, D.C. She earned her Ph.D. at Columbia University, a master's degree in planning and public administration from New York University, and a B.A. in government from Smith College. Previously, Dr. Schwartz was senior research scientist and visiting professor at Johns Hopkins University. She served four years as senior fellow and director of economic development at the Academy for Contemporary Problems in Washington, and earlier she was director of economic planning and development for the New York City planning commission. She also has been a research associate at Columbia University's Institute for Urban Environment as well as an advisor to local, state, and federal government bodies. Dr. Schwartz has authored and edited numerous books and articles on economic policy, economic and community development, and public administration. Among them are the first book on U.S. industrial policy, *Being Number One: Rebuilding the U.S. Economy* (1980), *Advanced Industrialization and the Inner Cities* (1981), and *The Work Revolution* (1983) with William Neikirk.

DEREK SHEARER is director of urban studies at Occidental College in Los Angeles. He is also vice-chair of the planning commission of the city of Santa Monica. During the Carter administration he was a presidential appointee to the Board of Directors of the National Consumer Cooperative Bank. He has also served as special assistant to the director, State Department of Employment Development, in California during the administration of Governor Jerry Brown. He is the co-author (with Martin Carnoy) of *Economic Democracy: The Challenge of the 1980s* (1981), and co-author (with Martin Carnoy and Russell Rumberger) of *A New Social Contract: The Economy and Government After Reagan* (1983). His articles have appeared in the *New York Times*, the *Los Angeles Times*, the *New Republic*, the *Nation*, and numerous other publications.

ROGER SKURSKI is associate dean of the College of Arts and Letters and professor of economics at the University of Notre Dame. He earned his Ph.D. at the University of Wisconsin where his areas of specialization were Soviet economics and comparative economic systems. He has published a number of articles on the Soviet economy in journals such as *Slavic Review* and *Soviet Studies* and has recently published a book titled *Soviet Marketing and Economic Development*. In addition, he is the editor of another book in this series, *New Directions in Economic Justice* (1983). He was a Fulbright-Hays Fellow at the University of Birmingham and is currently the executive secretary of the Association for Comparative Economic Studies and consultant to the National Institute for Trial Advocacy.

ROBERT A. SOLO is professor of economics at Michigan State University, where he specializes in organization, policy, and planning. He has taught at Princeton, Michigan, McGill, Rutgers, Johns Hopkins, City College of New York, and several universities in France. Dr. Solo has worked in Washington with several government agencies and has served as a public sector consultant there and elsewhere. He graduated from Harvard University and received his M.A. at American University. After studying at the London School of Economics, he earned his Ph.D. in economics at Cornell University. Solo is the author or co-author of thirteen books and more than 75 articles in a wide spectrum of journals and books. His most recent book is *The Positive State* (1982).

JAMES M. STONE is chairman and chief executive officer of the Plymouth Rock Company, a newly formed corporation founded to engage in the property-casualty insurance business in the New England area. He received both his B.A. and Ph.D. in economics from Harvard University, where he was then appointed lecturer in economics. In 1971, Dr. Stone began work as a part-time consultant for Fairfield and Ellis Inc., a Boston insurance brokerage firm, and in 1974 was promoted to vice president-economist. In 1975, he was appointed commissioner of insurance for the Commonwealth of Massachusetts, a position he held until 1979 when President Carter nominated him to become commissioner and chairman of the Commodity Futures Trading Corporation. Stone is the author of the book, *One Way for Wall Street* and numerous articles on finance, insurance, and economics.

WILLIAM FOOTE WHYTE is professor emeritus, New York State School of Industrial and Labor Relations, Cornell University. His A.B. is from Swarthmore, where he majored in social sciences and economics. He was a research fellow at Harvard University and attended the University of Chicago, from which he received a Ph.D. in sociology. Dr. Whyte has spent most of his professional life with Cornell University, but prior to that he taught at the University of Oklahoma and the University of Chicago. He has also directed a research project on human relations problems in Venezuela and was a Fulbright Fellow in Peru. Dr. Whyte was one of the early proponents of the concept of worker participation, and he recently helped found the Cornell Program for Employment and Workplace Systems—a program which will offer business and labor a set of tools to help increase productivity, forestall plant closings, and thereby save jobs. Professor Whyte has authored or co-authored more than a dozen books, including *Street Corner Society,* now in its third edition. Most recently he co-authored *Worker Participation and Ownership: Cooperative Strategies for Strengthening Local Economies.*

Preface

The papers in this volume are the end product of a process which began in the spring of 1981 with the conception of a speakers' series on new directions in economic policy. The Department of Economics at the University of Notre Dame has sponsored such a program annually since 1976, and its faculty have organized the lectures and edited the volumes emanating from them. This is the sixth book in the series, all of which have been published by the University of Notre Dame Press.

This year the basic premise suggested to potential participants was that neither traditional Keynesian policies nor the pure free-market approach would constitute a necessary and sufficient economic policy for the United States. The speakers were challenged to offer workable alternatives to these policies which were humane and democratic. The response was tremendous: during the 1982–83 academic year twenty speakers addressed the Graduate Public Policy Workshop; most were economists, but the group also included a lawyer, businessman, political scientist, sociologist, and psychologist. Each in his or her own way attempted to respond to our challenge and break new ground in the debate about economic policy.

The workshop participants were also invited to prepare and submit formal papers based on their presentations. Nine of them were able to do so within the time limits we set; the subject is both current and important, and therefore, we aimed for publication within approximately one year of the last visitor to Notre Dame in May 1983. The published papers represent very well the spectrum of all those given in the workshops, and do, we feel, contribute valuable ideas and analyses which push the policy debate forward. In some, issues are raised which clearly must be added to the research agenda before policy options can be evaluated.

We wish to thank all the participants in the Public Policy Workshop whether or not they were able to contribute a paper to the volume. A special word of thanks is due to Charles K. Wilber, chairman of the Department of Economics. The original idea for this annual visitors' program and the series of books built on it is his, and he has continued to supply inspiration and encouragement to these endeavors. Finally, without the cooperation of the University of Notre Dame Press and especially of its director, James Langford, this book would not have been possible.

Gar Alperovitz
Washington, D.C.

Roger Skurski
Notre Dame, Indiana
1983

PART I

Challenge and Response

1

Introduction: The Need for New Directions and a Progressive Response

ROGER SKURSKI

The purpose of this volume is to confirm the need for new directions in American economic policy and, more importantly, to offer the beginnings of a progressive response to that need. Our basic working assumption is that both traditional Keynesian policies alone and the newly revived free market approach will fail to deliver on their promises. It is our belief that economists must begin thinking about how to construct feasible alternatives to those policies. It is time to go beyond critiques, and to start restructuring a humane, democratic, economic policy.

I. The Need for New Directions

Why is a new economic policy necessary? Because, in a word, American economic policy is a shambles. To the extent that we have a policy, it is often unfair, ineffective, or inappropriate for dealing with the problems of the last decades of the twentieth century. The American approach to economic policy has been very pragmatic: "If it isn't broke, don't fix it!" Policy, therefore, arises from problems, or our perceptions of problems, just as a fire department responds to emergency calls. In effect, the United States does not have *an* economic policy; it has a large number of policy responses to particular problems. Generally, these are uncoordinated, imbalanced with little attention to their differential effects on different economic classes, and short-run oriented, and they do not add up to a well-

3

thought-out, consistent, and effective strategy. This failure has been recognized before, and proposals for alternatives such as government planning have been made. For example, in 1975 the Initiative Committee for
National Economic Planning, headed by Nobel Prize-winning economist
Wassily Leontief and then-president of the United Auto Workers, Leonard
Woodcock, recommended the establishment in the White House of an
Office of National Economic Planning because they felt planning had
become an economic and social necessity (*New York Times*, March 16,
1975, sec. F). Whether or not one agrees that an indicative planning
system is appropriate for this country, the committee's perception of the
problem appears correct. Yet, nearly ten years later, we are still trying to
muddle through with no real economic direction to our policy. A further
look at the planning issue may help explain this.

Planning is a misunderstood and mistrusted term in the United States.
When Americans think of planning, they usually think of the Soviet
Union with a rigid, hierarchial, authoritarian, Stalinist system. They do
not think of French or Japanese or Swedish planning. They do not think
of their own personal or business planning, and Galbraith (1973), for one,
argues that the corporate sector is *already* planned. They do not consider
family planning, budgeting, or setting a game plan in the same light as
economic planning. They forget about the American space program which
was an example of sophisticated and successful planning. Moreover, they
do not realize that Stalin has been dead for more than 30 years and that
even Soviet planning has departed at least somewhat from their stereo-
typed image of planning. In any case, Americans seem to have a built-in
bias against government economic planning.

We would suggest that the sources of this bias are: ideology, fear, and
lack of understanding. The ideological source consists of two components.
First: the USSR is our enemy, and it is a planned economy; therefore, we
are against planning. Second, we think we have a free market system
(which is considered good) and that planning is the opposite of this; therefore, again we are against planning. Next, we fear big government and
idealize the laissez-faire doctrine which probably never accurately described
the role of the American state, and which even Adam Smith assumed
would be applied within the context of a set of moral rules or ethical
guidelines (Worland 1983, 1). It is assumed that at best government planning would be bureaucratic and inefficient, and at the worst it would fulfill
the Orwellian vision of big brother. Finally, most of us do not understand
planning and have not taken the time to consider the possibilities for it in
our economy. The reason, in part, is that plan and market are considered
polar opposites, that is, alternative allocation mechanisms. Why not plan
and market? Other nations such as France, Hungary, Japan, and Yugoslavia have found ways of combining both (see Holland, 1979). Planning

could also be viewed as *one* of many tools or components of a fully developed economic strategy rather than the be-all and end-all of economic policy. Further, the common view of planning is from the top down, and thus, the key question immediately becomes who will do the planning for the rest of us? Why not consider ways to build a planning system from the bottom up which would be decentralized, truly democratic, and in tune with the needs of the people?

The intention here is not necessarily to build a case for planning but only to show the necessity of going beyond the present grab bag of policies and the enormous difficulty of overcoming our inertia. The range of people who see the gap in policy covers almost the entire political spectrum. The Left has been writing about it for more than a decade (see for example Galbraith's *Economics and the Public Purpose*, O'Connor's *Fiscal Crisis of the State* and Harrington's *Decade of Decision*), but now others are also speaking up. Recently, Robert Dole, chairman of the Senate Finance Committee declared that "we are drifting into an aimless stupor when it comes to economic policy," and he warned "if that continues, we may have a rude awakening indeed" (*Newsweek*, August 22, 1983, 46).

To some, the need for change is self-evident, but others may require more evidence. Other papers in this volume will deal with this in more detail, so a few of the main arguments will suffice at this point. In our opinion, any economic system faces a real problem when millions of its workers must be unemployed regularly to bring down the rate of inflation; nominal interest rates are in the double digit range and real rates at unheard-of levels; the federal budget deficit is at record levels while poverty is rising, social and educational programs are dying, and infrastructure crumbling; the distribution of income has remained essentially constant for nearly forty years; the plight of women and minorities is a serious problem; its corporations take over each other and move at will to different regions or countries, leaving a trail of decaying communities and discouraged workers.

The list could no doubt be expanded and documented, and these problems are chronic. They cannot be solved by the simple application of traditional macropolicy tools or by the trickle-down (supply-side) approach recently in vogue, and we refuse to believe that we must resign ourselves to accepting them as facts of economic life. Although a unified planning approach does not emerge from these papers, the need for coherent, long-run, forward-looking, equitable economic policy clearly is strongly suggested.

II. Why a Progressive Response?

There has been no shortage of critiques and proposals from the American Left going back to the *Port Huron Statement* of the Students for a

Democratic Society. However, "radical changes in policy and practice have never found a place on the official agenda" (Moody 1983, 18). Largely this is because of American attitudes and prejudices. Slogans such as, "America— love it or leave it" do not suggest flexibility and adaptability. Moreover, the United States may be a nation built by pioneers, inventors, and innovators, but when it comes to economic programs and institutions, we seem to demand telling proof in advance that they will work. And yet, as James Galbraith suggests in his paper, foreign experience with alternatives carries no weight here. As a consequence, unless our difficulties escalate to the crisis level, a major modification of our economic system as a whole is remote, and therefore grand schemes for a new American system receive little attention.

On the other hand, the current policy dilemma affords an opportunity to develop options in between the traditional liberal answers and full scale revolutionary reform. This is what we mean by a progressive response. Such an approach would be willing to place institutional and structural change on the national agenda, but yet would be realistic enough to ground its proposals in the ideological, political, and economic setting of the United States today. This point was brought out by Martin Carnoy and Derek Shearer in their book, *Economic Democracy* (1980, 32):

> The American emphasis on democracy and capitalism, the absence of a labor program and party, the hierarchical and compromised labor unions, American aversion to bureaucracy, and the strong two-party political system, all shape American political reality. Any structural reforms proposed for the United States must be formed by the context of this reality or they will have little chance of serving as the basis of a movement for change.

The opportunity for a progressive response exists, but whether or not it is forthcoming is an open question. The variety of ideas in the later chapters of this book constitute an excellent beginning for this task. Whether or not they find their way into a more completely developed program and whether or not such a program is accepted by the population remains to be seen. Many suggest that a new mass political movement is the crucial ingredient and hence, inseparable from economic deliberation (Harrington 1980, 316; Moody 1983, 21). Some insist that the Democratic party is the only conceivable vehicle for this, while others claim nothing will happen without an independent labor party. Either way the movement must be built on political democracy—not the surface appearance of democracy but a genuine participatory democracy.

In fact, the concept of democracy may emerge as the common ground and unifying element in this whole matrix, although that concept itself may change in the process. It clearly belongs to the basic or core values Americans hold important. Expanding the notion of political democracy beyond voting for our "representatives" would appear both logical and attractive if we actually do value this goal. Further, democracy need not, and many would agree should not, be restricted to the political sphere; the economy and the family are other sites where the practices of democracy can be applied (Gintis, 1983). The possible extension of democracy in these ways, no doubt, will raise other fundamental questions concerning democracy and capitalism. Radicals take the position that the two are a most improbable mixture (Weisskopf 1974, 53) while Keynesian liberals feel that they are a perfect match (Okun 1975, 120). Our view would be that if democracy and capitalism are to continue to coexist, both terms must be redefined and adapted so that political and economic power as well as participation in decision making are more equitably distributed (cf. Kann 1983). Progressive analysts have already been thinking along these lines. Examples include *Economic Democracy* by Carnoy and Shearer, Tom Hayden's *The American Future* (1980), and *Beyond the Waste Land* (1983) by Samuel Bowles, David Gordon, and Thomas Weisskopf. Although there may be disagreement among progressives on the amount and nature of participation in the democratic process, there appears to be almost universal agreement that the state must take the lead in the transformation of society. For example, in his essay here, Robert Solo suggests that *only* the state is capable of accomplishing the kinds of things that must be done to break out of the current malaise. Whether stated explicitly or implied, progressives are willing to utilize the government to attempt to serve the needs of the people. While progressives share the general concern over unfeeling and inflexible bureaucracies, they are not afraid of government as such and are willing to experiment with new types of public and private institutions and modes of public involvement. Perhaps this is the raison d'etre for a progressive response.

If the progressive, as defined here, is willing to bet on the state as the institution to lead the way out of the present situation, he/she is also careful to emphasize the importance of democracy in this process. The democracy theme plays itself out in different ways in the essays which follow: worker participation, tripartite industrial commissions, and Congressional control of the Federal Reserve, for example. The writers clearly are aware of the potential problem of interest group takeovers of public agencies or policies, but they do not agree on the institutional mechanism(s) for totally preventing it.

III. Outline of the Book

There are five parts to this collection. In Part I, Richard D. Bartel outlines the shift from the economic tranquility of the 1950s and 1960s to

the upheaval of the 1970s and 1980s along with policy issues implied by
the transformations of the past decade. The fundamental transformations
he sees include: "1) the oil price revolution; 2) the manufacturing revolution in developing countries and a corresponding shift in the U.S. international comparative advantage; 3) the technology revolution and global interdependence; 4) institutional aging and paralysis in decision making; and
5) a drastically altered market environment for economic policy." In light
of these, he argues that the countercyclical medicines of the past, monetary
and fiscal policy, are inadequate and, in fact, can have a destabilizing effect.
He suggests that conventional stabilization policies cannot solve the problems caused by real shocks to the economic system such as OPEC, and
they therefore need to be supplemented by more specific, targeted micro
policies. Bartel ends with a call for a structural policy to deal with the transformation of the national and global economy by creating new institutional mechanisms and strategies.

Part II, whose theme is the public and private role in policy, is made
up of two chapters by Robert A. Solo and Leonard A. Rapping. Solo's
essay in Chapter 3 is entitled "Lessons from Elsewhere" because the
Japanese experience is examined from the perspective of broad lessons for
the United States. Professor Solo's main point is that the state is the only
system or organization that could be capable of acting for, responsible for,
and accountable to the whole society. He believes however, that the state
must be a *positive* state—an instrument of collective choice able to deal actively with the problems of the whole—but that such a state does not exist
in this country (see also Solo, 1982). Japan is offered in his paper as a case
study of a positive state. Lessons are drawn, but Solo does not suggest a
duplication of the Japanese approach. Instead, it is necessary to find ways
of overcoming such handicaps of our current state as the denigration of
public servants and public agencies which prevents it from acting positively
on the structure of the economy.

In his paper, Professor Rapping echoes the view of Richard Bartel that
the basic economic problems of the present period are in a very broad
sense structural and not cyclical and that a viable national economic program to deal with them requires that important institutions - government,
corporations, schools, families—adapt and change. His essay focuses on the
corporation and argues that the very nature and *modus operandi* of this institution militates against innovation and change. Tax cuts designed to spur
entreprenurial drive have not produced the hoped for results because production is largely organized by highly bureaucratic corporations oriented
toward short-run profits used for increased executive compensation and
takeover warchests rather than innovation. Monetarism and industrial
policy face the same set of obstacles. Rapping suggests that despite the

popular image, private bureaucracies are not better than their government counterparts in terms of flexibility, motivation, or time horizon. For him, the issue of how to organize for technological advance and innovation is not just an efficiency issue but also a political one, and like Solo, Rapping sees the necessity of government coordination to break the corporate logjam. He concludes that the hope for America is a compromise between government bureaucracies accountable, however imperfectly, to the people, and corporate bureaucracies accountable to their boards, large stockholders, managers, and the market. The state must take the lead in forging this compromise and in including other groups in the decision-making process.

Part III includes chapters by Gail Garfield Schwartz and James K. Galbraith on industrial policy, a topic receiving considerable attention in the popular press, in academia, and in Washington (Blumenthal 1983; Bluestone and Harrison 1982; Reich 1983). It is clear that the question of industrial policy is already on the agenda as a possible component of future economic policy. However, what that policy ought to consist of and how it could be implemented are issues that have yet to be resolved. The two authors in this section take basically cautious positions with respect to industrial policy. Neither one wants to resurrect the Reconstruction Finance Corporation, set up an American version of the Japanese Ministry of International Trade and Industry (MITI) or say how to pick winners and losers from our industries. Instead, each recommends that industrial policy play a limited role within the total policy configuration.

Gail Schwartz in Chapter 5, "The Hard Realities of Industrial Policy," argues that no single industrial policy can solve the individual problems of all vital industries. If we are to have an industrial policy, she maintains that it should be worked out separately for each industry from the bottom up. Centralized schemes such as those of France or Japan would not be workable in the United States. In her view, the collective bargaining mode offers the best possibility for hammering out individual industrial policies if Congress decides one is needed in a particular sector. Policy would be formulated by experts from business, labor, and government, each bringing different chips to the collective bargain table. General enabling legislation would be necessary to allow such bargains to be struck, but the main "point is that industrial policies must be viewed as microeconomic policies within the framework of macroeconomic policies—and that the impact of the latter on the former crics out for closer attention." At the same time, industrial policies must face up to political realities such "that workers, creditors and investors who are negatively affected by industrial policies must be compensated for their losses or assisted to recoup them." A collective bargaining approach could do this. In the end, Dr. Schwartz concludes that we are a nation of pragmatists and that a pragmatic approach is needed to take industrial policy debate out of the realm of slogans and into the realm of political action.

Next in Chapter 6, "The Debate About Industrial Policy," James Galbraith reviews the industrial policy debate from its origins in the New Deal era through its reincarnation in supply-side economics and the expected Democratic response. In his view, "there is no reputable economic argument for the proposition that policies of direct intervention, through subsidy or otherwise, in the investment decisions of companies necessarily by themselves will alter the share of investment in economic activity as a whole, through effects restricted to the supply side of the economy," and "moreover, actual policy actions are unlikely to have effects restricted exclusively to the supply side." Galbraith goes on to raise serious doubts concerning the kinds of industrial policy being discussed today. For example, he sees no evidence that consciousness raising (á la Robert Reich) will increase savings or that general rules for intervention in planning flow from the desire to increase international competitiveness or that one can pick sunrise industries and forecast their eventual size. Thus, Galbraith remains very skeptical—more so than Gail Schwartz whose major concern seems to be that industrial policy be grounded in political realities. Nevertheless, he does not totally reject industrial policy but suggests a course of action which would incorporate the valid goals of industrial policy in the United States.

That course of action would be "organized around the idea of preparing for an uncertain future" and would be oriented to "policies designed to foster the two attributes of success in any evolutionary situation: diversification and adaptability." The steps he suggests are more general than those of most industrial policy proponents: 1) support for science and basic research; 2) support for education, training, and equal opportunity; 3) democratic access to venture capital; and 4) flexible procedures to restructure capital, retrain workers, and avoid waste of human and physical capital. These are modest proposals. Galbraith does not expect industrial policy to cure unemployment, inflation, trade imbalances, or low productivity growth. To deal with these, a full set of economic policies would be needed, and "industrial policy is no substitution for such measures."

In Part IV the focus shifts from industrial policy to "Money, Credit, and Economic Power." The section consists of two rather different chapters: the first is a brief essay on monetary policy by James M. Stone and the second is a longer paper by A. Allan Schmid on broadening capital ownership.

James Stone's piece, Chapter 7, "Monetary Policy: A Reconsideration," contends that "the United States has been running a tight monetary policy ever since inflation became a national issue." To him, the short-term impact on investment of employing monetary policy as a break on the fiscal situation has been negative, and thus justification for the policy must be sought elsewhere. Breaking the cycle of poor fiscal management and inflationary expectations provides the needed rationale. The costs are high in terms of capital formation and unemployment, but possibly worth paying if the long-run result is growth without inflation. Stone doubts that the desired result will be achieved (though there may be a brief period of satisfactory growth, unemployment, and inflation) because the root cause of inflation in the imperfectly competitive American economy of today is structural and thus immune to a tight money/high unemployment policy. In light of this, he suggests that "monetary policy should abandon its macroeconomic pretensions and concentrate on the allocative role it inevitably plays." Stone's alternative monetary policy would explicitly ask where capital is being directed: speculative or productive uses, with or against fiscal policy, to the place of highest financial return or to local community credit needs?

Chapter 8, Allan Schmid's "Broadening Capital Ownership: the Credit System as a Focus of Power," employs a property rights framework to argue "that part of our institutional failure to realize our productive potential lies in a too narrow control of the credit-debt creation process." He hypothesizes that creating ways of broadening capital ownership will "be instrumental in the realization of our potential as well as its distribution." Two ideas are proposed: zero-yield public debt to be issued during recessions for money supply expansion and financed capitalist plans for citizen access to new bank credit for the purchase of stock issued for new equipment. Professor Schmid admits those ideas are not new, but observes they have been subject to little scholarly analysis. His purpose is to rectify this and to argue that they deserve a place on our research and public debate agenda as "alternatives to even greater reliance on the tax system and direct governmental management or to reliance on governmental withdrawal from and benign neglect of the economic system."

The last section of the book (Part V) has been titled "Ownership, Participation, and Democracy," and it expands and develops the ownership theme of Chapter 8 by Schmid even further. Chapter 9 by Corey Rosen, William Whyte, and Joseph Blasi argues that employee ownership itself is valuable in terms of our democratic ideology and its contribution to economic equity, but that ownership plus participation is more successful and desirable. Studies cited by the authors provide evidence that firms with employee involvement in decision making and employee sharing of the gains generally are more productive and profitable than comparable conventional enterprises. Moreover, the idea is consistent with American values of democracy, individual ownership, and free enterprise, and it has received broad political support. Yet despite all this, the number of American workers involved in these efforts is probably under five percent and ownership of private wealth in the United States remains essentially unchanged—one percent of the population owns fifty percent while large private and public bureaucracies in which individuals have little control erode our democratic society. The obstacles are inertia and lack of understanding—the same things blocking most meaningful change in our society.

Rosen, Whyte, and Blasi feel that we desperately need a mechanism to energize our companies, broaden opportunities, and give people more of a sense of control—without resorting to large government programs. They summarize:

> It is our conviction that employee ownership and participation can provide the basis for this revitalization. The steps needed to accomplish this "profitable revolution" rest largely with the private sector, for it is a revolution that can be made entirely within the current system. The federal and state governments, however, have a significant role to play. By providing well-targeted incentives, by making more information available, by supporting needed research, and by financing a limited number of the most innovative ownership and participation efforts, government can do much to move these ideas along more quickly. The ideas have not yet penetrated the market to the degree they must to cause basic changes in the economy, but they have established some important beachheads in many growing, innovative companies. With proper nurturing, the possibility at least exists that in the near future they could become a standard way to do business.

The remainder of their chapter details alternative employee ownership mechanisms, policy options for the federal government and for states, and leads nicely into the final chapter of the book, "Towards a Democratic Alternative: Neo-liberals vs. Economic Democrats," by Martin Carnoy and Derek Shearer.

Carnoy and Shearer agree that there is a need to democratize corporations, but they believe it would be naive to count on such a reform as the sole basis for what they call economic democracy—a participatory approach "to promote balanced economic growth, greater equity, and above all, more democracy." Theirs is a wide-ranging essay which begins by examining and ultimately rejecting both Reaganomics and Neo-Liberalism as successors to exhausted New Deal liberalism. Reaganomics with its pro-business, pro-high income policies of supply-side economics and its reduction in hard-won entitlements will create serious resistence among the vast majority of voters. The neo-liberal response to the economics of the Right shares many of the views of progressives like Carnoy and Shearer, such as full employment as the answer to the poverty and welfare problem, but the authors cannot accept the neo-liberal reliance on experts, big business, hi-tech, free trade, and wage accords which primarily enhance profits. For them, democracy is the crucial link in the entire economic equation, and neo-liberalism comes up short on this score.

The remainder of Chapter 10 outlines the elements of a national economic policy. It touches on many of the ideas raised in previous sections of the book and asks how they might be implemented more democratically. Economic democracy means wider participation, increasing responsibility, and shared decisions, especially concerning sacrifices and tradeoffs. Carnoy and Shearer believe that these principles must be inbedded in our employment programs, growth efforts, investment decisions, credit allocation, and industrial policy, to name just a few. They feel the government must play an important role in these matters. They also seriously question the idea of the relative inefficiency of public spending and "argue that when 'employment efficiency' and 'equality efficiency' are included in social performance criteria, government has done much better than private enterprise." Thus, they agree with others in this volume, specifically Rapping and Solo, and they would add the guiding principle of democratic participation in the operation of the state.

IV. Concluding Note

This book contends that the principal economic problems facing America are institutional. What is needed to solve these are innovative responses in which we begin to question our old assumptions and modify our institutional givens. As Fred Hirsch wrote in *Social Limits to Growth* (1978, 190)

> Piecemeal expedients now have little to offer by themselves. This does not deny them their place but makes them secondary to a shift of view and understanding. We may be near the limit of explicit social organization possible without a supporting social morality. Additional correctives in its absence simply do not take. That is the decisive weakness of the purely technical approach to keeping the market economy to its social purpose. . . . For the overriding economic problem discussed in this book, the first necessity is not technical devices but public acceptance necessary to make them work.

We agree.

References

Bluestone, Barry, and Harrison Bennet, *The Deindustrialization of America*, New York: Basic Books, 1982.

Blumenthal, Sidney, "Drafting a Democratic Industrial Plan," *The New York Times Magazine*, August 28, 1983, 30, 40–43, 53, 56–59, 63.

Bowles, Samuel, Gordon, David M., and Weisskopf, Thomas E., *Beyond the Waste Land: A Democratic Alternative to Economic Decline*, New York: Anchor/Doubleday, 1983.

Carnoy, Martin, and Shearer, Derek, *Economic Democracy*, Armonk, NY: M.E. Sharpe, 1980.

Galbraith, John Kenneth, *Economics and the Public Purpose*, Boston: Houghton Mifflin, 1973.

Gintis, Herbert, "Social Contradictions and the Liberal Theory of Justice," in Roger Skurski (ed.), *New Directions in Economic Justice*, Notre Dame, IN: University of Notre Dame Press, 1983.

Harrington, Michael, *Decade of Decision*, New York: Simon and Schuster, 1980.

Hayden, Tom, *The American Future*, Boston: South End Press, 1980.

Hirsch, Fred, *Social Limits to Growth*, Cambridge, MA: Harvard University Press, 1978.

Holland, Stuart (ed.), *Beyond Capitalist Planning*, New York: St. Martin's, 1979.

Kann, Mark E. (ed.), *The Future of American Democracy*, Philadelphia: Temple University Press, 1983.

Moody, Kim, "Going Public," *The Progressive*, July 1983, 47, 18–21.

O'Connor, James, *The Fiscal Crisis of the State*, New York: St. Martin's, 1973.

Okun, Arthur M., *Equality and Efficiency*, Washington: Brookings, 1975.

Reich, Robert, "The Next American Frontier," *The Atlantic Monthly Review*, March 1983, 251, 43–58, and April 1983, 251, 96–108.

Solo, Robert, *The Positive State*, Cincinnati: South-Western, 1982.

Weisskopf, Thomas, "The Theories of American Imperialism: A Critical Evolution," *The Review of Radical Political Economics*, Fall 1974, 6, 41–60.

Worland, Stephen, "Adam Smith: Economic Justice and the Founding Father," in Roger Skurski (ed.), *New Directions in Economic Justice*, Notre Dame, IN: University of Notre Dame Press, 1983.

2

Structural Change and Policy Response in an Interdependent World

RICHARD D. BARTEL

When I looked back over the past twenty-five years while preparing the Silver Anniversary Issue of *Challenge*, I was struck by the dramatic shift from the relative tranquility and stability in the economy of the 1950s and 1960s to the extraordinary turbulence and uncertainty in the 1970s and 1980s. The unexpected turn of events undermined theories, shattered forecasts, and disrupted the intellectual complacency of some economists. Indeed, the profession had taken some considerable pride in the advance of economic knowledge and practice through the 1960s. Economic policy was so effective, some had concluded, that it even signaled the death of the business cycle. But those happy days ended. And with somewhat diminished self-confidence, economists turned to the search for better explanations and new solutions.

If I had to choose a date for the turning point, my recollections indicate that mid-August day in 1971 when President Nixon devalued the dollar, broke its link to gold for the first time since 1934, imposed an import surcharge, and announced a wage-price freeze. The indicators from 1970 (*Economic Report of the President, 1982*) give an interesting picture of the developing "crisis" that culminated in those decisive policy changes. That year GNP registered a recession with a 0.2 percent drop in real output, consumer prices were climbing at a relatively fast clip of 5.9 percent, and unemployment stood at 4.9 percent. Treasury bills yielded 6.5 percent, the prime hovered around 7.9 percent, and the federal government chalked up a budget deficit of less than $3 billion. That year both merchandise trade

15

and the current account registered the last of a long string of *surpluses* going back to 1946 at least. In retrospect, it is amazing that a president of the United States could muster sufficient congressional and popular support for such sweeping, draconian measures, when the economy—from the vantage point of 1983—doesn't look so bad.

One need only leaf through the charts and tables illustrating the *Economic Report of the President* or popular magazines such as *Business Week* to see the extraordinary upheavals documented in the economic statistics of the 1970s and 1980s. It is the quantum leaps in the numbers, the sheer breaks in the continuity of economic performance that impress. One pivotal change in an energy-intensive economic system was the jump in world oil prices during the 1970s. Two severe recessions followed those shocks with related gyrations in dollar exchange rates, and in rates of interest, inflation, and unemployment. Trade balances swung in pendulum fashion, capital flows were massive, and international debt grew astronomically. And government policy seems to have contributed more to instability than stability, especially in recent years. What has the past decade of turbulence led to?

The American economy now confronts the worst economic crisis in half a century. In early 1983 the broad economic indicators still documented a rather precarious state of U.S. economic health, despite the conventional optimism about a near-term revival, glimmers of hope for housing, a pick up in auto sales, and a welcome collapse in the rate of inflation. Nevertheless, an appraisal of the institutional foundations of our economic system and our structural problems in a global context is not very reassuring.

We entered 1983 with some 20 million Americans unemployed or involuntarily underemployed: nearly 12 million could not find jobs, 1.8 million had given up the search, and some 6.5 million were working part-time involuntarily. Real GNP remained roughly at the level of late 1979. One-third of our overall industrial capacity lay idle, two-thirds was unused in a basic industry like steel. Our money-center banks, the very foundation of a sophisticated and far-flung banking system, were staggering under the burden of shaky loans to developing countries and to the energy industry and manufacturing giants at home. Their traditional "prudence in lending," the "discipline of the market," and regulatory oversight by government agencies have apparently failed. Meanwhile, "exploding debt" has eroded the financial structure of our major non-financial corporations, bringing them to their weakest position in the entire post-World War II period. Corporate bankruptcies reached their highest level since the 1930s. The decline of agricultural incomes and the high frequency of farm foreclosures recalled the hard times of the Great Depression. The federal government budget is now regarded as "structurally unbalanced," with deficits expected to fluctuate around $200 billion over the next several years.

This picture of disarray in the world's dominant economy would probably be less worrisome if similar symptoms did not plague the rest of the globe. We might be hopeful if policymakers appeared to have some coherent picture of the problems and a strategy to work us out of the situation. But too prevalent among policy makers, forecasters, and economists is the view that this is much like the other post-war, 40-month inventory cycles, perhaps a bit more severe, a trifle longer, with one or two added complications. While major leaders among OECD countries talk about economic cooperation, their policy actions are propelling national economies along diverging paths.

I. The Great Transformations

If we are experiencing a conventional business cycle, it seems to ride the backs of far more powerful "long waves" of historical significance. What is disturbing about our experience in the past decade is the apparent failure to consider our cyclical problems, and policy responses to those problems, within a larger historical and worldwide context. For the countercyclical medicine of the 1950s and 1960s will have little curative power to overcome inadequate growth, recurrent inflationary bouts, and persistent structural unemployment in the coming decades.

If economists grasped the nature of the problems unfolding in the 1970s, they failed to persuade policymakers of the appropriate measures to meet them. Rather, it seems that by the late 1970s economists themselves were overwhelmed by the view that policies based on the unfettered operation of the "free market" would be adequate. They seemed to reject an earlier attitude that capitalism, even in its modified forms, suffered genetically from periodic market failures and, therefore, required government intervention of a more direct fashion to sustain stability and growth.

Because of the limited scope of this paper, I shall allude only to the fundamental transformations that I see boiling under the surface.[1] To list them briefly: 1) the oil price revolution; 2) the manufacturing revolution in the developing countries and a corresponding shift in the U.S. international comparative advantage; 3) the technology revolution and global interdependence; 4) institutional aging and paralysis in decision making; and 5) a drastically altered market environment for economic policy.

These transformations have some general features important for planning economic policy responses and carrying out policy measures. The first three, especially the oil price increases, can impart discrete and sizeable shocks to the economic system. These have the makings of historical discontinuities in economic life that not only shape in a critical way the performance of the economic system, but also provide a focal point for the responses of our social and political institutions. Voter reactions to the instabilities generated by economic shocks will influence whether Congress can reach a consensus on economic policy and whether those responses—changes in monetary and budget measures—will lead to economic policies which themselves will constitute endogenous shocks. These policy-induced discontinuities can set off the same abrupt transfers of real income and wealth that followed the initial economic shock. In this way policy itself can have destabilizing effects both on economic performance and on the political process. Here I shall elaborate on the nature of the oil price shock and then look at the policy responses to it.

The oil price revolution is clearly the most dramatic change to hit the American economy in the 1970s. OPEC catapulted contract prices of Arabian light crude in two stages: One quick leap from roughly $2 to $10 per barrel at the beginning of 1974 and the second from roughly $12 to $30 per barrel in 1979–80 (see Chart 1). Prices subsequently rose further to $34 per barrel from which they have begun what some analysts now ex-

Chart 1. World-market commodity prices: Oil

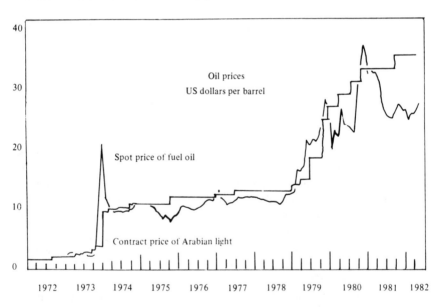

Source: *Fifty-Second Annual Report*, Bank for International Settlements, Basle, June 1982.

pect to be a collapse as precipitous and as large as the preceding jump. The increase in oil prices, operating like a huge tax, transferred income from oil consumers to producers, from consuming countries to OPEC, from the U.S. Northeast to Texas, Louisiana, Alaska, and other oil producing states. The locus of economic growth also shifted—between nations, between regions within the United States, between industries, and between GNP sectors from consumption to investment and exports. These adjustments led to remarkable changes in the U.S. and world oil situation. The growth of output from non-OPEC supplies in the North Sea off the United Kingdom and Norway, in Mexico and Alaska and in the developing world, greatly diminished OPEC's dominance in world markets. In the United States, however, massive investments in exploration, expanded drilling, and other exploitation have not altered the basic facts of domestic output: U.S. production, according to American Petroleum Institute statistics, peaked at 11.3 million barrels per day (mbd) in 1970 and in recent years has hovered around 10.2 mbd. Crude oil production alone (excluding natural gas liquids, shale oil, etc.) peaked at 9.6 mbd in 1970, recently leveled out around 8.5 mbd, and in January 1983 stood at 8.7 mbd, up from 8.6 mbd a year earlier.

On the other side of the oil equation, consumption in the United States quite remarkably declined much more than analysts expected even in 1980. After topping out at 19 mbd in 1978–79, it declined to 16 mbd in 1981. True, the years of recession and stagnation have cut into consumption. But the big surprise from the oil crisis is the fact that conservation efforts in the major industrialized countries caused the oil/GDP ratio to fall at an annual rate of 8 percent per year (Tussing 1983).

As a result, U.S. petroleum imports dropped from the peak reached in 1978–79 of 8.2 mbd to 5.7 mbd in 1981. In January 1983 we imported roughly 4.5 mbd, down from 5.5 mbd a year earlier. As a result, the share of imports in total U.S. consumption has fallen back to levels prevailing during the early 1970s. The decline in import volume, along with a modest drop in prices so far, shaved the value of imports to almost $63 billion in 1982, from nearly $80 billion in 1981.

A key feature of the oil price crisis in the 1970s was the widening of the U.S. oil import gap and its contribution to the structural shift in the current account of our international payments. The rise in the volume of oil imports until 1978–79 had covered both the decline in domestic production and the growth of domestic demand. That structural characteristic of the supply-demand equation gave the appearance of a higher U.S. income elasticity of demand for oil imports, as compared with other consuming countries that are not major oil producers (Bartel 1980, 96–97). The U.S. adjustment to major oil fluctuations may be more severe than Germany's or Japan's, quite ironically, because this country is a major oil producer.

Therefore, I do not share the unbridled optimism of those who see only benefits in the precipitous drop of oil prices. Even at these high prices, the United States has been unable to expand oil production back to the 1970 peak. New domestic finds are unlikely to be large, since domestic territories and offshore areas in the Atlantic and the Gulf have been intensively searched with little success. How will a precipitous drop in prices affect domestic production? What about the high-cost sources in the North Sea off Britain and Norway, in Alaska and Mexico? Will the search and development continue in the developing world outside OPEC? It was, after all, the new sources of supply outside OPEC (in addition to conservation and the global recession) which helped to develop the world glut that eroded OPEC's dominant supply position. Will this mean marginal supplies will be cut back in the United States and elsewhere, just as economic revival in the industrial world spurs demand, and oil companies rebuild their inventories? Are we setting the stage for a growing oil demand slamming against a faltering supply later in the decade?

I have no hard answers to these questions. But lessons from the 1970s show that a sizeable discontinuity in oil pricing will have major shocks on both the real and money economies. U.S. policymakers have the opportunity to cushion at least the domestic shock impact by imposing a variable duty on oil imports or a variable excise tax on consumption of gasoline. The taxes could be increased as oil prices fall. The purpose would be to stabilize prices or to manage a moderate decline. If prices later rebound, the taxes could be reduced to avoid any increase in consumer prices. We face a dilemma: The more successful we are in adjusting away from oil imports, the more oil prices tend to sag and the adjustment (new energy investment, for example) tends to be discouraged. Thus, our policies with respect to oil imports and domestic energy adjustment (including investment in alternative energy resources and conservation) may have to include explicit floors under oil prices to prevent periodic price reductions which may disrupt a continuous adjustment process.

II. Policy Response and Policy Interdependence

A. Adverse Shift in Terms of Trade and the Monetarist Response

For some economists the unprecedented jumps in oil prices, viewed together with periodic run-ups in food and raw materials prices, are part of a long wave, or Kondratieff cycle. Indeed, W. W. Rostow dates a turning point in 1972 (1978, 287–304) when the terms of trade turned against the mature, industrial countries in favor of oil producers in particular. The world economy began a period of relatively high prices for basic commodities after some twenty years during which those prices had fallen absolutely or relatively to manufactures' prices. The reversal of those relative price trends in the 1970s, in his view, stemmed from fundamental structural changes in the world production and demand of manufactures, foods, and raw materials. In the 1950s and 1960s, the favorable price trends for raw materials contributed to the growth and relative price stability of the manufacturing countries. After 1972 the adverse moves in price trends dragged down growth and reinforced the price uptrends. The adverse shift in real terms of trade against industrial countries was clearly the most abrupt and powerful destabilizing impulse in the world economy during the 1970s and early 1980s. It took a long time for policymakers to recognize the nature of this powerful, destabilizing force, and to design appropriate policies to cope with the instability. Since the most immediate impact hit the prices of oil products and energy, the consumer price index was the most closely watched economic indicator to alert the public, policymakers, and economists to the problem. In those episodes of oil price shocks, consumer prices shot up along with the leap in energy prices (see Table 1).

Policymakers went astray in the nineteen seventies because they mistook the oil price shocks, and the rise of the CPI that it caused, to be a

Table 1. Changes in U.S. Prices
(in yearly percentages)

	Consumer Prices	Energy Prices
1973	6.2	8.0
1974	11.0	29.3
1975	9.1	10.6
1976	5.8	7.2
1978	7.7	6.3
1979	11.3	25.2
1980	13.5	30.9
1981	10.4	13.5
1982	6.1	1.5

Source: *Economic Report of the President, 1982*, p. 55.

"monetary" problem that could be corrected by monetary restraint. Policy-makers and their economic advisers tended to focus on the consumer price index and respond to its movements as if everything that moved the index were symptomatic of monetary inflation. The shift in relative prices of oil and other goods instead was a fundamental shift in the real economy. Whether that shock was caused by a reordering of market power—cartels, monopoly, etc.—or basic changes in the relative supplies and demands of oil and energy around the world is not terribly important. The point is that a shift in relative prices requires a *real* adjustment in supplies and demands and in the structures of national and global economies. Those adjustments cannot be prevented or aided simply by changes in non-targeted conventional monetary policy.

For policymakers, then, it is important to distinguish between real and monetary phenomena in explaining the rise in price indices. Policymakers and economic advisers retained the mindset of the 1950s and 1960s when price inflation accelerated and decelerated within the context of conventional business cycles. Countercyclical demand management policy, of which central bank leaning-against-the-wind was a major foundation stone, was the rule of the day. Economic theory, econometric model building, and even the GNP-national income account data bases reinforced the conventional approach.

B. Interdependence, Monetary Policy, and the Overvalued Dollar

If monetary policy had primarily domestic impacts as seemed the case in the 1950s and 1960s when our economy appeared to be more closed, then the consequences from the errors of the 1970s may not have been so bad. But the policy environment had changed drastically by 1973 with the advent of floating exchange rates and increased capital mobility. Closed national economies became increasingly open and integrated into a global system. In this context, monetary policy became synonymous with exchange rate policy. Flexibly moving exchange rates powerfully transmitted monetary impulses to real impulses via international trade. Increasing interdependence meant not only that individual economies reacted to changing economic developments in other countries but that changes in economic policy itself set off strong international repercussions. While the familiar economic environment, anchored to Bretton Woods, dissolved in the early 1970s, monetarism gained increasing influence over monetary policy in major countries. Early 1970 marked the first time the Federal Reserve included monetary aggregates as targets under consideration in the Federal Open Market Committee Directive to the domestic securities desk of the Federal Reserve Bank of New York.

By mid-decade, monetarist ideas deeply influenced the thinking of central bank policymakers and economists in Germany, the United Kingdom, Switzerland, and Canada, as well as in the United States. So it came as no surprise that the momentum of monetarism's advance by the fall of 1979 should culminate in the Fed's adoption of hard rules to restrain the growth of monetary aggregates. It seemed reasonable to many that the Fed should learn from the Bundesbank's success and firmly establish its own anti-inflationary credibility.

Controlling more rigidly the growth of the monetary aggregates invariably meant greater volatility in money-market and long-term interest rates. That is clear from the data. But as a result, the increased risk and uncertainty meant the markets also had to incorporate a higher risk premium into the structure of interest rates. That contributed to a generally higher level of real interest rates. The increasingly high rates of interest and their wider amplitudes of fluctuation (see Chart 2, Tables 2, 3) had a two-pronged impact on the economy: 1) the usual dampening of business investment, construction, household spending, and government operations; and 2) exchange appreciation which dampens exports, encourages imports, and slows economic activity. Dollar exchange rates moved through extraordinary swings after 1973, and the volatility took on even greater significance after 1978.

While the oil shock demonstrated the high degree of economic interdependence, not just among industrial countries, but among the larger

Chart 2. Short and long-term interest rates.

Monthly date

..........Money-market rates[1]   _____Prime rates[2]   _____Bond yields[3]

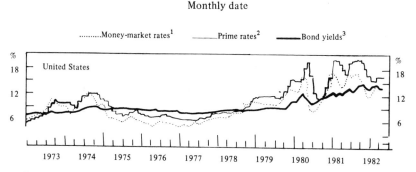

[1] Representative rates. (Three-month money-market instruments.)   [2] Minimum rates charged by commercial banks for cash credits to first-class borrowers.   [3] Representative rates. (For the United States, industrial bonds.)

groupings including OPEC and the LDCs, the policy response demonstrated the interdependence among policy instruments and their consequences. The monetarist interpretation of the oil shocks and the monetarist policy response soon generated extremely wide swings in dollar exchange rates. Those in turn had substantial impacts on U.S. trade flows, on production in import-competing and export industries, and on employment in the affected industries.

U.S. policy first resulted in a precipitous depreciation of the dollar during 1977–78. Depending on which weighted index of the effective exchange rate one uses, the dollar reached troughs in late 1978 and mid-1980 (Feldman 1982). At these troughs, the dollar was widely regarded among U.S. and foreign experts to be greatly undervalued. Following the advent of militant monetarism in late 1979, the dollar turned around and skyrocketed in late 1980 and 1981 in an unprecedented cumulative ap-

Table 2. Month-to-Month Variability of Interest Rates

Countries	January 1972 to March 1975				January 1979 to March 1982			
	maximum	minimum	mean	standard deviation[1]	maximum	minnimum	mean	standard deviation
	In percentages per annum							
Money-market rates[2] United States	12.1	3.5	7.4	2.5	18.0	8.3	13.1	2.9
Bond yields[3] United States	9.1	6.9	7.6	0.7	15.0	9.0	11.7	2.0

[1] Calculated as $\sqrt{d^2}/(n-1)$ where d denotes deviations of individual observations from the mean and n the number of observations. [2] Based on monthly measures of domestic money-market rates on three-month instruments. [3] Representative rates (see Chart 2).

Table 3. Day-to-Day Variability of Short-term Interest Rates[1]

Countries	15-month periods ending								
	28th September 1979			31st December 1980			31st March 1982		
	range	mean	standard deviation	range	mean	standard deviation	range	mean	standard deviation
	in percentages per annum								
United States	8.2–12.9	10.5	1.2	8.8–22.0	14.1	3.2	11.8–19.9	16.5	2.0

[1] Based on daily measures of rates on three-month instruments, Euro-currency rates.

Source: *Fifty-Second Annual Report,* Bank for International Settlements, Basle, June 1982 p. 61, 62, 63.

preciation against the currencies of other major industrial countries (see Chart 3). By 1983, the dollar had become even more severely overvalued than in 1970–71 when overvaluation brought the collapse of the Bretton Woods System.

Measured by the Federal Reserve Board index (based on a global tradeweighted index including the G-10 countries plus Switzerland, March 1973 = 100), the dollar's value climbed over 40 percent from 85.5 in September 1980 to 120.9 in September 1982. Changes in bilateral rates with the German mark and the Japanese yen were equally volatile. From mid-1976 to October 1978, the dollar dropped by about 28 percent against the German mark and by about 38 percent against the Japanese yen. Then in the subsequent upswing from September 1980 to July 1982, the dollar appreciated by over 40 percent against the German mark and by about 19 percent against the yen.

Chart 3. Nominal and Real Effective Foreign Exchange Value of the Dollar

MARCH 1973 – 100

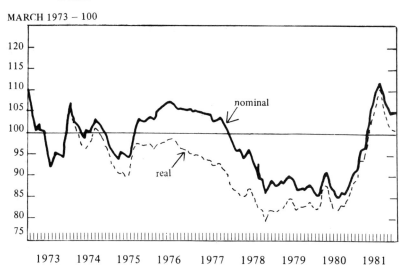

Note–The effective exchange rate is computed using multilateral trade shares of the G-10 countries plus Switzerland. The real exchange rate is calculated by adjusting the nominal index for relative movements in consumer prices (this is one among various ways to measure real exchange rates).

Sources: Department of Labor and Board of Governors of the Federal Reserve System.

C. Dollar Fluctuations and the Trade Impact

The extreme swings in dollar rates during the late 1970s and early 1980s only underscore the significant impact of changes in real exchange rates on the volumes of exports and imports and on the trade balance. First the extraordinary undervaluation of the dollar from late 1978 to mid-1980 was followed by a contraction in the U.S. merchandise trade deficit from $34 billion in 1978 to $25 billion in 1980. If oil imports and agricultural exports are subtracted from total merchandise trade flows, the shift was even more dramatic from a $21 billion deficit in 1978 to a $12 billion surplus in 1980 (Feldman 1982).

The story about the subsequent dollar appreciation is not yet completed, since the trade impact takes two years and more to work out. The lagged responses of trade to the dollar's appreciation will still be coming in for another year at least, but the consequences so far indicate the prospects for the trade accounts: On an annual rate basis, the trade deficit deepened from a deficit of roughly $22 billion in the fourth quarter of 1980 to some $50 billion in the third quarter of 1982. Once again removing agricultural exports and petroleum imports from the aggregate trade flows, the balance on merchandise swings from nearly an $11 billion *surplus* in the fourth quarter of 1980 to an $18 billion *deficit* in the fourth quarter of 1981 at an annual rate (Feldman 1982). As the lagged effects of overvaluation mount, the trade outlook grows even worse: By the end of 1983, U.S. exports were expected to be roughly $35 billion lower and imports about $10 billion higher because of the dollar's appreciation, according to calculations of the Federal Reserve Bank of New York (see Feldman 1982). Early in 1983, forecasters in the government and private sectors expected the deficit on merchandise trade to range from $60 to $80 billion for the year.

This is an astonishing picture for the trade outlook, in particular given the cyclical stage of the economy. Normally, a deep recession would move merchandise trade to a surplus, as after the first oil shock, when trade registered a turnaround from a $5 billion deficit in 1974 to a $9 billion surplus in 1975. In the current recession, the aggregate value of exports is declining markedly, whereas in the 1974–6 period, exports continued to grow. On the import side, the current value of aggregate imports is also dropping, but this is due almost entirely to a fall of nearly $18 billion in oil purchases (reflecting both the drop in volume and price). In contrast, the 1975 recession generated a big drop in total imports, even as petroleum imports pushed higher. Given the evidence that U.S. import elasticity with respect to income is greater than the U.S. export elasticity with respect to foreign income, the current trade performance is unusual. Certainly, even this casual analysis leaves little doubt that the overvalued dollar weighs heavily on U.S. trade performance.

D. The External Sector, Growth, Jobs and Prices

That the external sector is important for fluctuations of U.S. GNP is also borne out by the statistics (see Table 4). From 1978 through 1980, the sharp increase in the net exports of goods and services that had been spurred by an undervalued dollar, amounted to nearly three-fourths of the rise in GNP during that period. Later, when GNP turned down, the lagged impact of an overvalued dollar propelled a deterioration of net exports from the first quarter 1981 to the third quarter in 1982 that amounted to some two-thirds of the corresponding decline in real GNP.

The impact of changing trade flows on domestic activity and employment is clear, as the American industrial heartland can now attest. The U.S. export expansion during 1977–80, C. Fred Bergsten argued in congressional testimony (Bergsten 1983), was responsible for "80 percent of all new jobs created" in that period. On the negative side of the ledger, the trade deterioration of the past two years, he argued, cost the country "over one million jobs," and "a further, even larger, loss can be expected in 1983 as the trade and current account deficits soar to record levels." In terms of our unemployment rates, he estimates the external sector will have added over two percentage points during the 1981–83 period.

The dollar's appreciation, in Robert A. Feldman's analysis (1982), has resulted in a rise of import volume, which combined with a fall in export volume, will "directly reduce the level of U.S. real GNP at the end of [1983] by 1 to 1½ percent of its third quarter 1980 pre-appreciation level". In addition to the costs of appreciation in terms of lost growth there are also gains in terms of lower inflation. His evidence suggests that the "appreciation could reduce the level of U.S. prices by as much as 3 to 4 per-

Table 4. Net Exports and GNP
(Billions of 1972 dollars)

	Net Exports	GNP
1978	24.6	1,436.9
1980	50.6	1,474.0
IQ 1981	50.9	1,516.4
IIIQ 1982	27.5	1,481.1

Source: U. S. Department of Commerce, *Survey of Current Business,* December 1982, Vol. 62, No. 12. *Economic Report of the President, 1982.*

cent by the end of [1983]." Indeed, this anticipated result may well have been a primary motivation for pursuing a monetarist policy and extreme exchange appreciation to begin with.

But policymakers in an interdependent world should also consider the impact of appreciation on those industrial and developing countries which must buy oil and other raw materials with dollars. Our policy has directly contributed to their resurgent price inflation. Despite the recent drop in world oil prices, a country like Germany experienced *rising* oil prices because of the dollar's appreciation.

Finally, there is a time dimension to these policy choices concerning the value of the dollar. An overvalued dollar cannot be sustained indefinitely. This means future depreciation will once again give an inflationary impulse to the price level. And if the outlook for a yawning trade deficit in 1983 comes to pass, the dollar will be headed for a sharp fall thereafter—if history is any guide. Thus the gains from dollar appreciation on the inflation front may prove to be short-lived, even though they were won at a high cost.

E. From an Overvalued Dollar to the Rise of Protectionism

While militant monetarism has contributed to a severe global recession and financial crisis, its by-product—an overvalued dollar—has reinforced protectionist sentiment arising from a widening spectrum of American interest groups. Those protectionist pressures are particularly acute against Japan, in part because the dollar/yen exchange rate is greatly out of line: The dollar's value has climbed over 40 percent relative to the yen (from October 1978 to September 1982). This is contrary to what one would expect from underlying economic fundamentals, since U.S. consumer prices rose cumulatively more than twice as fast as did Japanese prices during that period, and changes in productivity have not compensated for the price differences.

Nowhere are the price and cost disadvantages more dramatic than in the automobile industry. According to James Harbour, a Detroit automotive consultant interviewed in the *Wall Street Journal* (August 26, 1982), U.S. auto workers are paid about $8 more an hour in wages and benefits than Japanese workers, and it takes 30 person-hours to produce a small car, compared with 15 person-hours in Japan. Considering the entire production process from iron ore to finished vehicles, Harbour estimates that the Japanese car contains more than 100 person-hours of labor, while U.S. producers require 190 hours. That gives Japanese car makers a $2,500 cost edge over their American counterparts.

This illustrates the kind of threat Americans perceive, perhaps to a lesser extent, to other basic industries, like steel, and to consumer electronics items. The typical response of voters, and therefore many legislators, is that U.S. producers face unfair competition from abroad and inadequate access to foreign markets. Rather, the public should understand that where the dollar now stands, it constitutes an "unfair" subsidy to importers and a tax on exporters. Rather than trade barriers, a more reasonable value of the dollar/yen exchange rate is called for. Somewhere between the late 1978 lows (for the dollar) and the highs of late 1982, could only be an improvement, and a major step toward appropriate adjustment. This would do much to help defuse the protectionist pressures.

Despite all the rhetoric about free trade and free markets, the Reagan administration in its first two years in office made major decisions which accelerated the slide into protectionism and weakened the international institutions which had presided over the growth of world trade in the postwar period. The administration imposed: 1) "voluntary restraints" against auto imports from Japan; 2) further restraints on trade in textiles and apparel under bilateral agreements within the Multi-Fiber Arrangement, an international, protectionist agreement aimed mainly at developing countries; 3) narrower quotas on sugar imports; and 4) voluntary restraints against steel imports from Europe. The economic effects of these measures far outweigh the administration's liberalizing steps on shoes and television sets.

Meanwhile, Congress is pushing legislation which would embody a new "reciprocity" strategy in our trade policy and include domestic "content requirements" applied to auto imports. The new attitudes on trade in the Congress and the administration are significant in the degree to which they run counter to the traditional principles which have guided the growth of free trade for over thirty years after the Second World War.

The new concept of "reciprocity" is a case in point. Reciprocity in the past concerned the equitable distribution of gains achieved through trade negotiations in exchange for reducing protectionist measures. Typically this was accomplished in the successful multilateral trade negotiations within GATT–the Dillon, Kennedy, and Tokyo Rounds as examples. Current American proposals in Congress actually seek reciprocity in the *level* of protection through *bilateral* negotiations concerning *narrow* ranges of goods. The objective is really aimed at retaliatory actions to achieve greater protections against *specific* countries and *selected* products. William R. Cline (1982) sees this strategy as "reciprocity enforced by retaliation," which would "violate the fundamental principle of unconditional most-favored-nation treatment. . . . " Another surprising feature of this strategy is the proposal for unilateral action by the United States to renege on trade agreements reached in international negotiations without resorting to international talks to settle trade disputes.

While the United States alone cannot be faulted for the breakdown in international trade cooperation, this country has clearly lost its preeminent leadership role. The United States had strongly supported reciprocity under the most-favored-nation principle for the last sixty years. The multilateral and non-discriminatory features were keystones of the GATT system. Resort to bilateral negotiations and agreements and to retaliation outside the framework of GATT constitutes a sharp departure from successful trade policies of the past. If not halted, the process will lead to worldwide proliferations of bilateral agreements and to competitive retaliation. The resulting strictures on world trade will reinforce the current decline induced by global recession.

F. Bilateralism in Economic Analysis and Policy

For years now, much of the concern in Congress for fair treatment in international trade has been prompted by the growing U.S. trade deficit with Japan. This is a result of bilateralism in economic analysis. The focus on bilateral trade balances has caused a cry for bilateral trade negotiations and unilateral actions by the U.S. or bilateral agreements between the two countries to correct the imbalance. Many congressional analysts typically point to the nearly $18 billion 1981 trade deficit with Japan and the $19 billion 1982 deficit as supporting evidence for a bilateral approach. Yet, the bilateralists neglect to point toward our persistent *surpluses* with Western Europe — $9 billion in 1981 and over $5 billion in 1982. In the case of Japan, so the argument goes, the deficit indicates markets closed to the United States and other exporters. Then for the sake of consistency, shouldn't Europeans argue that the U.S. surplus indicates unfair access to our markets. Bilateralism has never been a sound basis for analyzing international economic issues, nor is it a proper basis for setting trade policy.

Unfortunately, the dissension on trade policy among OECD countries has become a smokescreen for a major problem in U.S.-Japanese economic relations, namely a grossly overvalued dollar and an undervalued yen. A significant part of the price disadvantages faced by basic American industries vis à vis the Japanese could be legitimately corrected by appropriate exchange rate relationships. That requires both the U.S. and Japanese governments to change their monetary/fiscal policy mixes, allowing the dollar to fall and the yen to rise against all other major world currencies.

G. Exchange Rate Alignment and Future Trade Negotiations

Conducting commercial policy in a world of managed, but highly flexible, exchange rates adds uncertainty that did not confront policymakers working in the Bretton Woods System. Any across-the-board changes in trade restraints will have an impact on prevailing dollar exchange rates and induce short-term capital flows that can reinforce or offset the desired objectives of the trade measures. Misalignments of exchange rates can quickly erode the progress in dismantling trade barriers that have been achieved over the course of decades.

A general import surcharge, for example, will affect the short- and long-run views of exchange market participants towards the dollar's prospects. Exchange market participants invariably crank new policy measures into their computer models for a revised forecast of the U.S. current account and dollar exchange rates. Some traders will conclude that a uniform import surcharge will improve the trade balance and the current account and strengthen the dollar. Others may conclude that the import surcharge simply indicates the government's desperation in trying to turn around a deteriorating external position. Both traders alter their dollars' foreign currency positions accordingly.

Depending on the weight of market opinion, various outcomes in the foreign exchange markets are possible. If the balance swings in the positive direction for the dollar, the U.S. currency strengthens and capital may flow in. As a result, the tendency of the import surcharge to raise the price of U.S. imports is at least partially eroded by an appreciation of the dollar which makes U.S. imports less expensive. On the other hand, if the weight of market opinion reinforces a pessimistic outlook, the dollar weakens, capital may flow out, and the foreign exchange market's response reinforces the import surcharge. The depreciating dollar in this case makes imports even more expensive, in addition to the surcharge itself. Thus, in both cases the exchange market evaluation of the policy change is important, because market expectations may generate short-run capital flows that can either reinforce or undermine the effects of the policy decision.

In a world in which capital is far more mobile and exchange rates far more flexible than under the Bretton Woods System, these induced exchange rate changes and accompanying capital flows cannot be ignored. A new set of risks and uncertainties must be recognized. In one extreme, the effects of the policy change could be completely offset by contrary exchange rate movements. In the other extreme, the effects of the policy change on trade flows would be reinforced by exchange rate movements. This opens the possibility that short-run exchange fluctuations could have wider amplitudes than in the absence of the change in trade policy. The feedback between policy changes and resulting exchange fluctuations could thereby contribute to destabilizing speculation.

It is easy to imagine that disordered trade relations and uncertainties about the direction of trade policy can contribute to "over-shooting" of dollar rates. The quick, deep, short-run depreciations of the dollar that can result will generate inflationary repercussions in their wake, as the higher price of imports feeds back to the domestic consumer price index. Indeed, the combined effects of 1) the lack of an oil price policy to prevent wide swings in domestic prices, i.e., a resurgence of oil prices in the late 1980s; and 2) the inevitable correction of an overvalued dollar and a trade deficit soaring to $80 billion, i.e., a steep dollar depreciation in 1984, could set the dollar up for another massive swing in the next year or two. This possibility poses once again the question, will U.S. authorities continue to depend solely on monetary restraint to cope with external inflationary impulses of a non-monetary origin transmitted by the prices of key imports (oil) and also via excessive dollar depreciations? Overreaction on monetary policy is very likely to trigger another undesirable and avoidable cycle of interest rates and dollar exchange rates.

The cautious policymaker would therefore avoid general, across-the-board trade restraints. The alternative is to apply as a last resort *industry-specific* restraints to selected commodities. This follows from the fact that most individual commodities or industries comprise a relatively small weight in a country's total trade. Therefore, the induced reaction in the exchange markets and accompanying capital flows are likely to be of less consequence than if a general measure had been used. The specific measure, while avoiding some of the adverse effects of an across-the-board measure, may well achieve the intended policy objectives in the industry to which it is applied.

There is still the danger, however, that if industry-specific measures — tariffs, quotas, orderly marketing arrangements — proliferate, the collective and cumulative effects on exchange market expectations will be the same as if an across-the-board measure had been applied. The United States seems to have reached that ominous threshold already. To recognize that selective import restraints are more appropriate than general measures within a flexible rate system is not to recommend their widespread use. Furthermore, the greater the efforts focused on specific measures, the more likely that political interest groups for and against these measures will become increasingly polarized and strengthened. This complicates not only a rational formulation of policy, but its fair and effective implementation and enforcement.

IV. The Issue: Real Adjustment Needs a Structural Policy

Up to this point I have argued that policymakers misdiagnosed structural problems (the oil shocks) in the 1970s and then misapplied non-targeted stabilization policies in a conventional countercyclical sequence.

When the swings in unemployment and inflation grew progressively wider over the decade, policymakers had hoped to gain credibility and some measure of cumulative success by persevering with, and intensifying, the usual policy treatment. The end result—an extreme mix of monetarist restraint to halt price inflation coupled with "supply-side fiscalism" to spur investment and growth—produced global recession and financial crisis.

In response to questions about what to do, I don't suggest scrapping conventional monetary and fiscal policy instruments. A part of our difficulty is that we have an insufficient number of policy instruments to apply to all the policy objectives. Rather, we need to use non-targeted, macroeconomic policies appropriately and to supplement them with targeted structural policies. The latter approach is called industrial policy by some economists. But the label has imprecise meaning, because there is a variant of industrial policy for every gradation point in the spectrum of political-economic persuasion. Besides, structural policy calls to mind immediately the nature of the problems we must confront.

U.S. policymakers will have to begin thinking about changing economic structures to deal with the source of problems and also as a long-term objective of national policy. This country lacks experience in this area of policy analysis, compared with European countries and Japan which developed structural policy strategies and the institutions to carry out such policies. One thinks immediately of MITI in Japan. Similar national agencies developed in Austria, France, and other European economies in their efforts to use Marshall Plan aid after the Second World War. Chancellor Bruno Kreisky recalled, in my interview (*Challenge*, Sept./Oct. 1982), how Austria continues to use structural strategies in planning domestic economic programs, and even in developing Austria's foreign economic aid contributions. Indeed, out of the Marshall Plan emerged the institution of the OEEC, the OECD, and The European Communities which prepared the way for integration of national economies into a larger framework. Resource-poor economies had to plan consciously for the goods to be produced at home which could purchase essential raw materials on world markets. They had to build a conception of how a small national economy could fit into and prosper within a global framework.

American thinking within both government and academic circles, by contrast, has generally viewed economic structure as the end product of myriads of economic decisions in a competitive market, rather than an objective toward which resources should be marshalled and policy should guide us. In this view, American management tends to see firms and industries as permanent fixtures on the economic landscape whereas their European and Japanese counterparts recognize developmental stages from infancy to maturity. In such a dynamic, long-term context, economic sectors and industries may have to be revitalized to attain world standards of efficiency, or be allowed to contract and die.

An active structural policy cannot evolve in an institutional vacuum, as we can see from the European and Japanese experiences. A good first step toward an institutional foundation would be a research agency to assemble a data bank, comparable in scope and size to the GNP and national income accounts, for studying economic structure. Input-output data must be compiled and regularly published to stimulate research on intersectoral, interindustry, and structural change. Such an institute should monitor the nation's endowment of raw materials and energy resources, so that we can guage how structural change alters basic requirements relative to supplies of depletable resources. Similarly, we need a national catalog of public infrastructure to enable nationwide plans for maintenance, repair, and expansion when necessary. Here the policy question is not simply about changing economic structure, but concerns geographic and regional shifts.

Finally, such an institute should develop a nationwide manpower data bank indicating the quantities and qualities of American labor. We need to know how the labor force is likely to change as demographic structure shifts over the long term. Such a data bank should provide information on job openings and extinctions on a nationwide basis. Unemployment programs must begin with an understanding of how the labor force is changing relative to the labor requirements of the economy. The information would also help in planning expansion and contraction of education and training programs to meet the changing requirements of industries and regions. Research work with a long-term, structural focus has been going on in an ad hoc way for some years. Numerous examples include The Joint Economic Committee's Special Study on Economic Change (1978–80), The Global 2000 Report completed under the Carter administration and various congressional and presidential commissions.

Government policy along the lines of a structural or industrial policy will be difficult to initiate, simply because of the widespread fears about government planning, burgeoning bureaucracies and long-term regimentation. Nevertheless, there are clear indications that even this traditional political resistance is weakening as the nation's economic disarray worsens. Politicians with an eye on 1984 elections are already developing ideas for platform planks including the issues of industrial policy.

There are two areas that require urgent attention and provide opportunities for starting embryonic institutions: incomes policies and credit allocation for investment. Both institutions would come to grips with a major consequence of long-term structural change in the economy — redistribution of national incomes among expanding and contracting industries and regions of the country, as well as internationally. Both sets of policy decisions, incomes policies and investment credits, would have to come to grips with questions of economic efficiency and equity. Using inputs of information and analysis from research on long-term structural change, policymakers would be able to develop operating standards for judging economic efficiency and equity in these areas of policy.

So much has been written about the wide range of possible incomes policies, that I do not want to elaborate here. We have only to resolve to do something and to act. The time seems to be right, given the weak state of the economy and the lack of inflationary pressures. Labor and management seem willing to cooperate, especially given the desperate economic condition of our basic industries. Labor has demonstrated its willingness to make concessions on wages and benefits; now management must demonstrate its ability to innovate and work creatively with labor to preserve domestic production, rather than move production abroad. But it is in the area of credit allocation where some significant weaknesses in the economic system can be corrected while we establish priorities for capital formation in the private sector, on infrastructure, and on government projects where high risk and huge financing needs discourage private commitments.

The energy sector of the 1970s is a perfect example of the failure of huge corporations to translate profits from oil price hikes into capital formation. The record shows one extraordinary failure after another. Huge sums have been squandered in massive mergers involving mainly oil and energy firms: In 1982 alone, the fifty biggest merger transactions totaled $48.2 billion, compared with $49.9 billion in 1981. (*Fortune*, January 24, 1983). The results have contributed virtually nothing to greater productivity growth, new technology, expanding markets, or new jobs. To the contrary, the surge of conglomeration tilts our economic structure even more dangerously in favor of the giants and their enhanced financial and political power (see Adams 1982).

The oil industry provides the best example at present. According to a recent report by Dr. Milton Lower (1981) to the House Oversight Subcommittee on Energy and Commerce, net income of the Fortune 500 companies *grew* by $19.6 billion between 1978 and 1980. Almost all of that growth—$19.2 billion—accrued to oil and gas enterprises among the 500. This constitutes an extraordinary redistribution of income from energy-consuming sectors of the economy to the petroleum industry. But how was the growth in cash flow used? Testimony before the House Oversight Subcommittee shows that the single largest allocation was made for *acquisitions* of other firms and investments outside petroleum—nearly two-fifths of the growth in cash flow and more than the total spent to find oil and gas in the United States and abroad. In 1981 alone, Gulf acquired Kemmerer Coal, Sohio bought Kennecott (copper), Occidental won Iowa Beef

Processors, and Chevron pursued AMAX. One could extend the list of acquisitions in recent years to include enterprises engaged in mining, chemicals, shipbuilding, containers, real estate, fertilizer, agriculture, life insurance, and department stores, among others.

If the oil company investments had enlarged oil supplies, the benefits would have been clear. But, to the contrary, the *Survey of Current Business* indicates U.S. output of crude petroleum remained virtually flat, even though the number of oil wells completed rose spectacularly from 19.4 thousand in 1979 to almost 27 thousand in 1980, to 37.6 thousand in 1981. Meanwhile, many of the non-oil acquisitions are widely judged by now to be failures on a huge scale: Exxon's purchase of Reliance Electric and its operations in minerals and office machines; Mobil's venture into Montgomery Ward; Gulf's nuclear operations and Sun's shipbuilding. Poor judgment and economic waste abound, but discipline of the market is apparently fended off by oil's sheer financial giantism.

The steel industry provides another example of misallocated capital funds which were derived at least partly from governmental policies such as the trigger price mechanism to restrain imports. The *Wall Street Journal* (December 7, 1981) asks "whether it is fair to make American steel users . . . pay 25 percent to 30 percent more for steel than their European and Japanese competitors."

This policy, which transferred income from the pockets of consumers of cars and appliances, and of builders and manufacturers using steel, to steel makers, was supposed to increase the steel industry's cash flow so that it could modernize its plants and equipment. But the evidence shows that steel companies are diverting these funds into investments in other industries — buying savings and loan institutions and oil properties. U.S. Steel's frantic competition with Mobil to buy Marathon Oil is the most dramatic example. Steel's cash hoard assembled for the campaign could have gone toward modernizing that company's facilities. In effect, ad hoc public policy is subsidizing the self-liquidation of the steel industry and a highly inefficient conglomeration of unrelated business activities.

The incredibly bad performance of the nation's "best" and biggest banks to mediate between savers and investors in an efficient and responsible way is the other part of the story that leads me to urge the formation of new development banks outside the commercial banking system. The loan exposure of the nine major U.S. banks to Mexico, Brazil, and Argentina is so concentrated that even Paul Volcker felt the need to inform the public officially of the potential dangers, in formal testimony before Congress (Volcker 1983). The structural shift of economic activity toward oil and energy since the oil shocks of the 1970s has tipped bank lending in the same direction, at the expense of non-oil, non-energy sectors of the economy, manufacturing, construction, and agriculture. The increasing concentration of banking and the narrowing focus on international activities have drained financial resources from localities and "peripheral" regions of the economy to the major financial institutions, which profit tremendously as "leaders" in international loan syndicates. In the process, bank regulators in the Federal Reserve, the Comptroller of the Currency, and FDIC have lost control of the situation. Where traditional "banker prudence" and market "discipline" have collapsed, government regulatory oversight has proved ineffectual on both international and domestic lending.

If the United States is to progress toward structural policies, we need to establish a system of financial intermediaries much like the development banks operating in many industrial and developing countries (see Mueller and Moore 1982). It could be a network of state or regional institutions with a national center for administration and research. Initial funding for such an institution would come from Congress, state governments, and private institutions, but like development banks in other countries, or international institutions, its operations could become self-financing through bond sales in domestic and international markets. In addition, co-financing with private institutions could add additional resources. Whether lending for new ventures or converting old industries to meet world competition, decisions should favor projects contributing most to enhanced productive efficiency.

V. Conclusion

This paper has rambled far and wide to support a central argument: The U.S. economy is staggering under the combined impact of several dynamic, structural transformations in a global economic system. The oil price revolution of the 1970s is simply the most obvious in the public mind. Yet, our policy-making apparatus and policymakers themselves are not equipped to respond to structural change. The theoretical underpinnings, the national data bases, and the institutions are still constrained by the strategies of countercyclical demand management and the mythologies of nineteenth-century capitalism, characterized by atomistic competition and self-corrective markets. Our policy responses to the oil price crisis demonstrate how a rigid adherence to conventional monetary and fiscal policy only worsened the economic instabilities. The impact of monetarism and supply-side fiscalism produced results as calamitous as the original oil-price disease. The way out of this mess is to find supplemental targeted strategies for economic policy that can deal with structural change and economic discontinuities. Structural or industrial policy, together with an incomes policy, provide some promising approaches, though probably not a panacea. How much self-destructive agony can a political democracy endure before it ventures to try an alternative?

Notes

1. The oil price revolution, the emergence of LDC manufacturers, global interdependence, and the altered environment for policy are discussed in some detail in Bartel 1980.
2. Data from U.S. Department of Commerce, *Survey of Current Business*, U.S. International Transactions, Table 3, December 1981, 1982; balance of payments basis, seasonally adjusted.

References

Adams, Walter, "MegaMergers Spell Danger," *Challenge*, March/April 1982, 25, 12–17.
Bartel, Richard D., "Dynamic Transformation of the World Economy: The U.S. Policy Response," an introductory essay to Volume 9 entitled *The International Economy: U.S. Role in a World Market* (December 17, 1980), published as part of a 10-volume study by the Joint Economic Committee's Special Study on Economic Change during 1978–80.
Bergsten, C. Fred, "International Debt, the U.S. Economy, and the International Monetary Fund," Statement before the House Banking, Finance and Urban Affairs Committee, February 9, 1983.
Cline, William R., "Reciprocity: A New Approach to World Trade Policy?" Institute for International Economics, No. 2, September 1982.
Economic Report of the President, 1982. Washington, 1982.
Feldman, Robert A., "Dollar Appreciation, Foreign Trade and the U.S. Economy," *Quarterly Review*, Federal Reserve Bank of New York, Summer 1982, 7, 1–9.
Keisky, Bruno, Chancellor of Austria, interviewed in *Challenge*, September/October 1982, 25, 31–35.

Lower, Milten, "The Changing Distribution of Industrial Profits: The Oil and Gas Industry Within the Fortune 500, 1978-80," Report of the Committee on Energy and Commerce, 97th Congress, 1st Session, Serial No. 7-W, December 11, 1981.

Muller, Ronald E. and Moore, David H., "America's Blind Spot: Industrial Policy," *Challenge*, January/February 1982, 24, 5–13.

Rostow, W.W., *The World Economy: History and Prospect*, London: Macmillan, 1978, Parts Three and Six; *Getting from Here to There*: London, Macmillan, 1979, Chapters 1, 2, 8, and 9; *Why the Poor Get Richer and the Rich Slow Down*, London: Macmillan, 1980, Chapters 1 and 2.

Tussing, Arlon R., "An OPEC Obituary," *The Public Interest*, Winter, 1983, No. 70, 3–21.

U.S. Department of Commerce, Bureau of Economic Analysis, *Survey of Current Business*, December 1982, 62.

Volcker, Paul A., Chairmen, Board of Governors of the Federal Reserve System, Statement before the Committee on Banking, Finance and Urban Affairs, House of Representatives, February 2, 1983.

PART II

Public and Private Roles in Policy

3

Lessons from Elsewhere

ROBERT A. SOLO

It has been an aspect of our national character, and not one wholly devoid of virtue and charm, to suppose without question that our America is the richest, the greatest, the most powerful, with the most freedom, the highest standard of life, where the sun rises and the world turns, hence that we have everything to teach to and nothing to learn from the foreigner. In reviewing a report of a 1976 Woods Hole conference by a distinguished panel of corporate, academic, and governmental elites set up to deal with a nasty turn of events in the trend of U.S. productivity (Solo 1979, 379), I called it "arrogant insularity."

> Except for a few casual references quoted in this review, no interest is shown in, no knowledge is made manifest of, there is not even a pretense of any systematic inquiry into the policies and experiences of those other countries that have so spectacularly outperformed the United States in recent decades. Surely something would have been learned through even a superficial consideration, for example, of the technology-related role of state planning and the control of corporate investment overseas as developed and practiced in Japan. Alas, there prevails instead, even in these days of decline, the arrogant insularity of the habitual victor thinking of himself without a peer, who has everything to teach and nothing to learn from others.

That was in 1976. Since then, certainly, there has been a change. With the continuing precipitous decline in America's technological standing (one can no longer say preeminence), and the mounting evidence and painful consequence of ideological bankruptcy, there has been a certain looking abroad for answers, clues, and alternatives; and for some, Japan has become a kind of Mecca. In this paper, too, we will be looking to the experiences of Japan.

It is to be expected, and in this regard this paper is no exception, that what we are looking for will influence what we find; and hence I would make quite explicit the presuppositions and the interest with which I have undertaken the search.

My interest is in the role of the state in modern capitalism. And I would argue that neither the laissez-faire state of neoclassical thought, nor the manipulative Keynesian state operating on the economy from the outside through gross monetary and fiscal leverage, is up to the tasks at hand; and that our failure to develop an appropriate instrument of collective choice and control is the consequence of values and an outlook (sometimes commendable values, but a quite archaic outlook) that belong to an earlier stage of our societal experience and development. We are hung up on a heritage of ideological liberalism. Our thought dwells with the images of man in the world of man: but we exist, we twist, grope, and stumble in the universe of systems.

I. The Universe of Systems

But haven't we always, you are entitled to ask, lived in a universe of systems—the life-death system of the organism, the physiochemical systems of the biosphere, the Neutonian harmonies of the solar system, the systems of the cosmos, the market itself. . . ?

We, indeed, have always lived in a universe of systems. The difference is this. There was a time that belonged to the world of man when those great systems were or could reasonably be regarded simply as parameters of individualized choice; when they were or reasonably could be taken as given, as a framework for the choice and interaction of individuals in that world of man. The market, for example, was always a great system surely, but there was no need in the world of man for the choice-maker to comprehend or to control it. It was or reasonably could be considered as self-directing, self-equilibrating, and beneficient.

It is no longer so. In the universe of systems, neither the systems of nature nor the systems of society are independent variables and parameters of individual choice. They cannot anymore be considered as self-equilibrating or inherently benign, or independent of what we do or beyond the reach of what can be done. They are that which must be chosen, they have become the prime subject of choice. And not of individual choice. In the universe of systems, choice itself is a complex process that belongs to the genre of organization. It is within and as part of organizations that the individual plays a role and occupies a niche

In the universe of systems, there is only one system, one organization among all the organizations that conceivably could be answerable to the whole, that conceivably could be made responsible for the well-being of the whole, that conceivably could possess the power or develop the competence to act positively upon and effectively to resolve the problems of great social and natural systems that are deteriorating, dangerous, or endangered, threatening cataclysm, on the edge of collapse, systems that depend upon what we do and upon which we absolutely depend. That system is the state. And that in our time, only within the domain of the nation. We are now without any instrument at all that could conceivably act responsibly and effectively upon systems and their problems transcending the nation.

I do not contend that the universe of systems is better or that it is worse than the world of man, but only that it is what now exists, and because it exists we need a positive state—that is, we need some instrument of collective choice able to deal actively and effectively with the vastly complex and critical problems of the whole.

If socialism must learn that one system cannot encompass the whole, capitalism must come to know that some system must be equipped to act positively upon the problems of the whole.

II. A Positive State: Japanese Experience

We need a positive state. We need a system of collective choice and action capable of dealing for the community, with the great problems that afflict us.

But how to create it? What are its organizational prerequisites? Its implications? Its dangers? Its limits? It is in this light, with these questions in mind, that we examine the Japanese experience. For, compared to all other advanced industrial capitalist societies, Japan has in this regard a distinct advantage. It entered our universe of systems without ever going through the stage of individualized choice in the world of man. It hasn't the hangups of ideological liberalism to overcome in adapting its sytem of collective choice to the existential realities of modern capitalism.

Here we will confine our discussion to the problems of the economy and to the role and record of the state vis à vis Japanese industry and the agency of the Japanese state geared to the formation and implementation of its industrial policy. (For factual data I have relied on Vogel 1980 and especially Johnson 1982, as well as my own experiences in Japan. The interpretation of the facts is my own.)

The Japanese educational system is terribly demanding, excruciatingly difficult, and ruthlessly selective. It competitively weeds out its student body to successively narrower echelons in a hierarchy of talent. At the top are the universities; among the universities, leading universities; among the leading universities, *the* leading university—the Tokyo Imperial University; within that university, elite of elites, is the Tokyo School of Law where, incidently, the training is not legalistic, but geared to the public service. Each year perhaps 50,000 top university graduates sit for the Higher-Level Public Officials Examination. Perhaps 1,000 pass, with the bulk of these from Tokyo University, and most of them from the School of Law. The ministries then select from among the eligible their new recruits. Approximately the top quarter of the Tokyo Law School graduates thus enter the government service. The others from the Tokyo School of Law go into prefectural governments, public corporations, banks, and businesses of all kinds where they are destined to play a leading role.

Each year a cohort of 15 to 25 are recruited to join the 500 or so higher level public officials in the Ministry of International Trade and Industry (MITI). That agency has a total employment of about 3,000 including lower level officials, who also are brought in through competitive examination and who occupy the niche of the specialist.

Suppose the cohort of the class of 1984. Each new recruit will form a relation of junior to senior with one of the cohort of 1983. Henceforth, the senior will play the role of patron, supporter, guide, and teacher. That senior is himself a junior in relation to his senior in the cohort of 1982 who is in turn a junior to. . . , etc. These vertical relationships remain throughout the official's career.

Each member of the new cohort is sent "around the track" from task to task, abroad and in Japan, in bureau after bureau, to acquire the capacity to comprehend and to deal with all the functions of the agency, and to create or cement relationships with others at the same level within the agency or with those outside of it with whom the agency must deal. Under the observation of their seniors, the cohort demonstrates their talents and capacities. Each of its members will be promoted by seniority, to attain after some 15–20 years of service, a position as section chief. Since beyond that level there are not enough higher positions to accommodate them all, the members of a cohort will, thenceforth, be selectively thinned out and retired.

The head of the agency, the vice minister, in established practice, names his own successor. When a member of a cohort is chosen to the post of vice minister, then all of his classmates and all earlier cohorts resign or are retired so that none in the agency will be senior to the new vice minister. Nor does the agency abandon its retirees who, as they say, in retiring "descend from heaven." Nor do those who retire sever their link with the agency. As a superbly trained elite of elites, conditioned to tasks of great responsibility at the nexus of politics and industry, they move with ease into politics (ex-officials dominate the Japanese Diet) or into key positions in the big companies, public corporations, banks, or universities, thus creating a network linked to the agency center.

Nor is the younger cohort's role one of subordination. Taking as axiomatic that the "new vision" belongs to the oncoming generations, MITI has at the center of its policy formation process "a unique institution" operating at the lowly assistant section chief level, "known as the Laws and Ordinances Examination Committee. It is composed of the deputy chiefs of the general affairs or coordination sections of all the bureaus throughout the ministry. There, at that level and in that committee all major policies of the ministry are introduced and no new policy can be initiated without its approval" (Johnson 1982, 82).

MITI's powers are very broad and the agency has its own revenue sources so that it is quite independent of the Ministry of Finance and the national budget. Its officials are indoctrinated in a samurai-like code of values—to dedicated service, discipline, austerity, an unlimited work commitment, pride and self-belief, and the sense that they (alone) bear the responsibility for the future of the nation, that they speak for the nation, and that it is for them to interpret and specify the national interest.

Aside from its far flung network of informal relationships, MITI reaches outside itself through the instrumentality of "deliberation councils." Starting with the Commerce and Industry Deliberation Council in 1927, antecedent to the Industrial Rationalization Council in the 1950s and to its successor the Industrial Structure Council in the 1970s, it has brought business leaders and academics together with the industrial bureaucrats to deliberate on the problems of the economy. Those councils are, it would seem, the sole instrument of citizen participation in the deliberated formulation of Japan's higher economic policy.

There are personal, factional, and ideological rivalries within MITI. Between the ministries there are jurisdictional rivalries and sometimes deep policy conflicts. Nor is there in Japan any instrument for inter-agency coordination or subordination to a common line.

Each ministry is or strives to be an autonomous, self-perpetuating, internally-bound group, so that the ministries as a whole constitute a cluster of such autonomous groups, interdependent and competitive, held together by shared tasks and responsibilities. It is in the relationship between ministry officials on the one hand and the Diet with the Prime Minister and the Cabinet on the other, that the very great distinction in Japan between authority and control is made most explicit; while authority resides in the Diet, control is firmly exercised by the ministry bureaucrats. The Diet reigns; the bureaucracies rule. The Diet is not a truly deliberative body. It has no independent staff. In the normal course of events all important legislation originates in, and is executed through, the bureaucracies.

This includes taxation, tariffs, and financial appropriations, with the Diet wielding the rubber stamp. The Diet legitimizes the work of the bureaucracy and shields it from external pressures. But the Diet also, in its composition and character, reflects the balance of interests and coalition of forces that are currently the working basis of the socio-political system, which the bureaucracy accepts and to which it accommodates. In rare but critical instances, when built-in bureaucratic imperatives conflict with the changing needs and values of society at large, as in the 1960s when the pains of pollution conflicted with the bureaucratic goals of rapid economic growth, the Diet can and has initiated new policy and the transformation of bureaucratic goals.

In another sense the Liberal Democratic Party (LDP) that dominates the Diet is also an autonomous, self-perpetuating group, dependent upon, but also competitive with the public bureaucracies. Sometimes the LDP attempts to infiltrate or control those bureaucracies through its exercise of ministerial authority. But attempts to "politicize" the ministries (as for example when the politically appointed minister who nominally leads MITI used his authority to appoint MITI's vice minister, rather than accepting the nomination of the retiring vice minister) are profoundly disturbing and, in the case of MITI, fiercely and successfully resisted.

It is the same pattern throughout Japan, of autonomous, self-perpetuating, internally-bound groups that are both functional instruments and long-standing communities, in a matrix where each is dependent upon and competitive with its counterparts.

In the economy, balanced against MITI are the powerful, rounded industrial communities called Zaibatsu, once bounded by a family's ownership and now each with a kind of mother bank at its center; each includes a trading company and a more or less complete set of those industries that have been targeted by MITI for support and growth, along with small subcontractors and servicing satellites. Historically, power has shifted back and forth between MITI and the Zaibatsu and to a significant degree the record of economic performance has depended on the balance of power between them.

Japan crossed the threshold of modernity directly from a millenia of feudalism, i.e., from a system of tightly bound, autonomous, self-perpetuating groups that were at once long-standing communities and functionally oriented organizations, wherein the individual occupied a niche that determined responsibilities and defined prerogatives. It was a universe of intensely competitive and combative groups, some rising to, some descending from positions of dominance, interacting under an imperial reign whose authority was as absolute and encompassing and whose rule was as distant as that of the Christian's God. Priorities, goals, expectations, and the nature of individual rights and prerogatives have certainly changed, but an essential continuity in the mode of social organization is too clear to require comment.

The objective of the Meiji restoration was to modernize Japan. It sought to do so initially by establishing governmentally controlled industries. In 1880 it changed its tack to the active promotion of private capitalism. To that end it sold off the industrial facilities it had created and offered support and subsidy to private enterprise. The beneficiaries of this change in policy were the big trading companies, the Zaibatsu who bought up, and with government support developed, these industrial properties.

In 1881, the Ministry of Agriculture and Commerce (MAC) was established; subsequently it set up and operated Yawata Steel Company. However, this ministry was primarily interested not in industry but in agriculture—appropriately enough in a country that was then primarily agricultural, where even its major export industry, silk textiles, was an agricultural offshoot. Therefore in 1925 it became the Ministry of Agriculture and Forestry, with its commerce side split off into a new Ministry of Commerce and Industry (MCI). The Tokyo Law School graduates entering the new MCI belonged to the first cohort to be recruited through competitive examination. That selfsame cohort would control MITI and the economy of Japan in the mid-1950s, having learned their craft on the job during the intervening years.

In 1927 the new MCI, in search of its role, convened a deliberation council that included all the leading businessmen and academics of the time, to chart with them its tasks and priorities for the future. The theme that emerged was one of rationalization: through cartels, through the promotion of scientific management, the provision of information as a basis for business choice, and the subsidized production of import substitutes. All this was institutionalized in agency organization and internalized in agency thinking.

In 1930 the depression began and the period of laissez-faire ended. As elsewhere, Japan's first response to depression was fiscal austerity and deflation, which augmented the disaster. The following year, 1931, saw distinct and decisive paths of policy development emerge. The Ministry of Finance, under Takakashi Korekiyo, pumped a stream of incremental (deficit based) spending into the sagging economy, to which might be credited Japan's extraordinary economic performance during that depression decade. From 1931 to 1939, production more than doubled.

In 1931 the MCI launched the two-pronged Yoshino-Kishi program focused on the promotion of heavy industry and on government enforced cartelization where Zaibatsu policy took on the force of law. This new regime of "industrial self-control" would shift the balance of power over the economy to those industrial empires, where it remained until after World War II, much to the later consternation of MCI officials.

In 1931 Japan invaded Manchuria and the military began its bid for supreme power, with a terrorizing series of political assassinations against which there appeared to be no recourse. The military pace accelerated in 1937, with the war against China. This so-called China Incident was coupled with the mobilization of industry in preparation for a wider conflict. MCI officials were now the workhorses of the regime. Sent to Manchuko, they initiated, planned, and managed the building of great hydro-power dams, transmission lines, and a new aluminum industry in Manchuria. With the North East Development Company they managed a TVA-like regional development project and attached to successive economic "general staffs," they did the military's nitty gritty. They staffed the Cabinet Central Planning Board which was merged with the MCI in 1943 to become the Ministry of Munitions (MM). MCI or MM had among its tasks the control of stockpiles, the control of prices in strategic industries, the establishment of a synthetic petroleum industry, the accelerated development of strategic industries generally, and the control of resource imports and materials allocation. Under the 1938 Mobilization Laws, which were nominally a blank check for total economic control, MM was charged with converting *all* peacetime industries to the production of munitions. Partly to escape the self-control power of the Zaibatsu, it established and operated a series of public corporations.

By 1940, most MCI officials belonged to the party of "reform bureaucrats," allied to a military faction in advocating the New Economic Structure, which would integrate Japan, Manchuria, and China into something approximating Hitler's plan for a New Order in Europe, state-controlled, managed by professionals, doling out limited dividends and "profits," as a kind of pension to a displaced ownership.

Whatever their nominal authority, whatever the magnitude of their responsibility, whatever the depth of their acquired knowledge and the great complexity and difficulty and variety of the tasks to which they were assigned, real control did not reside with MCI officials. They were crushed between and subordinated to the inexpert but overwhelming power of the military and to the interests of an ownership that firmly maintained "self-control" over industrial operations, frustrating attempts at effective coordination.

After the Japanese surrender, and before the allies had taken over, MM vanished and, in its place, MCI, purged of military officers, reappeared. The policies and the ups and downs of economic performance during the American occupation need not concern us, save for their impact on that agency.

The army and the Zaibatsu had dominated the economy during the years of mobilization and war. The American occupiers dismantled and displaced both; but MCI, with the great power it had nominally acquired as the MM, was left intact. With its rivals eliminated and its powers no longer nominal, no wonder MITI bureaucrats look back to the time of the occupation as their "Golden Years." When the occupation ended, the American authorities turned their total control over imports and exports to the Board of Trade, which was merged with MCI to become the Ministry of International Trade and Industry (MITI). In 1952, by the end of the seven years of occupation, Japan had reattained its 1936 level of production; and with the Americans gone, MITI was at last in an unchallenged position to direct (or guide) Japan's industrial future. What followed was certainly the most spectacularly successful economic performance in recorded history. MITI was at the helm. It allocated resource imports, capital funding, and external loans, controlled the import of foreign technology, and jealously protected every part of Japanese industry from any foreign domination. Through its Industry Rationalization Council it formulated and, with suggestions that no private company could afford to ignore, achieved fundamental management reforms, as for example in the adoption of policies of life-long employment, wage and promotion standards, systematic employee training programs, and quality control

MITI also resurrected the rounded industrial communities of the Zaibatsu, now, however, rid of control by ownership, with professional managers of the stripe of MITI bureaucrats in charge. "Through its licensing powers and its preferential financing, it winnowed the approximately 2,800 trading companies down to twenty big ones, each serving a bank-centered *Keiretsu* or a cartel of smaller producers, with unaffiliated enterprise assigned to a particular trading company" (Johnson 1982, 206). To further facilitate exports, and to supply the requisite intelligence concerning foreign markets, MITI established the Japanese External Trade Organization with operations in 55 countries.

Japanese industry was financed through overloans by banks, one at the center of each industrial community, which, in turn, relied on overloans by the Bank of Japan and the Japanese Development Bank. Loan applications were screened by MITI with lending directed to targeted industries in a scheduled stage by stage development of the Japanese industrial structure. In each instance, this led to Japanese technological preeminence in the targeted sector: from the stage of light, labor-intensive industries to that of petro-chemicals and steel, automobiles, digitally controlled machine tools and ships, electronics, robots and computers, resource-conserving and non-polluting technologies for the medical and educational sectors. MITI always planned and provided a specifically tailored infrastructure and R & D support for each targeted development.

With the rising wealth and financial independence of Japanese enterprise, and with international demands for the liberalization of Japanese trade and investment, MITI's preemptive powers have diminished. Its influence in the role of "administrative guidance" has become less direct and more equivocal. In any case, the record stands.

In two short decades all-industry production increased by 1200 percent, and manufacturing by 1300 percent. An oil crisis that struck Japan more brutally than any other country was transcended with Japan rising to new industrial heights. In response to popular demand MITI shifted its priorities and achieved a remarkable cleanup of the polluted environment. A revolutionary relocation of a population and an industry now densely concentrated in a narrow coastal plain seems in the offing.

III. Lessons

What can we learn from all this? Something certainly concerning the character and potentials of organizations. In the Japanese model the organization should be developed both as community and as polity, not as the private domain of "the boss," nor simply as a functional instrument. *Qua* community it should serve as a basis for secure, cooperative, interpersonal relationships and a satisfying way of life, offering the opportunity for individual self-fulfillment and an outlet for collective purpose and dedication. *Qua* polity it should open itself to universal participation in the formation of policy, seeking consensus; and, to renew its "vision," it should look for and systematically open channels to the creative imagination of youth.

In these terms can be understood the practice of Japanese business enterprise (as well as public agencies) in offering, *qua* community: lifetime employment, where status and salary are functions of seniority, and task and responsibility are functions of talent; bonuses to cover up to half an employee's income, thus relating employee reward to company success and enabling the enterprise to survive intact as a community in the face of fluctuating demand; and botton-to-top processes for policy formation.

Evolved organizations appears as *the* critical social resource. More important than the costs of what the organization produces is the cost of producing the organization. The value of an organization is in the skills and capacities it has acquired, the solidarity and communication capabilities it has developed, the information it has accumulated, and the knowledge it has internalized and institutionalized. All these are the product of organizational learning, which above all means learning through doing. To learn and to retain what has been learned requires continuity, continuity of organization and a cooperative teaching-learning relationship between those who enter and those who are there.

Japanese experience demonstrates certainly the potential of the positive state in the universe of systems, and the lacuna that exists without it. It demonstrates as well that this is not a role for *any* state or for *any* agency of the state. An organization is required that is honed to the tasks, capable of independent initiatives, with a significant degree of autonomy in the formation of policy and in the choice of strategy, with a competence at least as great and a relevant knowledge at least as profound as that of those who control the organizational entities to which its powers relate. The managerial competence of MITI officials is at least as great as that of the management of their banking or business clients, and MITI knowledge of industries is at least as great as that of the industrialists. It demonstrates that the relationship between such an agency of the positive state and the organizational entities to which its powers relate, is generally symbiotic. Thus, the commitment of MITI officials to industrial peace, stability, and development – and the exercise of their high competence and sophisticated understanding in the planning of infrastructures, in extending and directing financial aid and support – are all enormously valuable to Japanese enterprise. Nor could MITI achieve its objectives without the efficiency and dynamism of Japanese business. Sometimes, nevertheless, the relationships between the two will be conflictual – there is no inherently stable balance of power between them. What the balance of power ought properly to be remains perforce a subject of political judgment and "eternal vigilance."

What is implicit is a system of dual management, each level vectored to a different set of tasks and responsibilities, each answerable to a different set of clients; *private management* answerable for financial integrity, effective organization, high productivity, consensus, morale, recruitment and training, income distribution at the micro level in the specificity of operations, and answerable to those who constitute the organization and who seek to survive and prosper as a part of it; *public management* answerable for industrial structure in its evolution and development, infrastructural supports, technological advance and economic growth, distributional equity at the macro level, full employment, price stability, resource conservation and the availability of alternatives to depleting resources, non-discriminatory opportunity, and environmental protection. In short, management answerable, through the political system of representation and surveillance, to society at large. A perennial problem will be to develop the relationship between these two levels of management so that each is autonomous and able to perform effectively its essential task and fulfill the critical responsibilities of its domain. The problem of balance and coordination will be less to the degree that there is an awareness of mutual interdependence. Japanese industry owes its prosperity, often its existence, to the initiatives, the effort, the competence, the protection afforded and support forthcoming from MITI. MITI could not have achieved its purposes without an independent, efficient, dynamic, industrial *cum* business community in Japan.

IV. The State of Our State

What of ourselves and our system of collective choice and action? What is the state of our state? Most of the critical functions of the American state are scattered over the land in the autonomous entities of local government (78 thousand in 1976, 65 thousand with tax powers), allegedly close to the people, but totally lacking any organizational rationale, impossible of coordination, without the capacity to conceive, comprehend, or act coherently in this universe of systems in respect to that which concerns the whole.

We do have at the federal level a powerful system of popular representation and surveillance that Japan lacks. But our Congress, alas, is not a body designed to do anything. By Constitutional intent it was designed *not* to do anything. Given the tenure and the tasks and the professional backgrounds of its members, it is quite unable to comprehend or control or to act constructively upon the structure and performance of industry, of the economy, of the complex systems of education, defense, transportation, energy, communication, health, etc. Given the incredibly high cost of campaigning and the institutionalized means of bringing money into the political tills, increasingly the weight of the dollar overbalances the power of the vote in determining what our Congress represents and to whom it answers.

Aside from military officers, diplomats, and the judiciary, the haphazardly selected civilian bureaucrats are offered neither responsibility, security, nor honor. Their service is ceaselessly denigrated. They are subordinated to a stream of defunct politicians and second-level executives borrowed from business—alike quick in-and-outers who occupy all the seats of power. Few of the able and dedicated who come into our public service remain or are allowed to remain. Those who survive and prosper are the timid and mediocre, clerks and super-clerks, wise in the way of the turtle who has learned never to stick its neck out.

The administrative policy-making echelons are devoid of career professionals, devoid of those who, like MITI officials, combine a mastery of industry (or of science, or of technology, or of the economy) with an intimate knowledge of the problem of the whole, who are sensitized to social priorities and understand the processes of collective choice and policy implementation.

The American state as presently constituted and manned is not capable of acting positively upon the structure of the economy or of comprehending and controlling the systems of our society.

References

Johnson, Chalmers, *MITI and the Japanese Miracle*, Stanford: Stanford University Press, 1982.

Solo, Robert, "The Dilemmas of Technology: A Review Article," *Journal of Economic Issues*, September 1979, 13, 733–42.

Vogel, Ezra, *Japan as Number 1: Lessons for America*, New York: Harper Colophon Books, 1980.

4

Economic Change, Bureaucracy, and the Innovative Process[1]

LEONARD A. RAPPING

The United States economy finds itself in worsening difficulties. Economic restructuring is clearly needed. This set of tasks is made more complex by resource scarcity, loss of American world position, inflexible government and corporate bureaucracies, and growing economic and social inequality. The basic economic problems of this era are structural, not cyclical, and in that sense they are not unlike those of the twenty-year crisis between the two Great Wars. Both excessive unemployment and economic stagnation have resulted from changes in the composition of demand, technology, relative prices, and international competitiveness. A viable national economic program must assist in adapting to the long-run changes in the price of oil, grain, and other resources; it must facilitate adjustment to the new international economic, military, and political situation; it must aid in adjusting to a new and less dominant role for America in the world economy, it must accommodate the replacement of old and obsolete plants; it must stimulate innovation and technology; and it must support the development of a new and less energy-intensive life-style. Each of these tasks is difficult. Each requires that important institutions—government, corporations, communities, schools, families—adapt and change. This essay is concerned with the prospects for changes in only one of these institutions, the American corporation.

As described over fifty years ago by Adolf Berle and Gardner Means (1932), production and distribution are primarily organized by large-scale corporate bureaucracies. These hierarchical social systems are coordinated internally by authority relationships which are more or less constrained by market realities. These institutions interact among themselves and with other institutions and individuals in a market context. Market exchanges are governed by both pecuniary and social considerations. It is in monopolized markets where social factors—e.g., friendship, visual familiarity, and social class—receive the greatest weight. However, even in competitive markets the social parameters of exchange are crucial. Trust and confidence are often as important as the "bottom line" in initiating market behavior.

If there is to be change, it is necessary that these bureaucracies are both motivated to act and capable of acting intelligently. Moreover it is necesary that their actions be coordinated through the market system in a tolerably efficient manner. To encourage investment and innovation, national economic policy must manipulate those factors in the external environment which influence these institutions, and/or it must eliminate internal organizational arrangements which block innovation and change. It is in this light that one might consider such matters as monetarism, supply-side economics, and industrial policy.

I. Monetarism, Supply-Side Economics, and Industrial Policy

Monetarism, the policy of sound money, has in recent years been afforded considerable attention. By accommodating to a market-induced restriction of credit or initiating the restriction of credit, the Central Bank attempts to cope with the speculative excesses of an overexuberant expansion. Slack demand creates unemployment and excess capacity. There results a struggle for financial survival which is assumed to rekindle the old virtues of frugality, hard work, and self-discipline. The weak are eliminated. The strong survive. Corporations and other social systems, not unlike individuals, are also coerced in this process. Confronted with excess capacity and declining markets, these institutions are expected to eliminate waste and inefficiency, to reorganize the decision-making process, and to proceed forward. Otherwise they will fail. The idea underlying this Darwinian process is summarized best in the motto of a 1930s advertising executive, "Progress Through Adversity." Of course in this approach to restructuring corporate and other institutions in society, financial panic and collapse are ever-present risks. Individuals and families might be immobilized by adversity. And the corporation as a social system might disintegrate, not restructure, under adversity. Excessive executive compensation—million dollar parachute clauses in the event of corporate takeovers is a case in point—white collar crime, creative accounting, unproductive merger activity, and the hard sell of shoddy products are all instances of social disintegration, not resurrection.

Moreover, at a time when there is excessive corporate, consumer, and government debt—not to mention Third World international debt—market contraction can trigger financial panic as cash flow problems develop. The financial authorities must walk a tightrope between their tight money efforts and their lender-of-last-resort responsibilities. At present, the outcome of this risky balancing act remains uncertain although the prospects for success are not encouraging.

Supply-side economics, which in its excessive tax-cutting incarnation during the early months of the Republican administration is now discredited as only a shameless raid on the public treasury, can in other guises be interpreted charitably as an incentive economic program based on the belief that corporations are structurally sound, that they are capable of effective long-run decision making and that through the unfettered market process they would respond appropriately and in a coordinated fashion to pecuniary incentives. They would eliminate waste, invest in new techniques, discover new processes, products, and markets, and create jobs and prosperity.

Since January 1981 when the new Republican administration was inaugurated, an executive and legislative effort has been made to "let the juices of capitalism flow." To initiate economic growth under corporate auspices, corporate taxes were cut, tax relief was given to those of means, and other tax arrangements that allegedly would create the necessary incentives for capital accumulation and economic growth were introduced. These tax proposals are, in fact, the basis of the administration's "supply-side economics," a new term for that not-so-new idea that when an economy has obsolete plant, machinery, and techniques, it must be reindustrialized—a concept used by those who think that old-style industrialization has a future—or rebuilt—a concept used by those who are willing to entertain the possibility of the need for a new direction. Their tax plan was combined in policy with proposals to roll back public efforts at protecting the environment and workplace, to eliminate many government jobs, to continue cutting public relief, to contain social security, to weaken unions, and to lower the minimum wage. Together, these policies made up what can be viewed as a proposed return to the social and economic conditions which prevailed in the years after the American Civil War, suggesting a willingness to reintroduce the harsh arrangements under which America was rapidly industrialized under robber baron generalship.

The administration's plan did not augur well for blacks locked in urban ghettos who are desperately in need of jobs; nor did it offer hope for workers in the industrial Midwest in need of extended unemployment benefits; nor was it reason for optimism on the part of those living in the decaying cities of the North; nor did it inspire the army of the generally disadvantaged. It has been painful for these groups to wait and see whether the coporations would use their newly-found tax bonanza to accumulate capital and provide jobs or whether they would simply absorb the tax relief in wasteful consumption, high salaries, corporate mergers, and other un-productive activities.

History's verdict on the recent incarnation of supply-side economics seems inevitable. Even if the element of greed and indiscretion in the 1981 tax cuts is ignored, it was a program that failed to take account of the basic unsoundness of the current corporate bureaucratic structure and that failed to recognize the difficulties of an unregulated market system to effectively coordinate independent decision-making units.[2]

There are some who believe that change can be based on a national economic policy which achieves consensus and broad support. Support and consensus will be facilitated by a program which promises a fair alloca-tion of the potential gains from economic stabilization and a not-too-uneven distribution of the discomfort which will inevitably accompany the retrenchment, readjustment, and reinvestment necessary to develop a new economic and social foundation for prosperity. Proponents of this view sometimes organize under the term "industrial policy," a generic term call-ing for both public regulation and direction of market processes.[3] Although proponents of this approach are not always sanguine about internal cor-porate decision-making capability, to date they have not chosen to deal directly with this problem. Industrial policy represents an effort to support financially potentially growing sectors, to coordinate corporate decision making, and to ease social and economic adjustments in declining indus-tries. To only a limited extent is it an effort at parliamentary participation in internal corporate decision-making processes. In this approach, the government is necessary to reduce uncertainty which can paralyze decision makers, to introduce an element of fairness into the adjustment process so as to minimize potential opposition to changes, and to protect the public against corporate decisions which calculate only private, not public net advantage.

II. The Structural Roots of Economic Stagnation

An economic recovery program must be based on a theory—or even perhaps an idea or an inkling—concerning the causes of economic stagna-tion. There is no simple explanation for economic failure. Karl Marx argued that labor power was crucial to production. When labor was scarce, an economy would stagnate. But surely this is not the problem in an economy where millions of black workers stand idle in the cities of the Northeast and Midwest, where the unemployed in the industrial heartland wait in long lines for their relief checks, and where millions of Latin American workers stream into the cities in the Southwest and West and along the Eastern seaboard.

David Ricardo argued that scarce resources— in his day land, in ours oil, grain, and other raw materials—set limits to growth, thereby inducing economic conflict as owners of the scarce resources appropriate an increasing share of the social product. This theory has some current relevance. Since the early 1970s, the prices of grain, oil, and other raw materials have skyrocketed. In part, these rises were caused by a combination of concentrated monopoly power in the southwestern United States and in the Middle East, along with the exhaustion of the earth's crust. These events have intensified conflict in the United States and around the world. Inflation is the monetary manifestation of this conflict. The resolution to the resource problem is usually sought in technology—meaning knowledge—and in innovation—meaning the application of knowledge—both of which can help in conserving scarce resources and in developing new energy sources. But it is a forlorn hope that immensely profitable energy conglomerates will find significant oil reserves in the United States, which has, after all, already been extensively explored.

Economic stagnation is sometimes seen as a failure of technology. In the 1930s it was popular to argue that innovative waves or technological revolutions were the forces behind long-term economic expansion. In this view, the innovation and innovator are crucial. Steam power in the early 1800s, railroads in the middle and late 1800s, and electric power and the automobile in the 1920s were all instances of technology-driven expansions. Similar views were not uncommon among American economists in the years after World War II, when economic survival was viewed as very much dependent on wits and common sense as embodied in science and technology.

One must concede that science and technology have postponed the gruesome biological tragedy anticipated by Reverend Malthus. But they have also given birth to nuclear bombs, launching the possibility of an equally gruesome nuclear tragedy. Despite this contradictory development, many American economists remain technological optimists and place great stress on technology as a source of growth and prosperity. While they stress the productivity-enhancing effects of machine-embodied innovations like the oxygen furnace, the diesel locomotive, the electronic computer, and the jet engine, they also recognize that the visual concreteness of these technical innovations sometimes inappropriately rivets our attention on the machine rather than the social organization of production and the motivation of the individual.[4] On reflection, one cannot help but appreciate the productivity-enhancing importance of such organizational and intellectual innovations as the multidivisional firm of the 1920s as described by Alfred Chandler, the rationalization of work and the "scientific management"

movement as conceived by Frederick Taylor, the social convention of using money and credit to circulate commodities and to store wealth as
analyzed so brilliantly by John Maynard Keynes, the assumption by Herbert Simon in the field of artificial intelligence that thought processes can
be simulated on a computer, and the remarkable effort by Sigmund Freud
to think rationally about the irrational.

III. The Post-World War II Prosperity

At the end of World War II the metalworking capacity of the United
States was globally dominant; this capacity helped sustain subsequent economic growth. The automobile and the continued "tractorization" of farming were the technological foundations of the economy. It is estimated that
15 percent of the work force was directly or indirectly employed by the
automobile industry. Over 60 percent of post-World War II investment
was in road building, suburbanization, and electrification, much of which
was automobile-related. While there were new technologies—the computer, the jet, and nuclear power—it was mainly the automobile, powered
by cheap fuel, which drove the economy. While we must stress the technological base of the post-war prosperity, it would be narrow-minded to
ignore cheap energy as well as supportive social arrangements, of which
the domestic "Social Contract" and the stable international monetary and
commercial order that existed between 1945 and 1971 were most promi-
nent and important.

The metalworking and agricultural sectors of the American economy
were at this time very productive. In agriculture, manufacturing, mining,
and transportation, productivity advanced as oil-intensive machine power
replaced people power. The surplus from these sectors supported expanded
service and government sectors. White-collar employment in both the
government and corporate bureaucracies grew rapidly. Service sector
employment in such industries as eating and drinking places, banks, and
insurance companies also expanded. The national income accounting myth
developed that these activities were always productive in some meaningful
sense. Certainly some white-collar work is productive. Certainly some service work is productive. But their productivity can be overstated. Employment (and profits) in these activities was an ingenious social arrangement
for distributing the bounty from the goods-producing sector among the
people. In a society inclined towards a Protestant work ethic, no other
device was likely to have worked to avoid the social disorder and chaos
which would inevitably have accompanied "jobless growth."

While recognizing the importance of cheap raw materials, domestic
social cohesion, and international monetary and commercial order, some

basis remains for a "waves of innovation" interpretation of post-World War II prosperity. Yet considerably less clarity is found with regard to potential innovations which might serve as the basis of still another expansion. The modern electronics industry, propelled by microelectronic developments making computers faster, cheaper, and more flexible, is sometimes mentioned as the technical base for a new expansion. In this scenario, word processors and other office equipment cause a major revolution in office efficiency; robotics cause a major revolution in factory efficiency; and a variety of telecommunication developments enhance the potential for greater energy efficiency as the movement of messages by transportation vehicles is replaced by electronic communication. If these and other technologies are developed and introduced, if they significantly assist in conserving energy resources, if they stimulate further innovation and discovery, then perhaps they might be the basis of another long expansion. One hopes that such an expansion would be distinguished by full employment and energy conservation.

IV. The End of the Post-World War II Boom

The long post-World War II expansion ended sometime in the early 1970s. Its conclusion necessitated the reconstruction and reorientation of the economy; but no consensus was reached on how to conserve and develop energy and other resources, restructure the lifestyle, or relate to an emerging world situation attendant upon the end of the American System, or, in general, on how to proceed or where to go. There were many possible paths. For example: synfuels, solar or coal; small cars, mass transit or recentralization; meat or vegetable protein sources; regional trading blocks and more limited currency areas than developed after World War II. Pursuing any one or several of these options involved great risks and uncertain results. Organizing the society to restructure the profligate way of life and to pursue new technologies consistent with the increasing scarcity of raw materials and grain, as well as the new international military and political situation, proved impossible.

The Carter administration lacked the political power to recast and redirect the economy. Such an effort would have entailed confronting a dark and cloudy economic future with honesty and optimism. This could be done only if the society had confidence in itself and its future. Without such confidence the political coalition necessary to embark on such an uncertain project could not be formed. Lacking sufficient political support, the Carter administration exercized the only politically feasible option: it finessed the problem by importing large amounts of oil and expanding credit. A mini-boom on the old consumption model followed. The 1976–1979 American expansion supported a large part of a world economy that was dependent on American consumption spending for markets. One must appreciate that the Carter administration, by bolstering the United States and world economies, probably averted an economic calamity in the latter part of the 1970s. Indeed, in an important sense American economic policy over the entire decade of the 1970s was a success in the sense that it might have prevented—but at least delayed—a second Great Depression.

V. The New Republican Administration

Following the 1980 elections, the new administration embarked on a new economic program. By tax cutting and other fiscal means, this administration wanted to increase the potential after-tax profitability of acquiring financial and physical assets. Presumably its members thought these tax cuts would stimulate innovation, facilitate the replacement of old and obsolete plant and equipment, encourage the development and extension of new forward-looking industries, and promote the training and retraining of workers. In time—so the argument went—the standard of living would improve.

The hypothesis that underlies this effort was that if profits are so extraordinary that the gains to risk-takers are wealth, power, and prestige, then men and women of entrepreneurial cunning will innovate, create, and solve the economic problems of our era. But production is organized largely by highly bureaucratic corporations; even entrepreneurs of enormous creativity and imagination would find it necessary to express and implement their ideas and plans in corporate offices and boardrooms. There they would be subjected to the customs, habits, and traditions of the American corporate bureaucracy. In these bureaucracies, individuality is suppressed.[5]

The administration's economic program presumed that these institutions suffer neither from sclerosis nor from bureaucratic shortsightedness. It also presumed that they are better long-run planning instruments than federal bureaucracies. Unfortunately, American corporate bureaucracies, like their government counterparts, are in need of important restructuring before they can deliver us from our current economic predicament. In their current condition and frame of mind, increasing their retained earnings by tax cuts simply encouraged excessive executive compensation and corporate takeovers, mergers, and acquisitions, rather than the innovation and creativity needed to develop new and useful products, new production techniques, and new ideas on conserving energy and other scarce resources.

VI. Managing in Times of Scarcity

Over the past hundred years the expanding American economy has benefited from a variety of fortunate geographic, geological, and political circumstances. Until recently it had abundant and cheap energy—first wood, then coal, then oil. It enjoyed abundant and cheap grain, due largely to a fortunate geographic situation in which the Great Plains normally receive sufficient sunlight and water. First it had the West as a frontier and safety valve for excess population; then it had the globe as a frontier and as a source of both markets and raw materials. American economic growth was fashioned in a psychological and physical environment of never-ending supply. Except in the years after World War II when circumstances were temporarily favorable, these opportunities were protected for American business by tariff policy. The skills necessary to exploit these frontiers and opportunities in an era of plenty are different from the skills necessary to survive in a world in which the global frontiers are contracting, in which the rule is scarcity rather than abundance, and in which competition has greatly increased.

In an environment of plenty, Americans have glorified efforts at personal economic success. Reflecting this national sentiment, American management has historically been pragmatic and rational in pursuing its economic objectives. Relatively unfettered by custom, tradition, and sentimentality, it has been instrumental, experimental, and willing to take risks. In an environment of abundance, this risk-taking has often yielded handsome returns. However, under current circumstances the payoffs may well be smaller than they used to be. Unless managerial attitudes and values are changed, unless the quest for excessive profits is tempered, these declining payoffs will discourage risk-taking.

With the cost of bearing risk unchanged and with the benefits reduced, American management has had its already greatly weakened enthusiasm for long-run—which of course means risky—decisions reduced even further. They have been encouraged by a more competitive and difficult environment to seek pecuniary advantage in finance and marketing rather than in production. This is not a promising development, especially when an economy must be restructured—an inherently risky task. Tax cutting and other fiscal stimuli will not, indeed cannot, compensate either for the increasing difficulty of extracting resources from the earth's crust coupled with OPEC's monopoly power or for a contracting global frontier.

VII. Developing Bureaucracies

Aside from management's attitude toward risk and the reduced prospects for large returns to risk-bearing, there are other reasons to question whether American management is adequately organized to meet the current challenge of economic restructuring. The long post-World War II expansion submerged the individuality, initiative, and discretion of many managers into corporate and government bureaucracies. These bureau-cracies developed as a rational response to the problems of managing a global system.

Bureaucracy is a useful way of utilizing human skills in the imperfect form in which they exist. When an organization's objectives are stable and clearly defined, when the means of success are well understood, and when the future is seen as little more than an extrapolation of the past, bureaucracy is a useful organizational arrangement for routinizing problem-solving and minimizing the need for discretion and initiative. Even change itself is sometimes programmed. In bureaucratic organizations, efficiency, change, and continued success are possible provided the problems of to-morrow will not be too dissimilar from the problems of today. But when the environment changes significantly, as it has in recent years, bureau-cracies bound by fixed routines and encrusted interests are sometimes in-capable of responding to new challenges.[6] In this event, they become dys-functional. This point was made by Peter Drucker (1980) who argues that in "predictable times" fundamentals can be ignored but in "turbulent times" they must be managed.

In the post-World War II years two bureaucracies developed in the United States. Federal government departments and bureaus multiplied, while corporate divisions, branches, and subsidiaries proliferated at home and abroad. Bureaucratization increased as efforts were made to rationalize both corporate and federal government structures. The business schools were important vehicles for training the corporate managers, while schools of public administration grew up to rationalize the public bureaucracies. Management techniques and ideas were exchanged between these bureau-cracies, on both a formal and informal basis. This occurred by the inter-change of administrators between public and private institutions and by numerous joint public-private ventures, the Apollo program being one of the more successful. Shared ideology, shared educational experience, shared world views, and shared interests bound these bureaucracies together in thought and deed.

The similarities in experience and organization between public and private bureaucracies would lead to some doubt as to whether it is ap-propriate to describe free enterprise as flexible, enterprising, motivated, and pragmatic, while describing government as apathetic, discouraged, im-practical, and tired. Perhaps these adjectives seem appropriate when one compares, say, IBM to some of the tired and besieged state governments on the Eastern seaboard. But they are not especially appropriate when comparing Metropolitan Edison, Chrysler, Lockheed, the old Penn Cen-tral, or the Penn Square Bank to such successful federal agencies as the pre-Reagan Environmental Protection Agency or the National Institute of Health.

Economists of conservative or New Right persuasion sometimes suggest that the difference between private and public bureaucracies is the profit motive, which incites private seekers of pecuniary success to efforts and achievements unparalleled by their public counterparts. But with environmental and workplace pollution—what economists call externalities—current prices which determine profits are no longer reliable guides. Moreover an uncertain future makes future prices, which also determine profits, uncertain and in principle unknowable. Consequently, current or prospective accounting profits can no longer guide the investment process in an efficient and socially beneficial way. Corporate bureaucracies can and do make decisions; but there should be no presumption that these decisions are in some different efficiency domain from the decisions of government bureaucracies. Nor can it be convincingly argued that the relative efficiency of private as compared to public bureaucracies is that those private bureaucracies which do not meet the market test will be eliminated by bankruptcy and failure while the strong (i.e., efficient) will survive. With the economy dominated by large corporations interlocked with other corporations in product markets in which they are borrowers from and lenders to each other, large corporate failures are almost impossible. And these failures are not allowed for good reason. In these unstable times, a series of failures could reverberate through product and financial markets, causing other failures and perhaps financial panic. Even in earlier years, when the potential for interlocking disaster was considerably smaller, large corporations rarely failed. Rigorous market tests of efficiency simply do not apply to the modern corporation.

VIII. The Quantitative World View

The professionalization of the corporate and federal government managerial class was achieved through formal schooling in which modern management techniques played an important role. These techniques were taught in an effort to introduce the scientific method—or to use a less formal phrase, "straight thinking"—into the training of managers. Herbert Simon (1977), in discussing this development, points out that such professionalization of management was simply an extension of the scientific management movement of Frederick Taylor. In addition, because of World War II development of both operations research and the modern electronic computer, modern management training was enmeshed in quantitative techniques to a greater extent than earlier. A similar explosion of mathematical technique occurred in other areas like economics. In management training a variety of quantitative methods were introduced—linear and dynamic programming, probability models, inventory, marketing and production models, economic discounting, marginal and cost-benefit analysis. In increasing numbers, the modern middle level manager was imbued with a quantitative world view (or if not imbued, at least firmly pointed in that direction).

This quantitative view has its place and purpose. It is a useful guide to solving problems which are amenable to a programmed resolution. In this approach there is required a careful definition of purposes or ends, what economists and mathematicians call the objective function, the arguments of which are usually quantified by attaching dollar magnitudes to possible outcomes. It also requires mathematical abstraction to build a model of the system under investigation, one which captures enough of reality to be useful. It then requires parameter estimates for the model. This necessitates a reasonably stable environment because the past is usually used as a guide to parameter values in the future.

But, the quantitative vision has certain weaknesses. Too frequently, numbers are made a fetish, and qualitative information and informed judgment are erroneously ignored. There are many examples of numbers blinding the observers. In the 1970s many economic indicators—the Consumer Price Index, census counts, corporate profits, and income itself—lost their usefulness as inflation made obsolete the index weights, as undocumented migrant flows invalidated the population counts, as inflation and the internationalization of business contaminated estimates of corporate profits, and as the underground economy left much of the national income unreported. Despite this undermining of the statistical intelligence system, economic data continued to be reported and interpreted with sanctimonious reverence.

The preceding examples can be easily expanded in number, but for present purposes only one more example is important. A quantitative approach to business decision making leads naturally, although not necessarily, to excessive attention to measurable short-term accounting profits. Along these lines, some suggest that the problem of American corporate decision making is that it maximizes short-run not long-run, profitability. According to this critique, too much attention is given to measurable, immediate returns, to instant gratification, while too little attention is given to the uncertain and distant future. There is some basis for this contention. Too much of American managerial talent has been devoted to exploiting existing markets by manipulative marketing strategies, to corporate portfolio management which uses techniques designed to make money with money, and to the development of merger and other takeover strategies. Far too little energy has been devoted to production problems and process development, R & D, and strategic planning. In the words of Robert Hayes and

William Abernathy, both of Harvard's Business School, "The conclusion is powerful but must be faced . . . They [American managers] have abdicated their strategic responsibilities" (1980, 70).

The effectiveness of quantitative decision making for long-run choices has been lessened because the time horizon over which measurement is feasible has contracted. Now only the present and not-too-distant future are subject to numerical description. This state of affairs has resulted from many developments which have disrupted confidence in the future and weakened or destroyed the usefulness or usability of prices, which are important in quantification. Inflation threatens almost everywhere, there are major global political changes, populations are on the move, war is frequent, and the threat of large-scale war is all too real.

To borrow a metaphor from Kenneth Arrow (1974, 33), the successful use of quantitative approaches depends heavily on the receipt and interpretation of signals from the price system. In a relative sense, the wage rate and the prices of oil, food, transportation services, taxes, and other important prices must be stable and predictable. Otherwise they could not be used for planning purposes and certainly cannot be inputs into a mathematical model. Moreover, these prices have to index or measure something about which we are concerned. Thus, for example, if price increases motivate conservation, the rising prices should index physical scarcities, not monopoly or other social contrivances.

There are two further important situations, other than when monopoly power is exercised, when prices are imprecise and unreliable signals. First, so-called externalities—e.g., environmental and workplace pollution—which are not internalized into the decision-making process will cause faulty choices because costs are not appropriately measured. Second, with the future uncertain, as it is when relative and absolute prices change rapidly because of inflation and other manifestations of social and political disorder, it is impossible to formulate an expectation of future prices; long-run decision making must proceed in an accounting vacuum. Here those trained to think numerically and to maximize profits will seek short-term, measurable advantages, not long-term unmeasurable ones.

IX. Decision Making and Uncertainty

In a period of uncertainty, the shift in emphasis from long- to short-run profits is characteristic of both industrial and financial institutions. In product markets, American industry attempts to continue using existing production facilities and techniques, not to develop new facilities; to concentrate on product lines in which production processes are understood, not to experiment in the development of new and risky products; and to intensify the sales effort relative to the production effort – not the socially most rational response to economic decline, but reasonable when individual financial salvation is the objective.

It is uncertainty which prevents industrialists from attempting to organize the bureaucratic infrastructure necessary to produce and distribute in new and untried ways. They behave as if the long-term profit rate on new investments and organizations is unknown. Under these circumstances individual industrialists and financiers and the bureauratic organizations with which they are associated are unwilling and unable to forsake profits today for larger but uncertain profits tomorrow.

Uncertainty about the profitability of future production and physical investment is a state of mind, not a state of the world, since the future can never be known, only estimated. In normal times there is a pretense at firm or probabilistic knowledge about a variety of events including: what is relevant for new investment, future price-cost relationships, and the extent of the market. This claim to solidity, this arrogation of future knowledge, is bolstered by numerical calculations of future profitability. There develop scientific predictive arguments in the form of formal economic mathematical – or less formal literary – models which are often amenable to numerical estimation. Calculation and model-building become a social convention which lends credence to predictions and provides psychological security to those who must make long-run production and physical investment decisions which will decide the financial fate of individuals, corporations, and nations. Such confidence is obviously essential if men and women are to proceed.

However, pretending as though one knows the future is not simply an issue of generating motion. To the extent that men and women control their destiny, confidence in the future does, in fact, generate outcomes consistent beyond random occurrence with our estimates of future developments. Indeed, it is the psychological stuff of which an investment boom is made and profits result. Of course, in abnormal times the pretense of firm knowledge about the future is untenable and decision making is paralyzed.

When uncertainty afflicts financial markets, the slow, patient, and steady working of compound interest is replaced by the speculative search for quick profits. Financial investors abandon long-term bonds. The long-term relationship between the interest rate and the "net productivity of capital" is severed. The long-term interest rate, and indeed the prices of other financial instruments which are subject to speculation, become social psychological variables subject to the "hidden forces" which buffet the hopes and fears of financial speculators. As Keynes often stressed, it is only in normal times that there is a widespread belief that tomorrow will not be too different from today. The recent past provides the conventional basis upon which to judge the future. Prices can deviate only temporarily from this strongly held view of the normal. Speculators activated by their concept of normal prices, profit from temporary deviations from normality, and by so doing they drive these prices back quickly and efficiently to their normal level or range.

But in abnormal or uncertain times there is no basis for the individual to engage in orderly extrapolation. The stabilizing concept of the normal no longer commands allegiance. Financial survival now requires the speculator to jump on the bandwagon, to follow the herd. The herd instinct, or mass psychology, dominates market behavior. In this instance, prices are the result of market processes, but these processes are only seemingly based on decentralized decision making. In unusual times the process is actually subject to a group mind and decentralized units behave as one. The prices of financial instruments, the exchange rate between domestic and foreign currencies, and the prices of other objects of speculation now swing wildly in one direction or another, with speculation intensifying rather than damping the swings.[7]

The effect of uncertainty on product and financial markets is similar to its effect on the formation of a national energy policy. Oil and gas reserves are underground and, like those who must guess at the future, those who estimate resource availability must make educated guesses at what lies beneath the earth's crust. Like any educated guesses, these estimates are often wrong and knowledgeable estimators can diverge widely in their estimates. Aaron Wildavsky and Ellen Tenenbaum report that in 1908 (1981, 13), the U.S. Geological Survey estimated the United States had total oil resources— the amount of oil that physically exists beneath the earth's crust without regard to the cost of recovery—of between 10 and 24.5 billion barrels and that this oil would be exhausted by 1943. These estimates proved inaccurate. Wildavsky and Tenenbaum also report (1981, 13) that in 1974, M. King Hubbert, an independent estimator, estimated total oil resources of 72 billion barrels, while Vincent McKelvy of the U.S. Geological Survey provided an estimate in the range between 200 billion and 400 billion barrels. It is obvious that these divergent estimates of how much oil is potentially available are not the hard substance on which a policy can be formulated.

Because we do not know how much oil is underground nor how accessible it is, we will always have optimistic and pessimistic estimates. It is wishful thinking to believe that if only better estimates existed then we could formulate effective policy. More likely, if and when a consensus on policy is reached, a set of estimates consistent with this policy will become the dominant or official estimates.

X. Conclusion

Technology and innovation may be the basis for prosperity. They may provide the means to conserve raw materials. However, there should be no presumption that future expansion implies propelling the United States on the same path that has been followed in the past. Metalworking and the automobile need not serve—indeed, probably will not serve—as the driving force behind the next economic expansion. Innovation coupled with social change may involve the development of new lifestyles rather than facilitate the expansion and extension of old ones.[8]

It is not a matter of efficiency, motivation, or ability whether corporate or government bureaucracies, or some combination of the two, decide and implement our technological future. These bureaucracies are not too different in their operational modes. Indeed, in the past many important projects were undertaken on a joint basis. The space program, Department of Agriculture efforts at plant and animal breeding and raising, and recent synfuel project proposals are all examples of the interface betwen public and private bureaucracies. Indeed, when the society finds it necessary to organize for massive change, the distinction between private and public loses all meaning.

The issue of how to organize for technological advance and innovation is both an efficiency issue and a political issue. How much regulation and coordinated direction are neccessary for the market process to function effectively? Who will choose among the many available options? Who will benefit and who will lose from the choices made? How democratic will the decision-making process be?

Some government coordination is necesary to break the logjam of corporate decision making. And in this regard it must be recognized that government bureaucracies are accountable, however imperfectly, to the people through the system of representative government. While the checks and balances of this system reinforce the status quo as parochial interests are defended, the system has proven sufficiently adaptable to facilitate important change. Without regulation—and I use this term in its broad sense to include income policies, traditional regulation, and government direction and support for both growing and declining industries—the corporate decision-making process is not constrained by the electoral process. It is accountable only to the market and to corporate boards, private managers, and large stockholders. The hope for America is a compromise between these two parallel decision-making bureaucracies, each accountable to different groups. In addition, in order to be fair and effective, future decision making must include other groups in society. An incomes program and an industrial policy are beginnings at such a compromise. The administration's program of supply-side economics has been an attempt to eschew compromise, and thus it was destined to fail.

Notes

1. I have benefited from numerous discussions about the problems of technology and economic growth with Eileen Applebaum, Steven Bennett, Peter Dorman, Kenneth Flamm, Carol Heim, Michael Podgursky, and other members of the Project on Economic Restructuring and the working group on technology and economic growth at the University of Massachusetts, Amherst. Much of my knowledge of the subject of the American corporation comes from my years teaching at the Graduate School of Administration, Carnegie-Mellon University. During these years I was introduced to the view that the modern corporation is best understood as a bureaucratic institution, not as a sole proprietorship.

2. There were other problems with the recent version of supply-side economics. The understanding that American society is organized largely (but not exclusively) on the basis of material and not moral incentives, provides only an imprecise guide to the formation of economic policy. It does not recommend the size of the differentials necessary to enlist appropriate behavior. Too large a differential begets ill-will, encourages social conflict, and fosters orgies of conspicuous consumption. Too small a differential discourages effort, blunts initiative, and disheartens the ambitious. The proper balance is the difficult goal of national policy.

Observed differentials vary considerably not only among capitalist societies at a point in time but for a given capitalist society over historical time as well. For example, compared to West Germany and Japan—two very successful capitalist societies—the United States has maintained relatively unequal distributions of income in the post-World War II years, yet each of these three societies would be described as relying heavily on material incentives. And, in the United States, the income differentials in the 1920s were much greater than in the 1950s, yet in each instance the underlying incentive system would again be described as a system of material rewards.

These examples clearly indicate that a capitalist society relies on more than just material incentives to motivate people, and that the stakes necessary to organize a system of material rewards can vary considerably. The cultural and historical circumstances of a society are not superimposed on an obdurate human nature dominated by greed and self-interest. Rather, the interaction between individuals and their culture gives rise to an ebb and flow in the importance of material incentives. As the sense of social cohesion weakens—as it undoubtedly did in the United States during the 1970s—monetary rewards admittedly loom large and important. Loyalty, a sense of workmanship, a sense of duty, charitable predisposition, and other non-pecuniary forces determining behavior were probably weakened as organizing factors during this decade. It does not follow, however, that talented people are unwilling to perform for a modest but secure income. Nor does it follow that the tax cuts of 1981 were accurately targeted toward those who would respond appropriately to the prospect of greater after-tax profits.

3. Ira Magaziner and Robert Reich (1982) have made a recent statement of the need for market regulation in the American context. For an old classic on this matter, the reader is referred to the work of Karl Polanyi (1944). It should be noted that many of the arguments in support of an "industrial policy" share much in common with the arguments by the late Sidney Weintraub (1978) and the late Abba Lerner (1973) for an incomes policy.

4. To be either developed or effectively utilized, new techniques must be embedded in a workplace or in some other social context. This involves the mechanical interface between people and machines as well as interaction among people, the so-called "human relations" aspect of production. It is in this sense that new investments in machine-embodied innovation go hand in hand with new organizational structures. Thus, changes over time in the organization of work are no less important than the changes over time in the machine-embodied techniques of production.

5. The suppression of that individuality steeped in self-indulgence and license is, of course, not to be bemoaned. Instead, it is that individuality which is the stimulus to creativity and imagination that is the costly loss to the American system. There are many historical precedents for systems that lose their dynamism as creativity gives way to bureaucratic repetition.

The great empire of Rome—with its highways and aqueducts, its theatres and temples, its navy and trade, its agriculture and manufactures, its preeminent arms and successful colonization—decayed and collapsed into the Western darkness. Gibbon, who in accidental irony published the first volume of the *Decline and Fall of the Roman Empire* in the same year that Adam Smith published *The Wealth of Nations* (pp. 50, 52), describes this Western tragedy and attributes the Roman failure to internal decay and corruption. Over time, " . . . the minds of men were gradually reduced to the same level, the fire of genius was extinguished, and even the military spirit evaporated." Blind deference to authority " . . . precluded every generous attempt to exercise the powers or enlarge the limits of the human mind." In the end, " . . . the Roman world was indeed peopled by a race of pygmies when the fierce giants of the north broke in and mended the puny breed."

6. There have been some efforts by large corporations to free themselves from the layers of inflexible managerial control and from the difficulties of providing an adequate incentive system. As traditional approaches to corporate growth have encountered barriers, some corporations have adopted new organizational structures in an effort to develop flexibility and entrepreneurship. Often this requires

the spin-off of technical cadres and the development of semi-independent corporate units, the objective being, among other things, to identify and reward individual and small group contributions and to increase the flexibility of decision making. However, more common than the internal development of entrepreneurial talent have been efforts to absorb the entrepreneurial skills of smaller firms by purchase or joint venture. It is too soon to determine the success of these reorganizational efforts.

7. A few instances of unstable market behavior might prove enlightening: The price of gold rose from $400 per ounce to $850 per ounce in a three-month period in late 1979 and early 1980; I would also include the 50 percent rise in gold prices in a two-month period in the summer of 1982. Or, turning from gold to common stocks, I would cite the two-week decline in stock prices in the fall of 1978 when the stock market suffered losses comparable to those inflicted on it by the OPEC oil embargo of 1973, the fall of France in May of 1940, and the collapse of industrial production in 1937–38. In this instance the Dow Jones average fell by almost 110 points, from 900 to 790, while the losses in "secondary" markets, the American Exchange and the Over-the-Counter exchanges, were larger, with the price of an average share tumbling by 20 and 30 percent respectively. We might also note the over-100 point rise in the Dow Jones in the late summer of 1982.

Instability, is also in evidence on foreign exchange markets. In the fall of 1978, the dollar fell 14 percent against the mark and 7 percent against the yen in a ten-day period. From January to August 1980 the exchange value of the dollar, relative to 15 major currencies, skyrocketed upward an index value of 95 to a value of 114, only to recede by 9 index points in the following three months.

Lastly, let us note that bond prices and associated interest rates have been remarkably unstable during the 1980–82 period.

8. The argument that our economic problems are structural is often made, and I do not claim originality on this point. For an especially articulate statement of the "structuralist" view, the reader would profit from reading the essay by Charles Wilber and Kenneth Jameson.

References

Abernathy, Robert and William Hayes. "Managing Our Way to Economic Decline." *Harvard Business Review* 58, no. 4 (July/August 1980).

Arrow, Kenneth. *The Limits of Organization*. New York: Norton, 1974.

Berle, Adolf, and Gardner C. Means. *The Modern Corporation and Private Property*. New York: Macmillan, 1932.

Chandler, Alfred D. *The Visible Hand: The Managerial Revolution in American Business*. Cambridge, MA: Belknap Press, 1977.

Drucker, Peter. *Managing in Turbulent Times*. New York: Harper & Row, 1980.

Gibbon, Edward. *The Decline and Fall of the Roman Empire.* New York: The Modern Library, 1932.

Keynes, John M. *The General Theory.* New York: Harcourt, Brace & Co., 1936.

Lerner, Abba P. *Flation.* Baltimore: Penguin Books, Inc., 1973.

Magaziner, Ira C., and Robert B. Reich. *Minding America's Business.* New York: Harcourt, Brace, & Jovanovich, 1982.

Polanyi, Karl. *The Great Transformation.* New York: Farrar & Rhinehart, Inc., 1944.

Rapping, Leonard A. "The Domestic and International Aspects of Structural Inflation." In *Essays in Post-Keynesian Inflation,* edited by James Gapinski and Charles E. Rockwood. Cambridge, MA: Ballinger Pub. Co., 1978.

Simon, Henry A. *Administrative Behavior.* New York: Free Press, 1976.

———. *The New Science of Management Decision.* Revised Edition. Englewood Cliffs: Prentice Hall, 1977.

Taylor, Frederick W. *The Principles of Scientific Management.* New York: Harper & Brothers, 1911.

Weintraub, Sidney. *Capitalism's Inflation and Unemployment Crisis.* Reading, Ma: Addison-Wesley, 1978.

Wilber, Charles K., and Kenneth P. Jameson. "Crisis in the American Economy." In *Alternative Directions in Economic Policy,* edited by Frank J. Bonello and Thomas R. Swartz. Notre Dame, IN: University of Notre Dame Press, 1978.

Wildavsky, Aaron, and Ellen Tenenbaum. *The Politics of Mistrust: Estimating American Oil and Gas Resources,* Beverly Hills, CA: Sage Publications, 1981.

PART III

Industrial Policy

5

The Hard Realities of Industrial Policy

GAIL GARFIELD SCHWARTZ

Industrial policy, which was first seriously considered in the United States in 1933 and faded with the troubles of the National Recovery Administration, became a policy option again in 1980 as the United States moved towards the worst recession since the Great Depression that gave rise to the New Deal. Dismissed somewhat off-handedly by the beleaguered administration of President Jimmy Carter, industrial policy was orphaned temporarily; but in 1982, a host of foster parents stepped forward with offers to put a political roof over its head. Interestingly, these foster parents are not confined to any one ideological group or even to the Democratic party, although more Democratic than Republican politicians have endorsed the concept. Still, adherents range from those who see industrial policy as long-overdue centralized government planning, to those who see it as justification for removal of all government regulation of business and industry. The fact that so many interests treat industrial policy as a bandwagon to ride indicates that it is more than an abstract concept. For industrial policy to be more than a slogan, however, we must be much more explicit than we have been up until now in defining its objectives, identifying the tools to be used to reach the objectives, and making explicit the political trade-offs needed to bring it about.

This article will state the reasons why industrial policy is needed and timely. It will then discuss the political realities of industrial policymaking. Finally, it will describe the approach to industrial policy that is most likely to command the necessary political support by satisfying the needs of interest groups having power to adopt it, without jeopardizing the welfare of other groups or interests.

I. Why Industrial Policy?

The purpose of industrial policy is to enhance economic growth – to make the economic pie of U.S. gross national product bigger. My explicit political-economic bias is that the purpose of a bigger pie is to make it possible to raise the standard of living of lower- and middle-income Americans. It is far easier to redistribute income from a larger base than from a stagnant or shrinking base.

From this perspective, business and industry are a means to an end: the end is the efficient allocation of resources to the production of goods and services that can capture a large share of domestic and world markets. American history is replete with examples of government assistance to businesses and industry to expand markets and to increase profits. In every example, the political response has been to a group or groups that insisted on government participation. Farmers pushed for the Homestead Act, for farm price supports, and for payments in kind; cattlemen lobbied for depletion allowances for cattle feeding investments; oil interests advocated oil depletion allowances to encourage drilling; the construction industry backed housing market subsidies of all kinds as well as accelerated cost recovery for real estate investments. Big and little business and industry groups supported investment tax credits for plant and equipment in all industries. The list can go on and on, and it includes programs that protect American producers and workers from the competition of foreign-made goods ranging from shoes to steel, from toys to motorcycles, and automobiles, soybeans, sugar, sweaters, hats, handbags . . . and much more.

The case for a partnership between business and government has been well made throughout our history. But these partnerships have not yet succeeded in meeting the challenges of a changing world economic order in which large corporations, some economically more powerful than many governments, control diversified corporate empires and demonstrate little loyalty to a particular place as they transfer capital from country to country. Both multinational corporations and domestic enterprises find "outsourcing" of parts and services to low labor-cost countries to be cost effective and politically expedient to gain access to overseas markets. The jobs the companies bring to the developing nations are a strong incentive for governments in those countries to assist them – or to leave them alone, as the case may be.

The realities of internationalization of production are not confined to manufacturing as is evidenced by word-processing shops set up in the English-speaking Caribbean islands. Technology is speeding up, not retarding, outsourcing. Satellite communication makes instant transmission of data from any part of the globe relatively inexpensive; therefore, the job can be brought to the worker, rather than the worker being brought to the job. Just as relatively low-paid workers in Mexico, Taiwan, Singapore, Korea, Yugoslavia, Brazil, Colombia, and a dozen other countries assemble the microchips in our computers, so they will assemble the data-bits for our service industries. The ease with which outsourcing can occur is strengthened by technology which deskills the work involved. As robots, computer-controlled design and manufacturing, and the electronic office become less expensive, more and more jobs will be so simple that they can be done by workers with minimal education and training, in almost any country. Although new technology will create some new jobs requiring high skills, it will deskill millions of operative, craft and clerical jobs. By combining high technology and low-cost labor, firms will be able to increase their profits dramatically, and they will certainly seek to do so.

These realities face not just the United States but all the advanced industrial nations. As a result we are well into a neomercantilist era in which companies seek to gain a foothold in foreign markets by building facilities there or by joint ventures in those countries with "native" companies. Mercantilism, of course, requires protection against unwanted foreign goods and services, through tariffs, quotas, and other means. Every member of the Organization for Economic Cooperation and Development (OECD) subsidises its exports indirectly if not directly, and overtly or covertly individual nations and the European Common Market discriminate against foreign goods and services of many kinds. Developing nations have closed markets to many overseas products. Some nations, notably the Japanese, seem to be particularly adept at creating invisible trade barriers, such as prolonged bureaucratic delays.

In this situation, when you start dividing America into its component groups, what is good for General Motors is not necessarily good for America. While consumers might be able to purchase cheaper cars if all the parts were made outside of the country, there would be millions more Americans who would not have enough income to buy cars. (Auto industry employment is now down to 685,000 from over 1 million in 1976). The argument that free trade in the long run will benefit everyone because each nation will specialize in what it does best and thus all products will be traded at the lowest possible price appears less viable in a world economy in which there are no sharp differences in production capability. With advanced technology, many nations will be able to specialize, as the United States once uniquely did, in mass production. Many nations will be able to replicate processes we once monopolized—especially if U.S. companies continue to finance the capital investment required to produce overseas.

One possible response is to lower our standard of livng; but we cannot lower it enough to compete with most developing nations. Another response is to revert to a fortress mentality and promote a tight little self-sustaining economic island, even at the price of high inflation; but we cannot do this without severely disrupting many export-dependent sectors, particularly agriculture, which would drown in surpluses without exports.

A third response is to abandon inefficient industries and encourage the so-called "sunrise industries" such as biotechnology, services, communications, and flexible manufacturing of small batches of goods. The arguments against this approach are numerous. We would endanger our national security, because the inefficient industries include those necessary for defense, such as steel. The cost in dislocation of workers in the inefficient industries would be extraordinary; for this reason alone, the "sunrise industry" argument does not carry much political clout. Most telling, the "sunrise industries" will not be as labor-intensive as advocates of this approach would have us believe, since many of them will utilize computers and labor-saving communications.[1] There is no guarantee that the jobs they create can be confined to the United States, either. In 1983, after the "Atari Democrats" made their pitch in Congress for more government subsidies for electronics research and development, Atari moved a large share of its production overseas.

The only realistic approach, politically speaking, is to continue to evolve policies for both growing and shrinking industries that take into account the domestic and international market potential, the competition from foreign and U.S. overseas producers, the opportunities for increasing productivity domestically in those industries, and the consequences for U.S. workers. The question then becomes, how will these several industrial policies work in relation to one another? Will they be coherent and mutually supportive, making the economic pie grow, or will they work at cross purposes?

II. The Politics of Industrial Policy

All effective policies require a convergence of interests such that narrow-focused groups perceive at least as much advantage from them as from the alternatives. Industrial policies ideally will yield some approximation of Pareto optimality: they will satisfy the needs of the interest groups that support them, without seriously jeopardizing the welfare status of other groups or interests. For politicians, this means that the policies have to reveal the winners to gain adherents without making it too clear who the losers will be, as they will likely be opponents. And industrial policies will not help every firm or every community, even if they do help an industry as a whole. Some industrial policies affect many workers in a few communities; some affect fewer workers but more communities. An industrial policy for the steel industry would affect some 20 or 25 communities; an industrial policy for the auto industry would directly or indirectly affect

75 to 100 communities. An industrial policy for textiles and apparel industries would affect many small towns as well as large cities. A machine tool policy would touch every major city. The bottom line, politically, is that industrial policies would not help all communities equally. Since it would be necessary to rationalize industries by closing some plants and modernizing others, inevitably there will be some short term dislocations felt in some places (see Schwartz 1983, 295).

Because industrial policy legislation must be passed by a Congress representing places, these differential impacts must be dealt with in framing the responsibilities and the scope of industrial policies. The first political requisite, therefore, is that workers, creditors, and investors who are negatively affected by industrial policies must be compensated for their losses or assisted to recoup them.

Policy for a specific industry must include a plan for assisting workers in each community negatively affected by the policy. Substitute employment must be found for workers displaced as a result of the policy, and training must be provided for them if necessary. Some workers may be willing and able to relocate to find different and better work in other communities, and industrial policy has to include a way to assist them to do so. But others will balk; since forcing relocation is not the American tradition, industrial policy may have to include subsidies to create stop-gap jobs in other industries or in the public sector to "take up" workers whose jobs are lost as a result of policy. It does no good to argue that the jobs might have been lost anyway; the consequences will be blamed on the policy, not on the economy in general. Adequate funding must be provided in the industrial policy budget to take care of the displaced workers, or provisions made must be through amendment of unemployment compensation laws or social security laws or public service employment acts to provide the necessary substitute work. It is important to emphasize that mere income support is not as desirable as substitute work; if the private sector cannot provide jobs, then subsidized jobs are preferable to subsidized idleness.

III. Financing and Industrial Policy

No single government finance "window" can offer prepackaged solutions to all the problems of all types of firms. The interests of creditors and investors in any given industry subject to industrial policy will vary from firm to firm, and the mechanisms for dealing with those interests will have to be negotiated in every particular instance. If the assistance given to the Chrysler corporation is taken as a model, it can be expected that a government finance corporation would guarantee the debt of firms in an industry that seem to have revitalization potential. But many other mechanisms could also be used, ranging from writing off the debt to paying off the accumulated debt, direct loans of government funds, declaring bankruptcy, and so forth. Some firms would need to restructure their debt; others might raise additional equity. Others might be assisted to merge with other companies or divest unprofitable subsidiaries. Some might go into bankruptcy, but there is often life after bankruptcy. A viable industrial policy will depend heavily on disinterested professional expertise to determine the options in a given instance and negotiate a financing approach acceptable to lenders, management, and employees. The trick is to assure that the decisions would be made on a business-like basis, free from political favoritism. Explicit goals that do not vary according to political winds need to be framed in legislation that endures beyond the electoral cycle.[2] Experience with the U.S. Small Business Administration loan programs, for example, indicates how Congress' intent to assist firms through financing aids is circumvented by conservative administrations in accordance with their underlying philosophy and approach to business: they do not disburse the full congressional authorization for loans, and lenders apply stricter standards in judging applicants' credit-worthiness than intended by the legislation. Conservative administrations judge the program's success solely on the default rate, rather than on the economic development effects such as job creation and tax base enhancement. These same sorts of value judgments would be greatly magnified in relation to industrial policies, which would have to make general types of assistance available to all firms within a specified industry, yet hand-tailor the particular package of finance tools to each firm's particular needs and potential.

IV. How To Do It

Many writers, myself included, have used the Japanese model in arguing for industrial policies. The Japanese Ministry of Industry and Trade (MITI) demonstrates the kind of mix of overall collective goal setting and individual corporate competition that can achieve long-term market presence, competitive costs, and high quality. But this is not to argue that we should create a sort of blue-eyed MITI in the United States. The spirit of consensus, the authoritarian and conformist upbringing that underlie the success of the Japanese system do not characterize the United States. For industrial policy to work here, we need a mechanism indigenous to our own political economy and our own culture. Rather than argue that Americans should change their spots and become collective-minded, it is more appropriate to create institutions and processes that reflect American individualism. Remember that the United States was created reluctantly by a group of separatist colonies, and that the labor movement in the United States was led by strong-minded individuals who explicitly rejected socialism as well as syndicalism.

In my view, the "philosophy" which would lead to an effective industrial policy implementation mechanism is that labor, management, and government are necessary, balancing adversaries with many different interests that, when adjusted, benefit all parties. With this philosophy, the collective bargaining model becomes the industrial policy mechanism. Once Congress has decided that a given industry is valuable enough to the American economy to qualify as an industrial policy target, the actual policymaking is turned over to a team of industry experts representing busines management, labor in that industry, and the government. Any firm of a minimum size can participate in the policymaking and benefits, voluntarily: some large firms might be obligated to participate. Solutions to the problems of participating firms in the industry would be worked out on a case-by-case basis, under the overall umbrella of objectives for the entire industry. The objectives would be set through discussion, negotiation, and compromise. Bargaining seems a far more realistic approach to industrial policymaking than consensus-building.

If the bargaining process is to work well, the participants have to have some specific information. All must know what the real production costs to the firms are. All must know what the firms' real market share is, and what their real productive capacity is, at specific price levels. This kind of information is not readily made public by companies; it would have to be a requirement of any industrial policy bargaining session that they provide the information. Naturally the negotiators would be subject to confidentiality restrictions, just as any private troubleshooting team must be. In any industry, however, all firms, not just those in the deepest trouble or with the most innovative leaders, could participate in industrial policy; and the additional powers at the command of government could be made available so that restructuring could take place sooner and cover a wider range of firms.

Another prerequisite for effective industrial policymaking is the ability to create useful scenarios on which the various action alternatives will be predicated. This is an effort that cannot by any stretch of the imagination be performed by government bureaucrats. It must be an integral element of the discussion and negotiation process. However, it would be feasible for the government to provide the technical backup for assessing the outcomes under different sets of assumptions. Existing technology makes it possible to do so almost instantaneously, and many different combinations of possibilities regarding costs, competition, and time frames can be compared in the process of setting realistic industry-wide objectives for the near term, middle term, and long term.

The purpose of collective bargaining in the industrial policy framework is not to guarantee that all firms in the industry will stay in business, or increase their output or profits, or maintain their current market share. Rather the purpose is to set the boundaries of competition among domestic firms so that together U.S. producers can remain viable competitors. The U.S. company that is number one in the market today would not be guaranteed the number one position by an industrial policy. Competition among firms within industries would be encouraged, and care would be taken that subsidies to one firm in the industry would not endanger the competitive position of others.

As the parties sit down to negotiate the specifics of industrial policy, each brings its own set of "chips" to the bargaining table. Management's offers could include fixing production levels; limiting price increases or lowering prices; promising specific new investments within a specific period; sharing profits with employees; adopting a policy of notification in advance of layoffs or plant closings; allowing workers to participate in management decisions. Labor could offer to stabilize wages; "give back" benefits; tie wages to profits; work longer hours at straight-time pay; alter work rules; take compensation in the form of profit sharing. Government could offer special investment tax credits; preferential treatment for capital gains in specific industries; guaranteed loans or direct loans; adjustment of compliance standards for various regulations; merging and pooling of resources that otherwise would violate antitrust laws; and temporary protection against the competition of foreign goods.

General enabling legislation would have to be passed to permit these "deals" to be structured; some existing legislation, particularly that involving investment tax credits and tax treatment of capital gains might have to be modified. These are not insurmountable barriers to enactment of industrial policy legislation. In fact, they are an incentive to Congress to look more closely than it has yet done at what the actual workings of industrial policy would involve. The point is that industrial policies must be viewed as microeconomic policies within the framework of macroeconomic policies—and that the impact of the latter on the former cries for closer attention.

In this proposed collective bargaining process, government would not set production targets. It would not set prices or wages. In fact, government does not dominate. No industrial policy in which government does dominate would be practicable in the United States, with its diversity of firms and its commitment to free enterprise. The federal government cannot, should not, and, under this proposal, would not, pick "plums" and "lemons" from among firms in any industry. Congress need only identify industries that because of their contribution to defense, their large employment base, their large income multiplier, or their growth potential, are vital industries. They may be shrinking, and still be vital. Nominations for such industries could come and would be expected to come from industry and labor. There is nothing socialistic about this notion: in fact, the Tax Recovery Act of 1981 was deliberately intended to benefit certain industries, such as the railroad industry, which were determined by Congress to be significant to economic growth.

Nor should Congress rush to create an agency to formulate a single industrial policy. It is too soon to do so: the organization would determine the limits of policy options, when, in fact, the policy options should give rise to the appropriate organization. During the New Deal, the National Industrial Recovery Board was created before it had a mission, thus contributing to all its problems and its eventual discrediting (see Schlessinger 1957, ch. 6). If a single agency, such as a development bank, is established, then industrial policy will be limited to financing. Instead, Congress should set up separate councils or commissions for specific industries, and give them a few months to see what they can come up with—much as it funds special commissions on special problems such as social security or criminal justice.

This limited, but specific, approach to industrial policymaking should appeal to enough interest groups to test the concept and the realities. Wall Street would not be scared by the creation of an exploratory agency outside of government. Labor would not be intimidated by the prospects of bankers controlling all policy decisions. A working group could trace out the impact that specific measures would have on given industries, without being, like Congress, under pressure to choose one measure and choose quickly. The real political trade-offs—between import protection and prices, for example—could be explored in the private atmosphere characteristic of contract negotiations, rather than in the frenzied public atmosphere of a legislative battle.

V. Conclusion

There is ample reason for the United States to give serious consideration to the benefits of a more explicit and coherent set of policies to enhance the competitive performance of American industries. This is preferable to either a protectionist stance vis à vis foreign competition or continuation of current ad hoc efforts to shore up firms that are losing ground in world and domestic markets. No single industrial policy can solve the individual problems of all vital industries. In a nation as large and diverse as the United States, with its multiple sources of capital, industry expertise, and management experience, industrial policies should be worked out separately from the bottom up, for individual industries or sets of related industries. The nature of our government as well as our philosophical underpinnings make centralized schemes such as French indicative planning or Japanese consensus building impractical; any industrial policy that depends on these centralized, government-dominated approaches will either never be enacted or never be effective. A policy-making mechanism that builds on our own traditions would make industrial policies "doable": that mechanism is the collective bargaining approach.

Congress should experiment with tripartite councils for specific industries which would include equal representation by management, labor, and government. These councils should assess the potential for U.S. performance in the particular industries, pinpoint the changes that need to be made to improve that potential, and map out a contract by which labor, management, and government could implement those changes. The council initially would have advisory capacity only; if the exercise is fruitful, it would point the way for legislation setting up permanent industrial policy organizations. The United States is a nation of pragmatists; a pragmatic approach is needed to take industrial policy debate out of the realm of slogans and into the realm of political action.

Notes

1. As little as 3 percent of all jobs will be high technology industries and as little as 15 percent of all jobs will be professional, technical, and managerial jobs in the high technology end of traditional industries and the sunrise industries combined. For further elaboration of this prognosis, see Schwartz and Neikirk 1983, ch. 5.

2. This is crucial, and the most politically problematic aspect of industrial policy. If the general goals are not long lived, firms will not participate because they will expect the rules of the game to constantly change.

References

Schlessinger, Arthur, J. *The Age of Roosevelt*. Boston: Houghton Mifflin, 1957.
Schwartz, Gail Garfield. "Revitalizing Cities through National Sectoral Policies."
    In *Transition to the 21st Century*, edited by Norman Glickman and Donald
    Hicks. Greenwich, CT: JAI Press, 1983.
Schwartz, Gail Garfield and William Neikirk. *The Work Revolution*. New York:
    Rawson Associates, 1983.

6

The Debate
about Industrial Policy

JAMES K. GALBRAITH[1]

The premise of this collection of essays is that neither traditional Keynesian policies, nor a return to laissez-faire, can be relied on to restore economic growth, high employment, and reasonable price stability. Fifteen
years ago, nine-tenths of all economists would have objected to the first
part of such a proposition. The remaining tenth would have objected to
the second. Today, sadly, the statement is non-controversial, and so it is
natural to ask what the alternatives to Keynesianism and laissez-faire might
be.

Industrial policy is an alternative economic policy which has been actively under discussion in Washington for the past two years. Among its
proponents are some of the most powerful and respected voices in American public debate.

- The Labor-Industry Coalition for International Trade, (LICIT)[2] has
  published a report entitled *International Trade, Industrial Policies and
  the Future of American Industry* which states: "America faces an international competitive challenge today unlike any that it has known
  in the post-war decades."

- Barry Bluestone of Boston College and Bennett Harrison of MIT
  describe, in *The Deindustrialization of America*: "a widespread, systematic disinvestment in the nation's basic productive capacity. . . . Left
  behind are shuttered factories, displaced workers, and a newly emerging group of ghost towns" (1982, 6).

- Gerald Adams and Lawrence Klein of the University of Pennsylvania open their book, *Industrial Policies for Growth and Competitiveness*, with this assertion about industrial policies: "Only in this way can the United States return to the sucessful pattern of macroeconomic performance recorded in the 1950's and the 1960's" (1983, 3).

- A panel of the National Academy of Sciences, including Robert Solow, Carl Kaysen, and Richard N. Cooper, concludes a report on *International Competition in Advanced Technology* with these words: "The United States must act now to preserve its basic capacity to develop and use economically advanced technology" (1983, 10).

- Finally, *America's Competitive Challenge: The Need for a National Response*, a report prepared for the president of the United States and published in April 1983 by the Business-Higher Education Forum, a panel including university presidents Derek Bok, Martina S. Horner, Richard M. Cyert, and the Reverend Theodore M. Hesburgh, states: "The central objective of the United States for the remainder of the decade must be to improve the ability of American industry to compete in markets at home and abroad" (1983, 1).

It would be churlish, certainly, to suggest that extra skepticism is due any idea with so much backing. Nevertheless: why have all these important people all come to this particular conclusion just now? Consensus is a rare phenomenon in a nation's politics. In ours, it is sometimes sparked by a great study, such as Keynes' *General Theory* or Myrdal's *An American Dilemma*, more often by deep social trauma (the Kennedy assassination), or war (Pearl Harbor). Such things have the effect of driving large numbers of diverse-thinking people to a common and durable set of conclusions, capable of sustaining action toward jointly held goals. When consensus is not based on a compelling and visible set of reasons, one may be entitled to doubt that the conclusions drawn will be lasting.

There is no *General Theory* or *American Dilemma* of the industrial policy movement. There have been traumas in recent economic life: plant closings and joblessness in hundreds of communities, increased import penetration in dozens of major industries, declines in the U.S. share of certain world markets and a perceived fall in our world technological leadership. But these events and perceptions do not by themselves explain why ideas are crystallizing around one particular course of action. We have had recessions, unemployment, and plant closings before. We have lost world market share in certain industrial sectors before. Once before, at the time of Sputnik, we also thought we were losing world technological leadership. On each of those occasions, the calls for action were different from what they are today. How is it, that instead of calls for reflation or protection, to mention two remedies with much less public credibility today than in recent times, there is such a focus today on industrial policy? The answer appears to lie in the political exhaustion of alternative ideas. Industrial policy has had its moment of ascendance, not chiefly because of intrinsic merit or the persuasive powers of a great exposition, but because fifteen years of debate and mismanaged policy have discredited most everything else.

I. The Origins of the Industrial Policy Debate

Industrial policy was not a term much heard in Washington until 1978 or 1979. Up until the end of the 1960s, many people thought that Keynesian macroeconomics had solved the fundamental economic problems of the American economy. It had, certainly, created a powerful faith in the minds of many in government's ability to do so. When inflation shook that faith from 1967 on, it was first deliberate recession (in 1970) and then incomes policies, Nixon's three phases, which were called on to effect a cure.

Nixon's incomes policies were what would now properly be called a "supply-side" measure. They worked by restraining costs as aggregate demand, output, and employment expanded. They resolved the conflict between the goals of low unemployment and low inflation, however temporarily and imperfectly, by shifting supply curves for labor and materials down and to the right, to keep prices level in the face of outward-moving demand curves. At the time, however, these measures were often wrongly viewed as operating on the "demand side," and they were in any case discredited by the political uses to which they were put. Not until the mid-1970s did the idea of supply-side measures as such begin to take hold.

The first truly supply-side/structural change economic policy debate was, after the first oil shock, over energy. Energy policy continued to dominate discussion of supply-side measures straight through from Richard Nixon's Project Independence in 1973–74 to Jimmy Carter's Moral Equivalent of War in 1977. A subsidiary debate over agricultural export and conservation policy also took place after the price explosion following the Soviet grain purchases of 1972, and resulted in the long-term trade agreements of the late 1970s and the creation of the farmer-held grain reserve.

Such measures were a profound challenge to the simpler Keynesian view. Contrary to what had been believed, a benign combination of macroeconomics and free markets was not enough to defeat the worsening trade-off between unemployment and inflation. Structural change, brought about through direct government intervention on a sectoral basis, was required.

Inept political management of energy policy led to loss of momentum in this area, despite real successes in conservation, alternative energy source research and development, and reduction of oil imports by 1979. But the supply-side message stuck: there was no return to favor of demand-side expansionism. When the second oil shock struck, it was not to energy or other resource-oriented policies, nor to macroeconomics, that the public and the national political leadership turned in a search for new and more attractive solutions. It was to industry and to investment.

As national attention turned toward the possibilities of structural change in industry, there were difficulties one might expect in any new intellectual endeavor. The United States has no cadre of industrial planners, no academic reserve specifically trained in the art of industrial policy. So it was necessary to deal with what ideas and people there were. That meant a subculture of specialists in industrial performance, in comparative management practices, and in the comparative politics of industry who had previously had little contact with the mainstream of political debate.

Several distinct perspectives existed among these groups. One, originating in the business schools, focussed on the management habits of American corporations and sought to define areas where those of the Japanese or (in a few cases) Europeans were superior: attention to quality control, labor relations, a longer time frame for corporate planning (see, for example, Abernathy and Hayes, 1980, 1981). But this view offers solutions to business, not to government. It suggests little that a politician can do, that can be framed in legislation or as a plank in an electoral platform. And so it has remained marginal to the political debate.

A second set of ideas about what to do stemmed from studies of what other governments have done.[3] Many mechanisms for intervention in industry do exist abroad. Sometimes, these were established under Social Democratic governments in Europe and were clearly identified for the purposes of U.S. political debate as left-wing strategies (the British nationalizations, for example), and were therefore taboo. In other cases, interventions were the handiwork of conservative or nationalistic governments. These were attractive models for American advocates of industrial intervention, partly because of their political camouflage, and perhaps also because they contradicted the idea that social conservatism is to be uniquely associated with free markets. Industry policy measures in France and Japan, which work through control of capital flows, seemed particularly applicable to the United States, since they avoid the ideological trap of advocating direct or visible state control of industry. However, for the politician even these measures were risky because of the strong bias in our political culture against appearing to draw lessons from overseas.

Republicans solved this dilemma in their own way. Their theorists accepted the core message of the supply-side—that there had to be changes directly affecting the economic performance of industry—but rejected explicit government intervention as a means to this end. Tax changes, affecting market incentives in only an indirect way, were the alternative. So the Republicans developed a tax-based variant of supply-side economics and, in the heat of the 1980 campaign, adopted the program of business and personal tax reductions which were later made the cornerstone of the Reagan administration's program. Whether the creed that eventually captured proprietary rights to the term "supply-side economics" came into existence before or after the commitment to massive tax reduction was made is open to debate. It certainly did reconcile the conflicting ideological requirements of Republican politics in a way that proved attractive to traditional Republican constituencies, including business, who were unstinting in their support for the Republican program in the 1980 campaign and after.

For Democrats, to whom the simple escape of tax-based supply-side economics was not open, a final option was retreat to the relative safety of precedent in U.S. political history. That precedent was embodied, for symbolic purposes, in the memory of the Reconstruction Finance Corporation.

Ever since the abolition of the Reconstruction Finance Corporation in the early 1950s, there have been calls to restore it. Such calls were a fixture in the belief structure of old New Deal Democrats in Congress in the 1960s and 1970s, for whom the RFC represented the worthy efforts of government to help businesses out of hard times. Further, the RFC had a certain respectability in business circles that other New Deal agencies did not have. It was a relief agency for *business*. It had been created, not under Roosevelt, but under Hoover. And in its heyday it provided an institutional link between strong governments of the Democratic party and the American business class that did not otherwise exist. Up until the middle 1970s, scarcely a day of congressional hearings and floor debate went by without a call by some aging veteran of the Depression years for a revival of the RFC.

The post-war generation of congressional leaders did not share this view. They remembered the RFC mainly for the irregularities of its operations. That generation of liberals set the agenda of the sixties and early seventies, in a time of general prosperity. Their work focussed on human, social, and environmental concerns, not on the remaining problems of economic growth. As the older, Depression-era generation passed away, so did the active political constituency of the old RFC.

Now, economic problems different in scale but similar in type to those of the early Depression have re-emerged. And there is an even younger set of politicians near the levers of power in Congress. This group, first elected in the sixties and early seventies, sees a need to de-emphasize the traditional liberal social agenda in favor of fostering economic growth. Preferably, new policy ideas should also be capable of reestablishing the Democratic party's deteriorated ties to business. In this view, social objectives can only be reached effectively after implementation of a strategy to restore economic vitality, "competitiveness," and growth. If such a strategy itself requires a slowdown in the pursuit of the final social objectives—good health care, assured nutrition, quality public education, environmental control, full employment—then that price should be paid.

It is thus not surprising that the idea of industrial policy appeals to the rising moderate political leaders in Congress. It is a "new idea," the identification with which distinguishes this generation from its immediate predecessor. It addresses the issue of economic growth, newly important again after forty years, and clearly secondary in the value structure of the older leadership. It is oriented to business, while remaining attractive at least to the industrial unions.

Advocacy of industrial policy is emerging as the answer offered by the centrist faction of the Democratic party to two challenges: the demands being made on Democratic officeholders by traditional Democratic constituencies, and the appeal to business constituencies of the Republicans' tax-based version of supply-side economics. Industrial policy preaches at both extremes from the center. To the liberals, it carries a message of limits to resources, and a counsel of patience while policy concentrates on the revitalization of the private sector. To conservatives, it offers an alternative to what sooner or later all must recognize as an outlandish fiscal program.

Unfortunately, sponsors of a new line of proposals often feel the need to match the advertising of their opponents. When tax-based supply-side economics was in vogue, it was a common claim that these measures would do as much, even more, for the poor and the unemployed as the traditional liberal social welfare programs. Some advocates of industrial policy feel compelled by comparably fancy claims about what such policy will do for economic performance. Two goals in particular are commonly cited. First is that of directly raising the rate of gross capital formation in the economy or the share of such capital formation in gross national product, and thereby increasing the secular rate of real economic growth. Second is that of improving the "international competitiveness" of the economy as a whole. Neither result can logically be expected from the policy changes under consideration.

II. Industrial Policy and Capital Formation

There is no reputable economic argument for the proposition that policies of direct intervention, through subsidy or otherwise, in the investment decisions of companies will necessarily by themselves alter the share of investment in economic activity as a whole, through effects restricted to the supply side of the economy.

To the idea that industrial policies shift the aggregate supply curve (e.g., lower the supply price of capital as a whole), the objection is that such partial equilibrium actions are likely in principle to have some offsetting effects on some other part of the curve. That being so, the direction in which the supply curve will actually shift in response to measures pushing part of it outward—if it shifts at all—is uncertain. A good part of the economics profession certainly believes that such selective intervention is more apt to move away from the production possibility frontier than toward it.

Moreover, actual policy actions are unlikely to have effects restricted exclusively to the supply side. Unless the economy is already functioning at full utilization of resources (in which case industrial policy would be pointless), any effort to mobilize resources for industrial investment is likely to have as large an effect on aggregate demand as on supply. However, stimulating output and investment this way is not a novel trick. And if one should choose to neutralize the demand-side effects of an industrial subsidy policy, the exercise of holding total demand constant would undo most of any increase in net investment that would otherwise have been achieved. One would be left with a simple reallocation of resources, and an open question whether the economy was functioning more or less efficiently than it would have done without the policy.

The political concern with industrial policy nevertheless remains shot through with the conviction that such policies are linked to productivity growth and capital formation. However, in the politician's mind, the nature of the perceived linkage is more cultural than economic. This accounts, among other things, for the ready acceptance of the thesis recently advanced by Robert Reich of the Kennedy School of Government at Harvard. According to Reich (March and April, 1983), the American corporation as a social institution is at fault. An emphasis on short pay-back periods and high rates of return, unwillingness to abandon outmoded methods of production and to face the global nature of competition, and, especially, failure to adjust to the flexible nature of high-technology enterprise have led to behavior patterns inimical to competitive success. Among these particularly are a diversion of capital resources from real to speculative investment ("paper entrepreneurialism") and inefficient use of those real capital resources which are already in existence.

In this decayed corporate culture, Reich argues, investment withers, technology lags, the way is laid open for, particularly, the Japanese with their technological flexibility, labor-management-government cooperation, and malleable workforce. The government may not be a paragon of efficiency, but it can be a dynamic force when the private sector is burned out and ineffective.

Reich's argument is an extension of the old controversy in economics about managerially controlled firms and profit-maximizing behavior. In that debate, it was the liberal position that there was a managerial firm, untrammeled by a sense of duty to stockholders, whose non-neoclassical properties negated the optimality implications of traditional competitive theory. Such firms would willingly engage in displays of technological virtuosity, research and development, innovation and growth, as exercises of managerial prerogative, irrespective of the effect on profit. Since there was nothing necessarily optimal about the nature or extent of such activity (automobile executives might as easily devote their energies to styling as to safety), government could feel justified to hold the corporation to a set of social commitments.

Reich's argument combines the liberal notion of managerial control with the neo-classical view of the individual as a utility-maximizer. Paper entrepreneurs maximizing their own take are the villains of his story. Reich has, in a sense, advanced the theory of the firm to the age of William Agee. For the politician, the appeal of this argument is straightforward. If habits and culture are the problem, then ideas can be the solution. Ideas are cheap. They do not require an appropriation of federal funds. Uniquely, they shift the supply curve without affecting the curve of aggregate demand. Hence they pose no risk of inflation. And the politician most closely identified as the advocate of such ideas can, in the imagination at least, expect a generous reward from a grateful public when the ideas begin to have their effect.[4]

The difficulty is that probably the ideas will not work. There is no practical experience of rising rates of saving and investment in response to greater self-awareness. Reich's contribution is to the analysis of the problem, not to the construction of a policy solution. It is implausible to suppose that great gains in capital formation will be achieved by anything so elusive as a cultural transformation.

III. Industrial Policy and International Competitiveness

The concept of "international competitiveness" itself is the key to the claim that industrial policy will directly aid the international competitiveness of the U.S. economy as a whole.

In the old days, U.S. manufacturing enterprises produced for domestic consumption and oriented their politics toward the exclusion of imports. The trade debates of the fifties and sixties were over the declining vitality of textiles and shoes, produced in the United States and sold to the American consumer. The great concerns of international economic geography had to do with assuring a secure flow of raw materials for our manufacturing industry. There was little concern with protection against our manufactured exports since both the exports themselves and the potential competition to U.S. sources were small compared to the flows of goods aimed at the American market.

The growth of the world economy doomed an inward-looking strategy by most of U.S. business. Certain industries, including aerospace, machine tools and capital equipment, and agriculture, began to require large export markets. The political consequence was the failure—for fear of retaliation in other markets—of efforts to secure general acceptance of protection for those industries, including steel, automobiles, shipbuilding, and consumer electronics, which came to be most strongly affected by foreign competition in the American market. While specific protectionist measures continued to be enacted from time to time, most were temporary or half-hearted (for example, "voluntary" restraints on imports of Japanese automobiles). Unions pushing stronger measures, such as local content requirements for the automobile industry, had to cope with political "allies"—liberal Democrats especially—whose public support was tempered by ill-concealed lack of conviction. The introduction of "international competitiveness" as an objective of government policy toward business can be seen as a conceptual device which repairs the potential divisions within the industrial community over trade policy. It makes what are in fact two different sets of interests—those of industries struggling against manufactured imports on one hand and those competing in foreign markets to expand U.S. exports on the other—appear to be the same. This has political uses, building joint constituencies for investment subsidies, protectionist measures, and export promotion at the same time. As a matter of public relations, the emergence of international competitiveness as a political issue is perhaps even a stroke of genius (see Diebold, 1979). As a matter of economics, the judgment must be different.

The phrase "international competitiveness" has no standard, technical definition. Its use in common speech relies for concreteness on the prior understanding and empirical judgment of the listener. "Everyone knows" that the automobile and steel industries are not, and that the aerospace and petrochemical industries are, internationally competitive. On the other hand, some individual companies, plants, or products "are" internationally competitive despite the low standing of their industry generally. And sometimes one hears a global reference: to the international competitiveness of U.S. manufacturing or of the U.S. worker as a whole. At least three distinct notions are confused together in the idea of international competitiveness.

At the level of the national economy, international competitiveness would appear to refer to the overall balance of manufacturing trade. When this is in surplus, we are competitive, when in deficit, we are not. Alternatively, the concept may refer to whether in a given period the surplus is increasing or receding.

At the level of the industry or large industrial corporation, international competitiveness would appear to refer to the trend of global market share. If a company is losing ground to competitors from overseas, in either domestic or external markets, then it has lost "competitiveness." If its share is stable or growing, then competitiveness remains.

At the level of the individual product or process, international competitiveness would seem to refer to the incorporation of the newest technologies and most efficient production designs.

None of these concepts withstands critical analysis as general rules for intervention into investment planning. First, it is a commonplace in economics that the balance of manufacturing trade at any particular time has little welfare significance. When trade in services and transfers are added to trade in goods, the U.S. record in recent years is close to equilibrium, and only seriously departs from it when the rest of the world economy is performing worse than our own (as in 1972, 1977–78, and 1983). Finally, given our unlimited access to financial capital on the world credit markets, even such disequilibria can be sustained for a long time.

At the level of industries and firms, it does matter to the managements and workers affected whether their companies and products are gaining or losing ground on world markets, particularly if total sales are not growing rapidly enough to keep labor and capital fully employed. But, so long as total sales of U.S.-made goods and services are high enough in the sum of all markets to sustain high employment and profitability, such issues are of only transient concern to the broader public. It may be that the Japanese, Koreans, and Brazilians will come to dominate the U.S. market for civilian supplies of certain steels. In the economy as a whole, there will always exist sufficient other potential activities to employ fully and productively those seeking work, although whether the potential is exploited is another matter.

Concern about international competitiveness at the plant or product level suffers from a similar fallacy of composition. It may happen that an older process using depreciated equipment will be run into the ground by its owner, until a new process installed elsewhere revolutionizes the industry—as happened between the United States and Japan with televisions, radios, and some parts of the steel business. So long as the capacity to innovate and the incentive to invest remain, it is impossible to imagine this happening across-the-board. So what if one particular industry declines, so long as another is rising? Since every anecdote about a collapsing U.S. industry can be countered with an example of one that is up-and-coming, one cannot construct a generalized argument of falling international competitiveness from the plant level upward.

The argument over whether a firm or industry or a product line is internationally competitive is at bottom an argument over whether that firm or industry is big enough. For one industry or several, it is possible to look at the issue this way—to argue that subsidies or protection or industrial policy can give us a bigger steel industry or a bigger automobile industry than we would otherwise have. But, in the aggregate of all industries, this issue is not one of subsidies or protection. One cannot reallocate resources to raise market share in every industry at once. The size of our industries is the consequence of our macroeconomic policies, our exchange rate policies, and our tolerance for inflation or for the measures needed to cure it. That we do not move to achieve the highest possible levels of employment and output is not due to inherent characteristics of American or foreign industry, as the concept of "international competitiveness" suggests. It is a matter of other priorities, and particularly macroeconomic policy.

IV. Winners, Losers, Basic and Sunrise Industries

Discussion of industrial policy seems to flourish when the political climate appears to be shifting to the Democrats and the economic climate away from recession and the immediate need to do something about unemployment. It is a time when business leaders open doors to the center and left that they would otherwise keep closed, and when labor leaders descend on Democratic politicians seeking subscribers to the particular variants of industry policy most helpful to the organized fourth of the workforce. At such times, it is easy to become absorbed in abstract arguments for and against a general program of industrial intervention, and to forget that in practice the motivations may be quite concrete. In principle, the auto executive and the labor leader want what we all want: a higher standard of living built on a better international economic performance. In practice, even a little unproductive reallocation of resources would do. When matters descend to this level, the arguments offered can cease to be subtle.

The most basic practical argument for selective intervention in particular cases is that some industry—steel, autos, semiconductors—is too important to be left alone. Such an argument, being purely subjective, is irrefutable. Opponents armed only with the abstract dogmas of free trade and free competition are at a disadvantage, despite the logical merits of their case. So practical arguments against selective intervention were devised that operate on the same rhetorical level.

The early public arguments for and against industrial policy turned on a rhetorical Hobson's choice, constructed by the opponents of protection, subsidy, and intervention to trap the advocates into an indefensible position. Industries come in two kinds: "winners," destined to succeed in the competitive environment of the future, and "losers," destined to fail. One should not assist losers, the argument went, since to shore up failing industries merely subsidizes inefficiency, retards adjustment to new and higher productivity activities, and condemns the population to a lower-than-necessary standard of life. And one cannot pick winners, since mere mortals are incapable of figuring out in advance which the winners will be.

Eventually, proponents of industrial policy figured out their rhetorical counterstroke. To replace the concept of "losers," the classification of "basic" industries was offered. And the term "sunrise industries" came to substitute for "winners," possibly because sunrises are predictable. These semantic innovations helped to reverse the burden of proof. There is no need to construct an argument around the proposition that losers should be abandoned. The proposition that basic industries should be left to their fate would seem to require one.

There is the problem of defining a basic industry. Is automobile production a basic industry? If so, why? If the reasons are size and importance to the health of the economy, then what about housing? Or domestic oil production? Or agriculture? If domestic oil production is basic, what about solar power? If agriculture as a whole is a basic industry, what about strawberries and kiwi fruit? We are in uncharted territory: there are no criteria for separating an industry from its close and distant substitutes, or for distinguishing within a generically "basic" industry between the essential and the frivolous. Most people would agree that national security provides a minimal case for basic-ness. On this criterion cases have been made for shipbuilding, for certain exotic metallurgies, for aerospace and atomic energy, and for steel.

The argument is not a good one. There are a few clear cases: nuclear bombs, high performance aircraft, ballistic missiles and atomic submarines, and some of the associated electronics. But within this sphere, there is obviously plenty of room to debate what is essential and what is not. And outside it, the national security cover does not fit neatly over industries which are primarily civilian. Consider steel. Leave aside, for the purposes of argument, doubts about the relevance of aircraft carriers and tanks to national security in the nuclear age, and forget that steel, compared to aluminum and other metals, has become a less and less important component of military hardware since World War II. Today, some modern and competitive steel-making facilities are devoted largely or entirely to the production of tin sheet for cans. If this is a basic activity, then what about the competition: glass, aluminum, and plastic? If those are basic industries, what isn't?

Moreover, programs to assist an industry, however basic, do not operate through the industry as such. They operate through the companies in the industry. A trigger price mechanism may be intended in principle to help steel. What it does in practice is raise the revenues of the United

States Steel Corporation (and the others). Reinvestment in steel may or may not be the result. U.S. Steel's acquisition of Marathon Oil was a widely noted counterexample. The problem is endemic to a system where companies are neither restricted to a particular segment of the industrial marketplace nor required to follow clear public guidelines in investment decisions as the price of government market intervention in their favor.

Lastly, preserving capacity for national security reasons may not be compatible with use of the same capacity for civilian purposes in the peaceful interim. Domestic petroleum production is the most clear case: one cannot both encourage the domestic production of oil (to reduce imports) and plan to have that same oil in reserve for an emergency. The surge capacity that some argue we should maintain in steel and shipbuilding is a financial drain on private corporations and a resource cost to the civilian economy. With some exotic forges and specialized machine tools, and the entire industry of munitions and ordnance production, there is simply no link between the basic (national security) industry question and the question of civilian industrial policy.

The case for "sunrise industries"—meaning help to the currently successful—is not more persuasive. We all know what a sunrise industry is. What we don't have is any idea what the appropriate eventual size of these industries should be. The semiconductor industry is already growing like Topsy. It does not follow that its growth should be faster. Sooner or later, indiscriminate subsidies will return to haunt the industry in the form of low rates of profit. Indeed, given the herd instinct of the venture capital market—witness the rush into so many bio-technology firms so far innocent of production or sales—this may happen without the benefit of subsidy.

V. Industrial Policy Overseas

Another case for industrial policy rests on comparison: since it worked for the Europeans and the Japanese, why not for us? Industrial policies do exist in many of these places, and considerable adjustment of export and consumption patterns has occurred. But the link between the two is not clear. The 1973–74 shock created a rapid shift in the world-wide locus of purchasing power, first to OPEC itself, and then, in the latter half of the seventies, to the Third World. This was because the industrial economies responded to the inflation induced by OPEC with contractionary policies; they slowed their domestic rates of growth and permitted rising unemployment. The principal economies of Latin America and Asia did not do this, at least not as much. The loans—recycled petrodollars—went where the activity was.

What we perceived as a "supply shock" with respect to the oil price was therefore also experienced as a "demand shock" by many of the industrialized economies of the world. There were changes in the pattern of demand facing the industrialized economies. Internally, these were away from energy-intensive consumption activities first, along with some decline in goods with higher income-elasticities of demand as real incomes fell. Externally, the shift was toward industries for export. It was apparent to some governments in Europe that faster adjustment and greater exports meant faster recovery with less eventual inflation. Thus the Germans and the French scrambled for export contracts in Saudi Arabia and Iran and Korea and Brazil, mainly selling the products of industries which had already been developed for the European markets: capital equipment, heavy engineering, nuclear power plants, and armaments. No doubt, some aspects of national policy were helpful in securing large contracts from government buyers. For the Japanese, the adjustment was to a changed United States automobile market, and here perhaps the government also played a role, though many would doubt it. The important point is that in no case did government policy invent markets or industries that did not already exist. And it is also true that certain components of U.S. manufacturing, such as the energy equipment and heavy machinery industries, did well in the new export markets without benefit of systematic government support.

In the United States today we look at the gains achieved by the French, the Germans, and the Japanese in the face of large induced changes in demand and in the pattern of world-wide growth in the mid-seventies, and we infer that similar results can now be achieved by industrial policy alone in the United States. This is a serious error. The situation is totally different today in OPEC and the Third World. Today, we would strengthen our Ex-Im Bank, rebuild our steel industry, perhaps subsidize aerospace and farm equipment and nuclear power, only to discover that these products could not be sold on the world market at any reasonable price. The balance of economic power in the world is again shifting, away from resource-producing and debtor countries and back into the hands of the creditor, manufacturing powers. Yet we ignore the most elementary consequence of this fact, namely that the power to induce demand shifts in our own economy without grievous international side effects is coming back into our own hands!

If it were clearly understood in the United States that European and Japanese industrial policies of the late 1970s were phenomena of adjustment—in part the result of policy but often a simple response to changing markets—a good result in U.S. policy design would be more likely but still not guaranteed. For the crucial difference remains that in the wake of

OPEC, the Europeans and the Japanese knew what they were adjusting to. We do not.

VI. A Course of Action

The valid goals of industrial policy in the United States can be organized around the idea of preparing for an uncertain future. Such an orientation leads to policies designed to foster the two attributes of success in any evolutionary situation: diversification and adaptability.

Who can say where the next shock is coming from? Will it be oil again? Or food perhaps? Or some breakdown of manufacturing trade due to financial calamity in Latin America? Or a Depression-style freezing over of the private economy in the United States itself? We don't know. And a sensible advance strategy conceived in ignorance of the future is likely to be quite different from one conceived as a response to an established threat.

Diversification is the pertinent objective, for example, when considering policy toward education, research and development, and support for basic science. The economic literature on the relationship between industrial structure and rates of investment in research and development and the rate of diffusion of new technologies stresses how little we know. Theory does not tell us how government policies affecting industry will affect the rate of creation of new knowledge. But this is an area where, unlike the question of corporate culture central to other hypotheses, what little we do know is enough to take action.

Policy which affects the creation and diffusion of new technical knowledge should not be concerned with speeding the process up. Instead, it can work to create a large range of opportunities for individuals and groups to foster new knowledge, in the confident hope that something will turn up. There are three arenas of policy which directly affect the diversity of technological opportunity. These are:
1. Support for science and basic research.
2. Support for education, training, and equal opportunity.
3. Democratic access to venture capital.

There is nothing novel about any of these three policies. A strong science base, abetted by national research and development projects like the space program or the Naval Nuclear Propulsion Program or the National Institutes of Health, is an established feature of our national scene. Government-university cooperation has a proven record of accomplishment. Not least, a strong commitment to science and technology research attracts the best scientific talent from overseas—a persistent glory of American intellectual life. Likewise education. One cannot specify in advance which among a population of workers and technicians will be best suited to which tasks. But it is certain that a broadly and well-educated population will be more productive on the whole than an ill-educated one, will be more receptive to constructive technological change, and will be a better electorate. There is no real mystery about how to improve public education. You spend money on it. The main thing about science, education, and training is that they compete with other uses for a limited pool of public funds. The danger is that in our enthusiasm for new and different means of implementing industrial policy we will divert resources from established strategies which are known to work.

Capital access is a more subtle problem, since the United States continues to have the most open capital markets in the world. This is partly because of our immensely diverse and unconcentrated financial structure, but also a side effect of the distribution of household wealth: it is possible for many new enterprises to get started on the strength of an uncle's second mortgage or a little partnership capital scraped up among friends. There may be no way to augment this network of personal relations directly. But it is certain that the relative openness of our capital markets will diminish with a continuing decline of the wealth and security of middle-income American households. This source of innovation and diversity may become an incidental casualty of tight money and high interest rates.

The pursuit of adaptability is in some ways more difficult than the pursuit of diversification, since in general it requires actual changes in the way government and corporations operate. But here too there are measures which are traditional functions of government which simply need to be attended to. In a mature society such as the United States, efficient use of social resources means conserving and reusing existing physical and human capital as the transition out of some economic activities and into others is made.

Our social capital is built up in our manufacturing cities. Streets, housing, water and sewer systems, schools, cultural facilities, urban transportation networks, and other public activities are as vital a part of the attractiveness of a city to investors as to those who live there. And such capital is uniquely vulnerable, under a federal system of government, to economic dislocation. It does not take much erosion of the tax base to force service curtailment and rate increases. These in turn depress the climate for new investment, starting a downward cycle leading to emigration and ultimately to a need to recapture what was lost with vast new public investments elsewhere. A first priority of industrial policy should be to avoid this waste of resources through the conservation of industrial sites, irrespective of the manufacturing activities which go on there.

The workers themselves are in an analogous position. They should be recycled, not thrown away. Retraining is only part of the answer. Work life in the United States is not well organized to facilitate mid-life transitions to new careers. It doesn't have to be this way. A great merit of the Japanese labor market is that workers are constantly being retrained on the job, so that they can move with relative ease between jobs of diverse skills. Since a focus on direct preservation of communities implies a relaxed attitude toward job transformation, a second but nearly equal priority of industrial policy should be to encourage reorganization of work life to make multiple skill development easier.

Another weakness of the U.S. political structure appears periodically when a large corporate entity—Lockheed, Chrysler, the Penn Central Railroad, or New York City—shows up on the federal doorstep on the brink of financial collapse. There is considerable admiration in the United States, perhaps among those who have not looked too closely, at the quiet and allegedly efficient way the French handled their steel crisis or the German banks the agony of AEG-Telefunken. Some wish for a quasi-public institution, flush with funds, which could handle comparable crises in the United States far from the klieg lights of Congress.

The enthusiasm for de-politicizing large scale bail-outs is misplaced. With any public financing vehicle, adverse selection is a major hazard. But there are few companies indeed who would voluntarily pass before the public humiliations visited on Chrysler, Lockheed, and New York by the banking committees of the House and Senate. And where bankruptcy and reorganization are clearly the preferable route, Congress occasionally finds the courage to say so, as it did in 1970 when it refused to rescue the Penn Central.

What Congress does need is a better ability to impose technical performance criteria on corporations it helps restructure with public money, and to monitor those criteria over the lifetime of a financial aid program. For example, when Chrysler came before the Banking Committee, where this writer then served as chief economist, there was no technical expert on whom I could rely to evaluate Chrysler's plans for future investment and return to profitability. Without this expertise, provisions written into law designed to ensure that public money was not wasted were unenforceable. Whether in the total absence of effective oversight Chrysler has in fact rejuvenated itself durably is just unknown at the present time.

Adaptability is served by selected bits of public entrepreneurship, particularly where large scale organizational tasks are required. In 1982, in its annual report to Congress, the Joint Economic Committee identified two such areas in the United States: passenger rail transport and the mining and transport of coal (U.S. Congress, March 2, 1982, November 3, 1981, June 4, 1982).

Major improvements in public or semi-public transportation networks, including freight rail lines, slurry pipelines, and ports, would be rewarded by large increases in U.S. coal production and export. As a member of the German Bundestag, Ulrich Steger, pointed out in *Challenge* (May/June 1982), it is all right to have level grade crossings in small towns so long as only one or two hundred-car coal trains go through each day. It becomes less practical when such trains are going through every few minutes. Greater coal production would, of course, reduce the market power of OPEC. It would also redistribute income from the greatest oversavers in modern history to the most prolific spenders (American workers) and so in a small Keynesian way alleviate the world economic crisis.

A program of high-speed passenger rail, similar to the Shinkansen of Japan and the Train de Grande Vitesse in France, could be constructed in up to thirty inter-city corridors in the United States where population densities are similar to those of Europe. Such a system or set of systems, with their great contribution to the efficiency of point-to-point transit, would help determine industrial location patterns for decades to come. Specifically, they would focus such investments on the end points of the rail corridors. As such, a high-speed passenger rail system would powerfully complement a community preservation strategy implemented in the major manufacturing cities.

VII. Conclusion

There is a valid role for industrial policy in the United States. It consists in generalized preparation for a future about which we know little. To meet it, we should be strong in science and research, broadly and well-educated, open in our access to employment and to capital. We need attractive cities with modern water and sewer facilities and plenty of good transport. Government and existing large corporations must develop flexible procedures to restructure capital and retrain workers.

These are modest steps. Industrial policy will not create full employment. It will not cure inflation. It will not raise the rate of investment in the economy nor the rate of productivity growth, nor will it lead to a permanently stable trade balance. To do these things, a program of generalized expansion would be necessary, accompanied by public employment for those least advantaged in the private labor markets. Also required would be low and stable interest rates, as well as strong incomes, energy, materials, and food policies to combat the innate tendency of a high employment economy to inflation. Industrial policy is no substitute for such measures.

Notes

1. These views do not necessarily represent those of the Joint Economic Committee or its members.
2. LICIT "is a coalition of industrial unions and corporations that was formed in 1980. . . . LICIT's charter states that the coalition 'seeks to represent the common interest of American workers and American business in promoting increased, balanced and equitable trade among all nations of the world.' "
3. For a survey of credit-oriented industrial policies, see U.S. Congress, Joint Economic Committee, June 26, 1981.
4. There is no apparent danger in this of a backlash from business for taking so uncharitable a view. In our peculiar corporate culture, criticisms of the Reich and Hayes/Abernathy variety seem to be what business people like to hear.

References

Abernathy, Robert, and William Hayes. *Business Management Practices and the Productivity of the American Economy.* Testimony before the Joint Economic Committee, Congress of the United States, May 1, 1981.
———. "Managing Our Way to Economic Decline." *Harvard Business Review* 58, no. 4 (July/August 1980): 67–77.
Adams, Gerard F., and Lawrence R. Klein, eds. *Industrial Policies for Growth and Competitiveness.* Lexington, MA: Lexington Books, 1983.
Bluestone, Barry, and Bennet Harrison. *The Deindustrialization of America.* New York: Basic Books, 1982.
Business-Higher Education Forum. *America's Competitive Challenge: The Need for a National Response.* April 1983.
Diebold, William. *Industrial Policy as an International Issue.* New York: McGraw-Hill, 1979.
Gunnar Myrdal. *An American Dilemma; The Negro Problem and Modern Democracy.* With the assistance of Richard Sterner and Arnold Rose. New York: Harper & Row, 1962.
Keynes, John Maynard. *The General Theory of Employment, Interest and Money.* New York: Harcourt, Brace & Co., 1936.
Labor-Industry Coalition for International Trade (LICIT). *International Trade, Industrial Policies, and the Future of American Industry.* Washington: 1982.

National Academy of Sciences, Panel on Advanced Technology Competition and the Industrialized Allies. *International Competition in Advanced Technology: Decisions for America*. Office of International Affairs, National Research Council, Washington: National Academy Press, 1983.

Reich, Robert. "The Next American Frontier." *The Atlantic Monthy Review* 251 (March 1983): 43-58; (April 1983): 96-108.

Steger, Ulrich. "Piling Up Social Dynamite." *Challenge* 25 (May/June 1982): 28–37.

U. S. Congress. Joint Economic Committee. *Report of the Joint Economic Committee, Congress of the United States, on the February 1982 Economic Report of the President*, March 2, 1982, Washington: U.S. Government Printing Office (USGPO).

———. *Case Studies in Private/Public Cooperation to Revitalize America: Passenger Rail*. November 3, 1981, Washington: USGPO, 1981.

———. *Case Studies in Public/Private Cooperation to Revitalize America: Coal*. June 4, 1982, Washington: USGPO: 1982.

———. *Monetary Policy, Selective Credit Policy, and Industrial Policy in France, Great Britain, West Germany, and Sweden*. June 26, 1981, Washington: USGPO, 1981.

PART IV

Money, Credit, and Economic Policy

7

Monetary Policy: A Reconsideration

JAMES M. STONE

Monetary policy was my academic field some years ago, and it is one of the few areas in economics with which I have tried to keep up. This attraction may result either from the importance of monetary policy or alternatively from the fact that it is among the most primitive fields in the profession. Economists really don't know very much about money, and this permits discussion of questions more fundamental and more interesting than those which consume most of economic study these days.

Milton Friedman is by any standard an influential economist. He has called fiscal policy useless for managing the macro economy, but he believes monetary policy to be such a powerful weapon that it can never be safely employed. Fischer Black, a professor of Finance at MIT, is one of the most perceptive economists of our time. His view, which (lest you think I exaggerate) I will quote from a recent (1976) unpublished paper, is as follows:

> I believe in a country like the U.S., government does not, cannot and should not control the money stock in any significant way. Monetary policy is passive, can only be passive and should be passive. The Federal Reserve Board monetary actions have almost no effect on output, employment or inflation. If a helicopter went around dropping money, there would normally be no force tending to drive up prices.

Any topic on which the debate is this basic is plainly ripe for discussion.

I. The Modified Keynesian Approach

The closest there is to a consensus view might be called the modified Keynesian approach. Keynes held that aggregate demand is derived from

111

consumption and investment. He looked at monetary policy as influential principally through the impact of interest rates on the investment component of demand. In its simplistic form, a Keynesian model would understate the role of consumer credit and overstate the influence of interest rates on capital formation decisions. Expectations with respect to real growth and inflation play a greater role in these markets than Keynes imagined, but the Keynesian framework nonetheless remains useful. It tells us that the best way to examine the impact of money is to trace its effects on supply and demand relationships in the real economy.

A familiar equation is often used to translate changes in the money supply into fiscal terms. The equation, $MV = PQ$, may be the most widely known identity in the profession. It is also one of the most difficult to use. It fits everyone's model of the world. Friedman looks at it and sees the relationship between money and prices. Fischer Black would see velocity as an equal and opposite reactive variable to nominal money supply. Keynesians like to ponder how a given change in M will affect each of the other three variables at various points in the economic cycle.

Among the problems in any use of the monetary identity is that M has proven impossible to define. When I was in school, it meant cash and demand deposits. Later it included certain time deposits. Today we ask whether it should encompass NOW accounts, automatic fund transfers, or American Express checks. The V term, velocity, was never defined as much more than whatever falls out when M is divided into the product of P and Q. P and Q, of course, we cannot measure either. Q should be in units of product, independent of price. But is a $4 haircut the same product as a $40 haircut? Few even pretend to know how to formalize quantity measurement. My advice is to understand the monetary equation as a thought device, not a measurement device. It is for use by rationalists more than by empiricists.

It helps illustrate, for example, how increases in the money supply can be lost in velocity or prices rather than reflected in real output growth. A good monetary policy is one which concentrates growth, both short and long term, in Q instead of V and P. Policies which reduce the ability of Q to grow in the long run are slow-acting economic poisons. Policies which reduce Q in the short run are acute toxins.

II. Inflation and Tight Money

Growth in M becomes growth in Q through investment. The impact on investment (whether in human or physical capital) is the first thing to consider in judging a monetary policy. The United States has been running a tight monetary policy ever since inflation became a national issue. Despite a change from an interest rate focus to a money stock focus and part way back again, the Federal Reserve has been constant in its desire to use monetary policy as a brake on the fiscal situation. The short term impact on investment has been negative. The policy must accordingly look further out along the time horizon for its justification.

There is a theory under which this regimen makes sense, and it holds considerable sway in the financial community these days. If we assume, first, that inflation would never have arisen absent poor fiscal management in the 1960s, and, second, that inflation feeds on expectations and its own momentum, we might conclude that a purgative would be a sufficient cure. Once the momentum was stopped and government's toughness established, in this scenario, inflation would halt. Future growth without inflation would then become possible.

These years of monetary restraint have, in fact, come close to purging inflation. The Federal Reserve is wagering that it will not return, that it was a creature of past sins and not a companion of modern industrial structure. No small stakes have been placed on that belief. The short-run decline in output put millions of people out of work in the United States and abroad. The impact on global capital formation may last for years. Would the public have approved this wager had it been presented for a referendum in advance? The trade of double digit inflation for double digit unemployment would have been a rough sell. Yet there must have been a public ambivalence or Congress would have taken a stand. People seemed to be just gritting their teeth, closing their eyes and hoping it would work. It took remarkable fortitude on the part of our monetary leaders to hold the course with so weak a mandate. If their wager proves sound, we will someday all thank them. If it fails and inflation returns, the cost having been borne for naught, we will look back on the policy as arrogance and paternalism.

The key question is whether inflation is structural or happenstance. The structural argument begins with the observation that a modern economy has little in common with Adam Smith's model of pure competition. In his world everyone would be a price-taker and no one a price-maker. Today it is hard to doubt that there are corporations and unions large enough to be price-makers; negotiated prices are common. And since the New Deal the government has increasingly sought to protect people from the harsh personal consequences of pure competition. All of this has contributed to the demise of untrammeled, atomistic competition and the price stability it embodies. It is certainly not obvious that a period of high unemployment will have more than a passing impact on inflation.

The Fed's wager is risky, but there is a safer side bet for the administration. The president, in his political capacity, does not have to worry about inflation's eventual return. A temporary victory is enough for reelection.

It must be a source of comfort for White House political strategists to know that, even if inflation is inevitable in a strong modern economy, a lag will occur between business recovery and reinflation. Should the Fed's theory be mistaken, there will still be a window of many-months duration during which production will have returned while inflation will not. There is good reason to expect this type of window in 1984, and this may explain why the White House is so silent now on monetary issues.

This paper will be best forgotten if the current monetary path does indeed give us decades of high growth with stable prices. If, however, inflation returns whenever production growth improves, it will be time to think about abandoning the policy of induced recessions once and for all. It seems that each time the nation is made to suffer a period of induced high unemployment to no avail, the public's belief in the power of inflation only grows stronger. As a consequence it takes a deeper recession to dampen inflation with each succeeding attempt. This is how rational expectations work. After all the muscle applied in recent years, the reaction will be fierce if inflation shows itself capable of appearing yet again.

Perhaps monetary policy should abandon its macroeconomic pretensions and concentrate on the allocative role it inevitably plays. Not all uses of credit are equally valuable to an economy, and free market theory provides little comfort on the question of selectivity. Our profession is surprisingly ignorant about the market's ability to balance investment and consumption. Trade-offs between present and future are hard to weigh, and we can barely frame the questions when unborn generations have a stake in economic outcomes. Even if aggregate investment were sufficient, which I doubt, there would be no assurance the free market could allocate properly between private and public investment or between human and physical capital.

III. An Alternative Monetary Policy

A monetary policy I would be comfortable with would ask explicitly where we want the next dollar of capital to go. I would not, for example, be thrilled to see an increasing tilt toward speculation. Although defenders of speculation insist that it has no effect on the funding available for investment growth, their assertion should not be accepted lightly. There had to be an impact on access to ordinary loans, for instance, when silver speculators took a sizeable share of all the new bank credit extended in February of 1980. And although only dramatic cases like this capture the public fancy, the effect is similar when a large enough number of small speculators are active. Regardless of size, all speculators must constantly maintain liquidity in case markets turn against them. Every line of credit extended for this purpose reduces the banking system's ability to commit credit elsewhere and pushes the composition of assets toward greater liquidity. Since long-term growth requires a willingness to accept illiquidity, this is not good news.

Unproductive financial activity also expends human resources. No other economy in history has put so much of its talent into such marginal pursuits as we do. Too much of finance and too much of law, both of which professions draw heavily from the dean's list at our best economic institutions, are concerned with matters of scant societal import or real resource consequence. Brainpower is not a glut on the market in any society. In ours its allocation is uniquely skewed away from the real investment sectors.

Monetary policy is among the strongest allocational tools in the government's arsenal. Today, however, financial deregulation is in vogue; and the reigning thinkers regard credit preferences as indicia of barbarism. The issue is *not* really so simple. Deregulation encourages rapid and frequent diversion of money and credit as notions about available returns change. This is a dubious benefit at best, and especially dubious when the financial sector is highly concentrated. Do we want credit patterns to change more rapidly than human beings can realistically be expected to alter their training or residences? Do we accept the implications of funneling the savings of millions of individual American households through half a dozen decision centers and then off to wherever in the world the return appears greatest at the moment?

One is told that people want the highest possible interest on their savings, and this requires pushing the money to the highest earning sectors and locations. Yet I have long suspected that virtually any community would prefer lower rates of return on savings if this assured local credit availability for mortgages, small business expansion, or other such needs. There is a case to be made for a bit of sluggishness in the system. An entirely deregulated banking structure reminds me of a rowboat with a cannonball in the bottom. Every little shift of wind or water sends the cannonball slamming into one side or another of the boat. I would never defend permanent subsidies for economic relics, but there is nothing wrong with putting a little sand in the bottom of that rowboat to slow down the cannonball.

Historians will someday find it strange, I suspect, that this country's economic management depended for decades on a policy of purposely induced recessions. It will appear stranger still that these recessions were focused on essential capital markets. Economists of that future day may wonder why our economists thought monetary policy could be run out of synchronization with fiscal policy. All the more so, they will puzzle over our commitment to non-intervention in credit flows, to our mysterious indifference between unproductive finance on one hand and human and physical capital development on the other. It is true, of course, that selective government participation in credit direction has many costs. We will soon be able to judge whether tight money everywhere has been a constructive substitute.

8

Broadening Capital Ownership:
The Credit System as a Locus of Power[1]

A. ALLAN SCHMID

Let us begin with some of the striking facts of the current U.S. economy. There is over 10 percent unemployment and over 30 percent unused plant capacity. Wealth remains highly concentrated. There are substantial unmet public and private needs. Our public infrastructure of roads, bridges, sewers, etc., is deteriorating, and waste disposal is becoming life-threatening. Significant numbers of people are ill-housed. The combination of unused resources and unmet needs is prima facie evidence of institutional failure. The social system fails to organize production.

It shall be argued that part of our institutional failure to realize our productive potential lies in a too-narrow control of the credit-debt creation process of our capitalist system. One of the major property rights creators is not government but the private banking system, and when access to rights in future production is held too narrowly, some of our productive potential is wasted. Broadening the ownership of capital creation is hypothesized to be instrumental in the realization of our potential as well as its distribution.

The plan of this essay is to first review the familiar credit-debt system in perhaps less familiar property rights terms so that the sources of power to allocate resources and share in their benefits can be identified. The problem then is to find institutional changes that can make the system perform differently. Two ideas for broadening capital ownership will be proposed for the research and public debate agendas. The first is that of zero-yield public debt to be issued during recessions for money-supply expansion.

The second is a financed capitalist plan allowing citizens access to new bank credit for the purchase of stock issued for new investment. Both have to do with ownership of new debt and subsequent production. Both might contribute to full employment and a more equal income distribution.

These are not new ideas, but they have received little scholarly analysis. Perhaps it is because they are so ridiculous that they should be rejected out of hand. Or perhaps they have been rejected too soon because they do not fit the prevailing paradigm and conventional wisdom of economics. My purpose is not to argue that these are conclusively valid instruments to achieve full employment and a wider distribution of income, but rather to argue that they deserve a place on our research and public debate agenda.

I. The Credit System as a Locus of Power

Before changes in the credit system can be suggested, it is necessary to develop a picture of it as a locus of power. Banks are the central institution of a capitalist system. They are brokers facilitating trades between individuals with different time preferences (channeling individual savings). But, more important with respect to unemployment, banks serve to energize the future. I take it that growth is often a matter of roundabout production— that is, it involves the creation of producer goods. The creators of these producer goods need to eat before there is anything to sell and thus there must be some system for them to share in current output.

One way for this share to be obtained is from the decisions of individuals to reduce their use of current output and trade it to creators of producer goods for the promise of an interest in the future consumer goods. As already noted banks act as brokers in these transfers of existing demand deposits, and banks live off the margin of what they pay for savings and what interest they can obtain for loans. But, in addition, banks have the power to create new demand deposits.

In property rights terms, banks have the power to transfer claims on current output without the permission of its former claimants. Banks are institutions of nonvoluntary saving in the sense of bringing new people into the current flow of production. Let's look more closely at this familiar process of new demand-deposit formation in perhaps somewhat unfamiliar property rights terms. An industry sees an opportunity for profit in an expected future sale of a physical output. Industry goes to the bank and offers an interest in the future output in terms of a promise to pay. Industry sells its debt due in the future at a discount. Industry needs a claim on current output in order to pay its suppliers now. This can be provided by banks who buy industry debt due in the future with bank debt past due (this conception is from Commons 1934, 449). The bank's debts past due are new demand deposits which are general purchasing power over ongoing production. To capitalize future expected output is to obtain a claim on present output via bank debt demand deposits.

Thus banks force the economy as a whole to save in the sense that some of current output is diverted to making producer goods instead of being consumed. Banks can cut in new users of current output without asking anyone—subject only to the rules limiting the amount in proportion to existing deposits. In order for this saving to occur, it is not necessary for any individual to buy a savings account or bond or receive *any* payment for this enforced abstinence.

Today's loans pay for inputs to producer goods which also generate the income necessary to purchase today's output and validate (repay) yesterday's loans. Debt pays off debt in a repeating process.

The creation of more demand deposits by banks increases the money supply relative to the existing flow of goods and is thus inflationary. This is functionally equivalent to the government issue of greenbacks by which the military was cut in on current production to fight the Civil War. Claims on current production are reallocated by the credit system whether by private banks or government issuance of paper. We have carried over this analogy, and today, when governments want the money supply increased to cover public deficits, we speak of running the government printing presses. But nothing so crude is necessary. Banks have the right to create money by writing numbers after the names of anyone, including, as we shall discuss below, the name of the government, labor, or AFDC mothers.

For now, the point is that the method by which creators of producer goods obtain access to current production is by inflation. Of course, if the borrowers are successful in expanding production, supply increases to offset the greater money supply. And, if the ongoing process is stable and continuous, there is new supply of goods coming on line from past investments so the consumer may not notice any real decline in consumption, but rather an increase over time.

In current practice, a primary method of financing new plant and equipment is via retained earnings rather than bank borrowing. There are two sources of these earnings. One is increased profit from input-saving efficiencies. This requires no increase in money supply. The second source is raising prices which is only possible in total if consumers have more money via consumer debt. Consumer borrowing is an alternative to producer borrowing. Consumers expect higher income in the future and then pay more for goods today providing profits for investment. This is an alternative to producers expecting a profit in the future and borrowing for investment. While the function of shifting current output to producer goods is the same either way, the claim to shares of future output is quite different. Consumers pay the interest rather than producers.

Another difference is in the ability to fulfill expectations. When consumers lose confidence in growing incomes, the demand for consumer loans drops, particularly for costly items such as we see now for houses and cars. While organized labor can do something to fulfill its prophecies of future income, it is less than the ability of concentrated industry to increase prices. This means that sectors financed by consumer borrowing are much more unstable that those financed by producer borrowing. Thus there is some reason to support public policies of selective credit availability other than the usual bow to housing ownership having external social benefits (Silber 1972).

The purpose of this introduction is to see the credit system as a locus of power. We are used to seeing legislatures as distributing property rights, but banks also do it. Banks can redistribute rights to current production as surely as any government tax and transfer payment. The individual has no veto over either one. The key question in either case is who gets what shares in ongoing and future real output. The person who recieves the bank-created demand deposit for investment gets control over the residual net profit margin after the input suppliers and the bank itself get their shares. Note that when new demand deposits are created by loans everyone contributes in reduced consumption, but only a few get claims on the profit margin from the future output—just the owners of the borrowing firm and the bank.

II. Zero-Yield Public Finance

Unused labor and producer goods are the factual starting place of this analysis. This means that it would be possible to increase the rate of current or future production without reducing current consumption. Whether current production claims are reallocated is a policy matter. There is no opportunity cost for an unused resource, so its use cannot reduce total output. The claim that these nonworking resources make on current output can be altered. From any given starting place of resource owners living from transfer payments or starvation, this claim may be increased and current output reallocated, but it is in any case unaffected in total.

The point is that saving in the sense of reduced total consumption is unnecessary to achieve investment if there is unemployment, whatever the distribution of claims to the available output. When banks increase loans, and *if* the money is paid to the unemployed at going wage rates, there is a shift in claims to the current output whose total is unaffected. This appears as savings for some, but in total, consumption (Y_1) remains constant even though investment increases. And *if* the unemployed are employed in existing unused plant, there is little waiting for increased consumption (Y_2).

The problem is that during periods of falling aggregate demand, inventories accumulate or are sold off at losses, and no entrepreneur wants to borrow to create more or make producer-good investments when there is unused plant capacity. This is the current situation, and it appears to be the classic case for which the Keynesian policies were designed (Thurow 1982). Yet current policymakers hesitate to use deficit spending for anything but the military. Military production is the poorest choice to achieve full employment via government spending because its supply is relatively inelastic (causing inflation), and because of its relatively low employment multipliers. Part of the hesitation is an ideological objection to an enlarged role of government. Part is a concern with public dept service costs. Interest on the debt was $57 billion in 1980 and was expected to be $110 billion in 1982. It is a major category of federal spending after social security and the military, and about the same as spending for health. In 1981, the net interest budget outlay was 4.3 percent of GNP, compared to 5.6 percent for national defense (Fuerbringer 1982). A similar situation exists in the United Kingdom where interest on the public dept is 10.6 percent of government current expenditure in 1980 (Economic Research Council 1981).

It is time to ask what functions this interest serves. Government gave the right to banks to create rights in current output and thereby energize future output. When no one wants to take advantage of this, then government does the borrowing and increases aggregate demand. But, why does it pay banks to create demand deposits when it gave the banks this creative power in the first place? I must conclude that it does so out of pure habit, or that it has a distributive objective in mind which is served by taking taxes from general taxpayers and giving it to the banks and a few others who own government bonds.

As an institutional alternative, we need to find a way to put demand deposit numbers after the government's name as the commercial banks do for private borrowers without creating interest-bearing debt.[2] The demand deposit so created (no printing press needed) at no interest cost to government would be no different from the demand deposit created by banks for a fee. But, it would affect income distribution and remove one of the inhibitions to public debt expansion. Bringing unemployed resources into production at no real cost does not require creation of an asset for financial institutions and investors, nor does it require adding to the reserves and loan capacity of banks. It need not interfere with the Fed's money-supply objectives.

It should be noted that the Federal Reserve System creates interest-free debt when it does use the printing press for currency. What we call currency is the debt paper of the Federal Reserve which commercial banks needing currency pay for with their reserves. The Fed in turn takes these private bank reserves and buys government bonds. The interest on these bonds is returned to the Treasury (after the funds necessary to run the Fed are taken out). This means that a small proportion of the public debt is interest-free. It is payed for by selling currency to banks. This is debt paying for Federal Reserve system debt paying for government debt. Debt pays for debt pays for debt, and so on.

The payment of interest on public debt does not draw much comment from economists but seems to infuriate less-scholarly observers. Thomas A. Edison wrote, "It is absurd to say our country can issue thirty million dollars in bonds but not thirty million dollars in currency. Both are promises to pay. But one promise fattens the usurers, and the other helps the people" (Mayer 1974, 34).

To be sure, not all of the $110 billion current interest payment is for new debt because some of the borrowing represents savings. But the increase from the $57 billion of 1980 to the $110 billion of 1982 took place in the context of rising unemployment, and the rising debt had no opportunity cost in terms of reduced total consumption when government used resources otherwise wasted.

Now government creates new money by monetizing the public debt. The Fed buys government bonds from banks by creating demand deposits for banks at the Fed. There is no reason it cannot create its own debt past due (cash) and give it to the Treasury to buy things owned by a wider spectrum of the population (rather than just selling cash to banks). The prime candidate is labor. This can be done directly by hiring labor to produce useful goods such as roads, parks, and sewage treatment plants—anything whose supply can be increased.

Government also could give cash to all citizens declaring a social dividend. The only problem with that is if the debt expansion is for any purpose, some may be used where supply can't be increased. Thus the government might issue vouchers usable only for goods with unused capacity such as housing and cars. This presents a political problem because all producers would like more demand even if supply is inelastic, because it increases their incomes relative to others. There must be a careful evaluation of unused capacity. Even those producers of goods not eligible for vouchers would benefit once the economy begins to move again.

Another version of zero-yield public debt is for the Fed to buy debt directly from the Treasury. The Treasury would write checks on the Fed and make deposits in banks to be used to buy goods and services (or the Fed pays suppliers directly by checks drawn on the Fed, in which case bank deposits are increased as before when the checks are cashed). Both direct purchase and direct distribution of currency increase high-powered bank reserves and interfere with money management (though the Fed could sell bonds to reduce the reserves without concern for what that would do to Treasury cost of borrowing).

In the first case, the Fed creates its own debt in the form of cash, while in the second it is in the form of a demand deposit. Both are non-interest-bearing claims on current output of the economy to the benefit of the Treasury.

A third version of zero-yield public debt could require banks to create demand deposits for the Treasury (with no corresponding cash flow to the banks). The Treasury could proceed as above to write checks to input suppliers and for the vouchers when presented for payment. This version has the advantage of not changing bank reserves. The new debt is a Treasury-owned demand deposit which is debt past due and is not discounted (earns no interest) but is a new energizing claim on unused resources.

There is an advantage to putting the unemployed to work via vouchers producing public or private consumption goods. Since investment has been slow for some time, the rate of new output coming on line from past investment is also slowed. If the unemployed get a larger claim on current output because they are paid at the going wage (above current transfer payments) there is a reduction in consumption for others. This sharing can be eliminated very quickly if total output for consumption is increased by putting unused labor and existing plants together. The combination of government employment and directed vouchers has the best chance of increasing output so that the increased money supply is non-inflationary.

One of the current anomalies is that the money supply continues to grow, but investment in new plant and equipment is nil. Where does the money go? Some goes into inflation of consumer prices; some into inflation of producer goods such as land; some into mergers and more recently into the stock market (at least for the moment). During rising interest rates, more must be borrowed just to keep even. Existing plant is undervalued relative to new, so corporations borrow money to buy them instead of building new. If government can't direct some of this to productive investment, just increasing money supply will not suffice.

To summarize, interest-free debt could be implemented by (1) the Fed creating cash and giving it to the Treasury; (2) allowing the Treasury to sell public debt directly to the Federal Reserve; or (3) requiring the banks to create demand deposits for the Treasury. The amount is to be determined by the amount of unused resources which the government estimates could be employed by some combination of direct government employment and vouchers issued to consumers. In terms of broadened capital ownership, zero-yield public finance gives the unemployed effective control over their own capital-forming work rather than letting it go to waste.

Also, everyone who benefits from the governmentally produced goods gains from the reduced waste of resources. Conservatives may object because it provides a means whereby citizens express a demand for government vs. private production outside of the tax system. The government appropriates some of the growth potential for the private sector without it first going into the pockets of entrepreneurs and then trying to get some back in taxes. Incidentally, this is the only method of paying for public output that I know of that does not distort relative prices including the leisure-work trade-off as taxes are claimed to do.

Academic discussion of zero-yield public finance is limited. Among those who have noted it are John R. Commons (1934, 589–90) who argued that "In order to increase the purchasing power of labor the unemployed must be put to work by *creation of new money*, and not by *transferring* the existing purchasing power of taxpayers to laborers . . . nor by borrowing money by government which *transfers* investments but does not augment them. . . . In order to create the *consumer demand*, on which business depends for sales, the government itself must create the new money and go completely over the head of the entire banking system by paying it out directly to the unemployed, . . . to farmers, the business establishments, and practically all enterprises. . . . " He doesn't specifically speak of zero-yield public finance but that is consistent with going "over the head of the entire banking system."

Clarence Ayres (1974, 276) also observed the destruction of money in a depression when credit is contracted. He recommended the re-creation of money via deficit financing and suggested that "there is no good reason why such a program should not take the form of the outright issue of currency . . . up to the amount of purchasing power necessary to absorb the product of industry at full employment. . . . "

The most widely discussed and detailed suggestion for new monetary institutions came from Irving Fisher of Yale (1935). It combined and added to the first two approaches discussed above. Fisher called his book *100% Money* and its essence was to remove the rights of banks to create money via the fractional reserves system and return this right as specified in the Constitution to the government in the form of a Currency Commission (CC). The 100 percent reserves would be established during a depression by the CC buying government bonds from banks so that the banks would have a cash reserve deposit equal to their demand deposits. Professor James Angell (1936) of Columbia suggested that instead banks should give a general prior lien on their total assets equal to the value of the new currency (reserve deposit) received. The liens would carry no interest and would probably never be extinguished. Banks hold the reserves only in trust for demand depositors. The bonds are payed for by the interest-free debt of the government's CC. This does not increase banks' loan capacity in a 100 percent system. With the right to create demand deposits withdrawn, all banks become investment bankers, making their profit wholly on the margin between the cost of borrowed funds (including their own capital) and interest received, and charging for processing checks on demand deposits.

After the 100 percent reserve was established, the CC would regulate the money supply by further open-market operations buying and selling government debt. The money supply is adjusted to maintain constant price levels. As the economy grew, the CC might have retired all existing public debt as it increased the money supply by buying government bonds. At that point, the CC would increase the money supply, when needed to maintain constant prices as output increased, by buying government debt directly from the Treasury.

The Treasury could use the money to reduce taxes or to issue a "social dividend." Fisher doesn't specifically speak of paying cash for direct public employment, but this obviously could be done. Fisher (1935, 208) suggests that "the Government's main receipts would eventually come from the Currency Commission, merely by virtue of its efforts to prevent deflation by putting new money into circulation as business grows."

Fisher's objective was to reduce the wild swings in the business cycle and prevent bank credit contraction and failures such as was experienced just before he wrote in 1935. The creation of interest-free public debt was incidental to regulation of the money supply. Contrary to some monetarists today who advocate a constant fixed rate of money growth, Fisher's system would increase the growth of money as prices fall and decrease it as prices rise. He argued that the fractional reserve systems added to inflation. As demand for loans rose, the banks created additional demand deposits faster than output rose, thus causing inflation. Nominal interest rates rose, but because of inflation, real interest rates fell. This works just the opposite to the theory that would have interest rates rise to increase the supply of savings and decrease the demand for loans. As we have recently seen, if real rates fall, people buy goods rather than save, and even more demand for loans occurs as profit expectations are fueled by rising prices.

Under a 100 percent reserve system, increased demand for loans cannot result in new demand deposits unless the CC thinks output can be increased so that new money doesn't raise the price level. Otherwise, loans must be supplied from real savings, switching demand deposits to investment instruments. This would establish the conventional equilibrating role of interest rates as in current macro theory models. These models now pretend that the rate of interest plays this role, but ignore the ability of banks to create claims on current output independent of individual decisions to save.

It is not clear that it would be desirable to make savings and the resulting investment and growth rate wholly a market result of individual savings decision. This is why in the third alternative above, the right of banks to create money (force savings when new demand deposits are created) is retained but shared with the government in times of depression. Full discussion of Fisher's 100 percent money takes us too far afield from the focus of this paper, but it does serve to raise questions about interest-free debt in the context of the functioning of the macro economy. A variation of Fisher's approach has been proposed in the United Kingdom by the Economic Resource Council (1981).

It is one of history's ironies that Fisher took his basic idea of 100 percent money from Henry C. Simons and others at the University of Chicago, the home of the conservative monetarist Milton Friedman. Some of Simons' ideas are now carried by James Buchanan, a Chicago graduate. Buchanan and Flowers (1975, 335) argue that "interest payment of the 'debt' created in this way [creating additional currency] is largely unnecessary, and does not serve at all the same purpose or function as interest payment on real debt [savings transfers]." Robert A. Solo (1967, 269) says a large part of the interest on the Federal debt is "the cost of a social tabu." These few modern comments are rare. Is it because this is such a wrong or impractical institutional change or because it does not fit the prevailing professional paradigm?

III. Financed Capitalist Plan

The Financed Capitalist Plan (FCP) is the brainchild of the lawyer Louis Kelso. His objectives are full employment and increased aggregate demand through broadened capital ownership (Kelso and Hetter 1967, 1973). The essence of FCP is that corporations would be required/encouraged to finance a portion of new plant and equipment by stock issued to workers (and others) who borrowed the money from banks and repay with dividends. This would replace a certain amount of current bank borrowing by corporations.

Currently, the average worker would find it difficult to borrow money to buy corporate stock. First he or she has little collateral and the dividends seldom exceed the interest on borrowed money since corporations keep a large share of earnings for further investment, as noted above. Kelso notes that it is the going concern encompassing the productive capacity of the entire firm (workers as well as machines) that is the collateral and reality behind the expectation of future output which is capitalized when bank loans are created. Yet, under current property rights, it is only the corporate management and current stockholders that hold title and control over the newly created capital. Kelso would give the workers a share of that new capital and thus create new capitalists.

If workers borrowed money for new plant and equipment, the repaying capacity is the same going concern as before. But if the banks accept the workers as borrowers it is a recognition that they are part owners. The bank could evaluate a corporation's proposed stock issue and accompanying loan application by the workers in the same fashion as when the corporation management applied for a loan. The difference is in the distribution of the profit margin. Kelso claims his plan does not alter ownership of past capital formation, only of the new. It is a forward-looking distribution of rights. But, in a capitalist system, to alter future claims is to alter present value.

Let us look at the details of the plan as proposed by Kelso and interpreted by Speicer (1977, 72-73). First Kelso would apply FCP only to the largest successful corporations who in 1976 made $120 billion of new expenditures for plant and equipment. Legislation would require 100 percent of capital outlays to be financed by FCP. The corporation which wants to obtain investment funds makes available to the FCP mutual fund a number of stock shares equivalent to the desired funds at the then market value of its stock. So if it wanted $1 million and its stock were selling at $100/share it would issue 10,000 stock shares. Corporations are required to pay all earnings not necessary for operating capital as dividends (at least the new capitalist share). Either the corporation tax is eliminated or dividend payments to new capitalists are tax deductible. In 1976, he estimated that the average large corporation earned 20 percent return on investment capital which would more than cover cost of borrowed funds.

Eligibility to be a new capitalist would be determined by Congress, but Kelso suggests that priority be given to those with little capital now. Kelso and Speicer emphasize that capital ownership must be broadened even beyond those working for the large firms. Eligible persons go to banks and apply for their alloted shares. The new capitalist owns a proportional share in a pooled mutual fund. Banks loan the full amount of the stock purchase and create the usual demand deposits for corporate investment. These loans can be rediscounted by the Federal Reserve System. The loans are nonrecourse and no risk for the new capitalist. Banks hold stock in escrow until paid for in dividends. If dividends are insufficient to cover amortization, banks can sell stock in the market. If that is insufficient, the loans are insured by the government with fees of one-half percent per year paid by the banks (similar to FHA mortgage insurance).

Kelso estimates that at 20 percent dividends, the loans are repaid in 7 years and the stock's future dividends are paid to the new capitalists. If Congress prefers that the new capitalists have some immediate income from the stock, the repayment period could be extended.

FCP changes ownership of the returns to new bank-financed investment and thus eliminates the use of debt leverage. Leverage is the financial mechanism reflecting the property right of current stockholders to gain from new debt creation (after the bank gets its cut, of course). Mature corporations seldom use new stock to finance investment because it dilutes earnings per share. The explicit cost of capital via stock issue is usually higher than cost of debt since the new stockholder by law gets the same dividend as the old. So the old stockholder has to share all of any new net returns rather than just pay the tax deductible fixed interest. Investment is desirable if expected returns are greater than the market interest rate charged by banks. Earnings per share increase up to that point.

FCP redistributes claims on growth by eliminating leverage. What then is the objective of management? It is still to invest as long as returns exceed the interest rate. The effect on earnings per share depends on the number of shares which is now a variable. Kelso suggests that shares be priced at their market value. The stock market tends to equate capital returns in all stocks. If a firm earns more on its capital goods expenditures than the market rate of interest, the earnings are capitalized into stock price and the returns relative to stock price are forced to the market rate of interest. The capital gains are to the benefit of the previous stockholders, which is not Kelso's objective. So if stability holds, the FCP stock fund would earn only what it paid banks for the money. This capitalization of future expected earnings into present-value stock prices is one of the reasons that when mature corporations do sell stock it is usually below its current market price in order to attract buyers.

It would appear that if the objective of the FCP is to raise the income of new capitalists, the new capital provided must be issued shares (priced) at the same relationship between shares and cost of capital goods which characterized the previous capital inputs. When this is the case, and the new investment goods have the same return as the old capital goods, the earnings per share (even with more shares) remain constant. If the firm's returns on new funds exceed the interest rate and exceed the rate of return on the previous investments, earnings per share will rise to the benefit of old and new stockholders compared with the no new capital case. Of course, the existing stockholders would have received even more if debt leverage were part of their property rights. Instead, the new rights acknowledge that workers and the rest of society also contribute to the firm's ability to expand production or in any case have rights to part of that new production. It would be possible to price the new shares so that their owners get all of the new profit and none is shared with the old stockholders. The key to distribution is the number of shares per dollar of new debt money created by FCP borrowing.

If share of returns is proportional to the share of capital cost contributed, then if the return to capital is falling but still greater than the market interest rate, earnings per share must fall to the detriment of the old capitalists. The old stockholders had high returns in part from capturing past growth in debt, so it should not be surprising that this cannot be sustained if others are cut in. There is no conflict here between growth and a more equal income distribution (there is the same investment criterion as before), but it is redistributive as earnings per share decline. It is unlikely that we can give everyone access to the new debt and bring everyone up to the income of the old capitalists in the short run.

In the discussion above, it was suggested that the firm's managers should issue new stock (as they now issue debt) until expected returns equal the cost of bank borrowing. But, the firm under FCP has no fixed obligation to pay the market rate of interest for their risk class. What is the discipline that makes management try to avoid investing too much if there is not the fear of bankruptcy from not being able to meet fixed debt obligations? Perhaps some penalty could be exacted on the firm by the government if the dividends do not cover the FCP mutual funds cost of borrowing. Future capital access could be restricted (growth does seem to motivate managers). The banks might be expected to withhold loans to the FCP for firms that are judged to be over-extended. But, the banks' incentive is limited if loans are guaranteed. Why does Kelso suggest the government guarantee? Why shouldn't the firm pledge its collateral as a going concern as before? The only difference in FCP is that people other than existing stockholders are regarded as owners who may pledge part of the plant and equipment. Since the workers and the community contribute to the total productive capacity of the firm, it may not be unreasonable to regard them as part owners of the capital goods to the extent of pledging some of them as collateral. Before, only existing stockholders could promise the firm's total productive assets as the ability to produce future output and to pledge that part of the total comprising capital goods as collateral, and thus they received all of the net returns. Certainly if the managers make a mistake and the firm's survival is threatened, the workers and their community have as much to lose in terms of their other fixed assets (and maybe their pensions) as the existing stockholders who are usually better diversified. The fact that the bank only wants the plant and equipment if there is a default does not mean others have nothing at risk. A city cannot recover its debt for public infrastructure when a firm dies and stops paying taxes any more than stockholders can recover their asset values.

Kelso speaks of the loan being nonrecourse for the individual citizen-borrower. This needs further elaboration. The assets of the firm obtaining money from the FCP can still be at risk. If it defaults, the value of the FCP mutual fund portfolio is reduced and the bank loses. The assets of the firms obtaining the money are at risk, not the personal assets of the individual new stockholders. They are borrowing as part owners of the firm, not as owners of cars and homes. The corporation's credit is based on the same reality as before, only different people have a claim. That reality is capital goods in place, the work force, and the community.

As indicated, the key to distribution in this scheme is the pricing of the stock (shares per dollar of new debt obtained). One existing financial instrument that could be adapted to FCP is the convertible bond. The bond is a device for sharing in the growth of stock value. This bond states a price at which the bond can be converted to stock. This could be chosen by government as part of its rights redistribution process establishing the share of new debt to be allocated to old and new capitalists (rather than the above described process of setting the price of new stock so that old and new shares are proportional to contributions to the cost of capital goods).

If the new bond-financed investment adds to stock value, then the bond holder can convert to stock and share in the growth instead of being limited to a fixed-interest rate of return. Firms could be required to finance a certain proportion of investment by convertible bonds bought by the FCP mutual fund. As with the Kelso approach, the bonds could be financed by citizen-borrowing for the firm. If there are no new net earnings and no advance in stock prices, the bond is not converted and the citizen-owned mutual fund breaks even by paying the bank just what the firm paid in interest to the FCP mutual money fund. The required convertible bond is recognition of rights to growth by those other than existing stockholders. The cost of capital to the firm in terms of interest rates would be the same on the convertible as on the regular bond (which is not now the case). The interest rate could be determined in the usual way and banks could evaluate the bonds in the usual way. If the conversion price is tied to existing stock prices, the convertible feature would have value only if the investment does better than the market expectation of leveraged earnings. The point in raising the convertible bond concept is only to suggest that different instruments could be chosen effectuating various splits between old and new capitalists.

Community Claims

The rationale for broadened capital ownership rests in part on the fact that more people contribute to a firm's output than the stockholder or even the workers. The community provides many inputs of services and environment which are now leveraged into earnings per share. The new claims on debt-created money for new investment need not be wholly individualistic. Organized collectivities such as local governments could be issued shares in the FCP mutual fund or even, specifically, in those new stocks issued by firms within their boundaries. A portion of new stock issued to the FCP could be given to the local government in which the new capital spending is located.

To put this in perspective, consider how local governments now participate in corporate finance. The rapidly growing device is the issue of municipal bonds to provide low-cost investment funds for industry. This is done in the name of producing jobs. It is a tax subsidy from the federal government which is in effect a payback of part of the wages of workers to the employer. It appears as if going-wage-rate jobs are created, but after all workers pay the necessary taxes, they have really offered to work for less. This real wage reduction is further reinforced by competition between local government for corporate investment which results in property tax reductions—services provided at less than cost by removing full-rate taxpayers. Some states are using Federal Community Development Block Grants to provide public infrastructure useful to industry.

All of this capital input into new investment results in no equity interest by individual or collective taxpayers. It is the existing stockholders who reap any profits, though the taxpayer-contributed capital is also at risk. One way to acknowledge the community input would be to offer municipal bond-raised money to firms only in exchange for equity stock (or for a convertible loan as described above). If local government were represented on boards of directors, firms might consider the loss of local fixed assets when evaluating relocations.

Pension Plans

A discussion of broadened capital ownership must include reference to the growth in employee pension plans. This rapid growth has come from union wage bargaining in the form of future income obtained by investment of "wages" into stocks of the employer and other firms. This bargaining power is aided by substantial tax subsidies.

In a qualified employee-deferred benefit plan, the corporation gets an immediate tax deduction for any payment to the plan (as it would if it were a wage). Employees pay no taxes on these contributions or on any earnings or capital gains they earn until they are paid out upon retirement. Some plans are limited in the amount that can be invested in the employer's own securities but there are no such limits for employees' stock ownership plans (ESOPs). Only ESOPs can use leverage to borrow money to buy employer securities (1974 Employee Retirement Income Security Reform Act).

This latter feature was stimulated by the lobbying of Kelso, who with Senator Russell Long has been looking for a nonrevolutionary way to start toward his vision of universal capitalism. The leverage feature of ESOPs allows the corporation to get tax deductions for both principal and interest payments on money the ESOP borrows to buy stocks. Even so, the new stock issues are dilutive and direct bank loans are still more remunerative for most firms. ESOPs have had some modest successes. One use is as a vehicle for rescue of a troubled firm. Its employees can buy the firm on credit, repaying loan principle and interest as tax-deductible expenses. This is primarily a tax transfer to selected companies. It does put employees in the position of access to new debt issued by banks, but if the company is financially troubled the banks are only interested if grants from others are large. And the original owner would never have relinquished control if the operation were profitable. One of the oft-cited applications was in the rescue of the South Bend Lathe Co. in 1975.

ESOPs benefit the employees of a few firms, which leaves out many people. As Speicer (1977, 186) puts it, "We've got to diffuse ownership of stock in the successful large corporations, not in their discards." Speicer notes that most ESOPs involve small or closely held businesses, and the few large corporations which use it are special cases. While ordinary pension plans are owning a lot of stock, they benefit the employees of the most successful companies with strong unions and not the full spectrum of those most needing a stake in American capital.

Kelso's vision of universal capitalism caught the interest of Senator Russell Long. Long seems to have seized upon pension plans as a modest and saleable first step. In the 1975 Tax Reduction Act (and 1976 Tax Reform Act), Long tied ESOP contributions into the investment tax credit. This version is called TRASOP. A corporation could give one percent of capital outlays as stock to an ESOP and receive an equivalent tax credit. This one percent free stock at government expense for the benefit of the employees of the largest corporations may be a partial offset to the 10 percent investment tax credit to stockholders, but it does little to help those who need it most. According to Speicer (259–60), Long is aware of the limits of TRASOP but hoped to embed it in law and then make more of the investment tax credit dependent on use of TRASOPs and move on from there. I am not so sure that the idea of private property rights redistribution is furthered by increasing tax transfers.

To close this section, it should be emphasized that while the ESOP is what made Kelso well known—and rich as a consultant—it is not the vehicle he proposes for universal capitalism.

Professional Economist Reaction

The profession has greeted the idea of FCP with a profound silence. The only public academic response has been that of Paul Samuelson. The occasion was a 1972 legislative proposal made by the governor of Puerto Rico, Luis Ferre, with input by Kelso (Speicer 1977, 105–21). The Puerto Rican version was a Proprietary Fund Co-Investment Plan open to workers who earned between $800 and $7,800 per year. Each worker could buy $50 of fund stock annually matched by $50 contributed by the government. The $50 worker purchase was to be financed by a non-recourse bank loan guaranteed by the government. All of this is pooled in the diversified Proprietary Fund (PF). The fund would buy stock from voluntary sellers.

The PF differs so much from FCP that its relationship is tenuous. This is probably unavoidable at a level of government less than a large nation. First, there is no requirement that corporations pay all earnings in dividends so that the normal return would unlikely be sufficient to pay for the borrowed money even with the 50 percent government subsidy. To subsidize it further, the corporate income tax paid on earnings proportional to PF-held stock would be paid to the fund. The dividends paid on fund shares are tax-exempt for the shareholder.

Second, there is no prohibition of leveraged debt finance. As was noted above, mature corporations seldom dilute present stock with new stock when debt is an alternative. If property rights in new debt are not altered, there is no way to get corporations to issue new stock except with subsidies. In the PF proposal, incentives to sell stock to the fund were provided by making capital gains so realized tax-free. This sounds as if it would only transfer existing stock at great profit to existing stockholders rather than make firms issue new stock to obtain funds for new investment. The proposal limited this tax-free sale to $100,000. It is not a device to change ownership of new debt finance. Citizens borrow from banks to buy stock, but it is largely paid for by government subsidy and not new claims on new output.

The Proprietary Fund bill passed the Puerto Rican House, which was controlled by the governor's party. The Senate, however, was controlled by another party, and the president of the Senate asked Prof. Samuelson for his analysis of the bill. Samuelson's analysis appeared in the *San Juan Star* (reprinted by Speicer 1977, 111–14). Samuelson presented a scathing critique. The main focus of the critique was an attack on an economic theory propounded earlier by Kelso rather than on the bill itself. Kelso had argued that capital contributes 75 percent to output while labor contributes 25 percent (Kelso and Hetter 1967). Kelso reasoned that since labor receives 75 percent of income, its wages are excessive. This offense against modern factor-productivity studies seemed to lead Samuelson to the conclusion that Kelso could not have any other valid ideas. Samuelson said, "Because the basic economic principles underlying the proposal are faulty, it is likely in practice to prove a cruel disappointment. . . . " He seems to be referring to Kelso's mistaken view of factor productivity rather than any consequences of property rights redistribution. But, since there was so little of Kelso's new property rights ideas in the PF bill, Samuelson might be excused from analyzing them.

Samuelson does obliquely touch on the notion of access to new debt in a statement about bank loans for purchase of stock: "You cannot get something for nothing in economic life," referring to the scandal of John Law's inflation of the French currency. He added, "If the Commonwealth guarantees bank loans to purchase Patrimony stocks, it has less credit to expend in other directions of development."

The image of "something for nothing" is one that must be dealt with by anyone proposing a full blown FCP. Kelso makes the point that loans for new investment are paid back with earnings from the newly created debt money, regardless of who owns the debt-repaying capacity and who borrowed the money. The fact that the PF bill does not provide claims on this new output sufficient to repay the workers' borrowing is not part of Samuelson's analysis. The issue is not "something for nothing," but who owns the "something." The reference to John Law is irrelevant. The same borrowing by a corporation from banks to the benefit of existing stockholders is no more or less inflationary than if that borrowing were done in the name of workers for their benefit.

The fact that there is an opportunity cost if the Commonwealth guarantees bank loans to purchase PF stocks is true but not enirely to the point. One wonders why Samuelson does not take the same opportunity to indicate the opportunity cost of government loan guarantees often used to encourage private loans in high-risk areas. To determine the relative payoff to public funds would require an analysis of the spillover of different kinds of new investments and not who is the equity owner obtaining the loan. The real failure of the PF proposal in terms of the opportunity cost of scarce institutional reform resources is that it largely uses subsidies to buy existing stocks for the worker rather than to reallocate property rights in the future benefits of new credit and investment. But then, one would not expect a scientist to enter that distributive fray. In any case, the PF bill was defeated, and economists looking for research topics will probably remember that Samuelson was extremely negative on "Kelsoism."

The only other serious professional examination of FCP (albeit nonacademic) was by the staff of the Joint Economic Committee (1976). Staff member Robert Hamrin seriously discussed an approach proposed by the Sabre Foundation called the Capital Formation Plan. It is less ambitious than FCP in that it does not prohibit debt leverage, and it only provides incentives for paying out earnings as dividends. Eligible investors with some savings would be allowed a tax deduction (or tax credit) up to $3,000 per year for purchase of shares in public- or private-managed mutual funds who buy only new shares issued by corporations. To encourage corporations to sell their stock, the tax law would allow dividends paid on this stock to be tax deductible. But we have already seen that treatment of "principal" repayment as tax deductible has not caused a stampede to ESOPs where this provision is already available. It cannot overcome the disadvantage of stock dilution if current stockholders have the right of leverage. The plan further provides tax incentives to reduce the use of retained earnings for investment. A split-rate corporate tax now used by Germany, Japan, and Austria could be implemented. Hamrin suggested a 20 percent corporate income tax on distributed earnings and 50 percent on those retained. The report suggests this is a strong incentive to do more equity financing . This seems doubtful as long as debt finance is available.

The capital formation plan has so little of FCP in it that it is closer to the Puerto Rican plan. It is primarily a tax subsidy to allow purchase of stocks. Even if it increases dividend pay-out, this does not allow new buyers to bank-finance stock purchase, as the stock price would just rise capitalizing the higher pay-off. Timid plans rely on diverting the use of tax funds while the real FCP redistributes private rights to future earnings without going through the Treasury.

IV. Conclusion

The institution of zero-yield public debt and the financed capitalist plan have a common feature. Both change property rights in credit-debt creation. The one allows government to put unused resources to work when no one else wants to, without incurring an obligation to redistribute money from the general taxpayer to the banks. Government need not compete for savings, but rather can create new symbols to direct the unused resources which have no opportunity cost.

The financed capitalist plan also changes ownership of credit-debt by denying the right to leveraged debt by current stockholders. It redistributes claims on future output not via the tax system, but by changes in private property rights. It implicitly recognizes a right of workers and the community when the total assets of the going concern are promised as the reality behind the ability to produce new future goods which supports a loan. Again, the issue is not allocation of savings, but rather ownership of new money-debt creation.

These are not marginal institutional changes for the timid. But neither are they disruptive of the on-going capitalist system of production. Capitalism is retained, but its ownership is broadened, and thus the claims on its fruit are broadened. A more universal and stable capitalism seems possible. These institutional ideas seem worthy of further scholarly analysis and a wider public discussion. If scholars continue to ignore them, men and women of affairs may just implement them anyway. The body politic seems to be searching for alternatives to even greater reliance on the tax system and direct governmental management, or to reliance on governmental withdrawal from and benign neglect of the economic system.

Notes

1. Michigan Agricultural Experiment Station Journal Article Number 10767. Paper presented to the Public Policy Workshop, University of Notre Dame, November 5, 1982. Thanks without implication to Warren Samuels, James Shaffer, David Reisman, James Generoso, Bob Rasche, and Jim Johannes.

2. Prior to Volcker, the Fed bought a great deal of government debt on the open market to keep the interest cost of public borrowing down. This was not zero-yield public finance. The purchase is after the obligation to pay interest was incurred (or its realization in present-value bond prices). None was regularly bought directly from the Treasury. Wright Patman frequently suggested abolishing interest on the Federal debt held by the Fed. But this is mere cosmetic accounting since any surplus of the Fed is already returned to the Treasury. The original bond buyer has received the capitalization of its interest whatever the net taxpayer cost of interest courtesy of the Fed creating its own debt.

References

Alperovitz, Gar and Jeff Faux. "Beyond Bailouts: Notes for Next Time." *Working Papers for a New Society* 7 (November/December 1980): 14–18.

Angell, James W. *The Behavior of Money*. New York: McGraw-Hill, 1936.

Ayres, C. D. *The Theory of Economic Progress*. New York: Schocken Books, 1962.

Bazelon, D. T. *The Paper Economy*. New York: Random House, 1959.

Buchanan, James M., and Marilyn R. Flowers. *The Public Finances: Introductory Textbook*. Homewood, Ill.: Richard D. Irwin, 1975.

Christ, C. F. "On Fiscal and Monetary Policies and the Government Budget Restraint." *American Economic Review* 69 (September 1979): 526–38.

Commons, J. R. *Institutional Economics*. New York: Macmillan, 1934.

Dillard, Dudley. "A Monetary Theory of Production." *Journal of Economic Issues* 14 (June 1980): 255–73.

Economic Research Council. *Government Debt and Credit Creation*. London: Economic Research Council, Research Report No. 9, December 1981.

Fisher, Irving. *100% Money*. New York: Adelphi, 1935.

Fuerbringer, Jonathan. "Ways to Look at Deficit Vary." *New York Times*, November 30, 1982.

Galbraith, John Kenneth. *Money—Whence It Came, Where It Went*. Boston: Houghton-Mifflin, 1975.

Generoso, James. "Social Credit 1918–45: An Essay and Select Bibliography." *Paideuma*, forthcoming.

Helfert, Erick A. *Techniques of Financial Analysis*. Homewood, Ill.: Richard Irwin, 1977.

Hiller, Brian. "Does Fiscal Policy Matter? The View From The Government Budget Constraint." *Public Finance 32*, no. 3 (1977): 374–89.

Joint Economic Committe. *Employee Stock Ownership Plans (ESOP's)*. Hearings, 94th Cong., 1st sess., December 11, 1975, Dec. 12, 1975 (Washington: U.S. Government Printing Office, 1976).

Kelso, L. O. and P. Hetter. *Two-Factor Theory: The Economics of Reality*. New York: Random House, 1967.

———. "Corporate Social Responsibility Without Corporate Suicide." *Challenge 16* (July/August 1973): 52–57.

Leontief, W. W. "The Distribution of Work and Income." *Scientific American 247* (September 1982): 188–204.

Mayer, Martin. *The Bankers*. New York: Ballatine, 1974.

Minsky, Hyman. "Capitalist Financial Processes and the Instability of Capitalism." *Journal of Economic Issues 14* (June 1980): 505–23.

Robinson, Joan. "Solving the Stagflation Puzzle." *Challenge 22* (November/December 1979): 40–46.

Schmid, A. A. "Symbolic Barriers to Full Employment: The Role of Public Debt." *Journal of Economic Issues 16* (March 1982): 281–93.

Shaffer, J. D. "Power in the U. S. Political Economy—Issues and Alternatives." *Increasing Understanding of Public Problems and Policies*. Chicago: Farm Foundation, 1975.

Silber, W. L. "The Excess Burden of Monetary Policy." *Journal of Money, Credit and Banking 4* (May 1972): 414–18.

Solo, Robert A. *Economic Organizations and Social Systems*. Indianapolis: Bobbs-Merrill, 1967.

Speicer, S. M. *A Piece of the Action*. New York: Van Nostrand Reinhold, 1977.

Thurow, L. C. "The Great Stagflation." *New York Times Magazine*, October 17, 1982.

Voorhis, Jerry. *Out of Debt, Out of Danger*. New York: The Devin-Adair Company, 1943.

PART V

Ownership, Participation, and Democracy

9

Creating a More Participatory Economy[1]

COREY ROSEN, WILLIAM FOOTE WHYTE, AND JOSEPH BLASI

According to a recent study by the New York Stock Exchange (1982), if American companies were to embark on a serious effort to involve employees in decision making at all corporate levels and were to reward employees with a share of the gains such participation would create, productivity in the United States would increase by 20 percent in one year—more than it has increased in the last ten altogether. A recently reported study in the *Journal of Corporation Law* (Marsh and McAllister 1981) found that companies with employee stock ownership plans (ESOPs) had annual average productivity increases twice those of comparable conventional firms. These findings tended to corroborate another study of employee ownership, this one by the University of Michigan's Survey Research Center (Conte and Tannenbaum 1980), which found that employee ownership firms were 150 percent as profitable as their conventional counterparts.

These impressive data are not the only sources of support for employee ownership and participation. "Quality of Worklife," "Theory Z" and related concepts have become the darlings of management consultants, and not an insignificant number of companies (see National Center for Employee Ownership [NCEO] 1982). Ronald Reagan thinks employee ownership is a fine idea; in fact, the Republican Party put it in its 1980 platform. But Tom Hayden, Gary Hart, Ted Kennedy, and even the Pope like the idea too. Russell Long has been its ardent champion in the Senate (Long 1982).

It is not a new idea that the economy—and the polity—would work better if employees owned and participated in the management of their workplaces. John Stuart Mill (1965) said it was the only way the economic

141

system could survive in the long run; Albert Gallatin, secretary of the Treasury under Jefferson and Madison, said that "the democratic principle upon which this nation was founded should be applied to the industrial operations as well" (Mason 1982, 148).

It has only been in the last few years, however, that American companies and unions have begun to take these ideas seriously—none too soon, we would argue, in light of our continuing economic problems. Over 5,000 companies now have employee ownership plans, and even more are said to have quality of worklife programs (estimates are not too reliable, however). At least 500 companies have a majority of their stock owned by employees and together employ well over 300,000 people (NCEO 1982).

Yet despite all the political support, and despite the increasing evidence that ownership and participation work, the number of American workers involved in these efforts is still very small, probably under 5 percent. This is an idea which can improve productivity, has the broadest kind of political support, and is entirely consistent with American notions of individual ownership, free enterprise, and personal initiative. Yet it is still something of a curiosity, and very much a newcomer.

At the same time, existing ways of doing things have left us with an economy in which 1 percent of the population owns 50 percent of the privately held wealth, which is about the same as it was 100 years ago (see U.S. Congress, Joint Economic Committee 1976). Moreover, the democratic society which we cherish is increasingly eroded by large private and public bureaucracies in which individuals have little control. Socially, politically, and economically, we desperately need a mechanism that can energize our companies, broaden opportunities, and give people more of a sense of control. And we need to do all this without reliance on large government programs.

It is our conviction that employee ownership and participation can provide the basis for this revitalization. The steps needed to accomplish this "profitable revolution" rest largely with the private sector, for it is a revolution that can be made entirely within the current system. The federal and state governments, however, have a significant role to play. By providing well-targeted incentives, by making more information available, by supporting needed research, and by financing a limited number of the most innovative ownership and participation efforts, government can do much to move these ideas along more quickly. The ideas have not yet penetrated the market to the degree they must to cause basic changes in the economy, but they have established some important beachheads in many growing, innovative companies. With proper nurturing, the possibility at least exists that in the near future they could become a standard way to do business.

I. Participation and Ownership: What They Are

Because we have focused our own efforts on employee ownership, we will similarly focus this paper on that subject. Many of the steps the government can take to encourage employee ownership, however, can also be taken to encourage employee participation programs—quality of worklife, joint area labor management committees, participatory management, etc. Participation programs (programs in which employees are given significant control over the organization of their jobs and/or the right to participate in management decisions) and joint area labor management committees (where union and business leaders meet together to plot strategies for community revitalization) have been exceptionally successful. Those interested in pursuing the subject further should consult the best book on the subject, *Working Together*, by John Simmons and Bill Mares (1983).

Employee ownership has been around for over 100 years, but it is only in the last decade that the idea has had a potentially significant impact on American buisiness. Over 5,000 companies have employee stock ownership plans (ESOPs), and several thousand others have some other form of widespread worker ownership, including at least 800 worker cooperatives. The typical ESOP, about which we have the most information, owns about 15–30 percent of company stock. In at least 10 percent of the ESOPs, the plan owns a majority of the stock—and this percentage is increasing (NCEO 1982). Employee ownership companies are found in all types of businesses, and are established for a variety of reasons. Contrary to popular impression, however, relatively few employee ownership plans (less than 1 percent of the total and less than 10 percent of the majority-owned companies) are the result of employee buyouts of failing firms (NCEO 1982). Most are set up as an employee incentive, with another large percentage coming from profitable independent businesses in which the plan is used to transfer ownership from a retiring owner to the employees.

Only an estimated 25 percent of the employee ownership plans (but 57 percent of majority employee-owned companies) provide workers with full voting rights on their stock. In many employee ownership companies, in fact, ownership is little more than an uncertain right to a relatively small amount of stock at termination or retirement. Nonetheless, there are many other companies where ownership has been the basis for a complete restructuring of labor-management relations. The success that these firms have had suggests the enormous promise of employee ownership.

Three examples illustrate the point. W. L. Gore Associates is a high-technology manufacturer ("Gore-Tex" and other products). It is 95 percent employee owned and almost totally democratically structured: there are no hierarchies or job titles, and employees vote all their shares. This may strike many as a recipe for chaos, but Gore has used the creative energies the plan has unleashed to grow 40 percent per year for the last several years. It now has 2,000 employees and is building seven new plants (Rosen 1982–83). People's Express Airlines advertises that its employees, after just two years, already own an average of $55,000 worth of stock each. Employees work in self-managing teams, with many jobs rotated. In a tough market, People's Express has grown very rapidly and has the lowest cost per seat-mile in the industry (Rosen 1982–83). Science Applications, a 3,600-employee R & D firm, is 85 percent employee owned, as it has been from the outset. The employees vote all their shares, and their active participation in the company is considered a key to its considerable success—a 1200 percent increase in employment and a 2000 percent increase in its share earnings over the last decade (Rosen 1982 – 83).

In part, the recent growth in employee ownership stems from the publicity these and other success stories have revealed. For many companies, employee ownership is just good business. Also of considerable importance are the tax incentives Congress has provided ESOPs since 1973. ESOPs are a kind of employee benefit plan. Companies set up a trust and make tax-deductible contributions of stock or cash to it. Employees thus can acquire stock, and even entire companies, without buying it out of their paycheck or savings. Stock in the trust is generally allocated to accounts for all full-time employees either according to salary or some more egalitarian approach. Employees gradually acquire vested rights to their stock, generally becoming fully vested in ten years or less. In publicly held companies, employees must be able to vote their allocated shares; in closely held ones, they must be able to vote only on a few major issues (but about 15 percent of these firms allow full voting rights anyway). ESOPs can also borrow money, making it possible for companies to deduct both interest and principal on loans; they also are very attractive as a means for business owners to sell out their shares to employees. The tax incentives of ESOPs have acted primarily as sweeteners—they encourage companies to consider employee ownership but are rarely the primary factor in setting up a plan.[2]

A third reason for the growth of employee ownership has been employee buyouts. Although comprising only a small percentage of all employee ownership plans, their dramatic nature, and the fact that many of the most important innovations in plan structure have come from these buyouts, have given the idea of employee ownership wide publicity. Their remarkable success (over 90 percent of the 50 or so buyouts are still in business, and many are very profitable) has given employee ownership considerable credibility (NCEO 1982).

Recent worker buyouts fall conveniently into two periods: the 1970s and 1980s. In the 1970s almost universally the prime movers in the shift to employee ownership were members of local management. Workers cooperated simply to save their jobs and made no demands for participation or control. Furthermore, in most of these cases, workers did not have to make substantial sacrifices in order to save their jobs. In some cases, the plant had been yielding a profit, but not enough profit to satisfy the conglomerate decision makers. In other cases, local management people correctly concluded that the unprofitability of the plant was due primarily to mismanagement by remote control so that establishment of local autonomy would make the company profitable.

In the 1980s, with the deepening recession, we found major changes in both the principal actors and in the financial arrangements. In cases such as Rath Packing Company (Whyte 1983) and Hyatt-Clark Industries (Sokoloff 1984), it was union leaders who initiated the buyout, and the financing arrangements involved workers sacrificing part of their pay and benefits in return for ownership. In the 1980s a union also pioneered in establishing the first investment fund to finance worker cooperatives. The fund was the result of a wage concession package between A & P and the United Food and Commercial Workers in Philadelphia (Philadelphia Association for Cooperative Enterprise 1982). With the concessions, A & P was able to reopen 40 Philadelphia stores under the "Super-Fresh" name, and the UFCW was able to secure an agreement to dedicate 1 percent of the gross sales of the new stores for an investment fund. Thirty-five percent of the fund will be used to open new worker-owned supermarkets, two of which, under the O & O name (owned and operated by workers), are already underway.

II. Employee Ownership and the Economy: Areas of Potential Contribution

The most obvious contribution employee ownership can make to the economy is its ability to improve profitability and productivity. We have already cited some of the evidence on this point. As we write this, in fact, one new study, done by the National Center for Employee Ownership, is being completed showing that majority worker-owned firms generate three times the average annual employment growth of comparable conventional firms (NCEO 1983).

We are also finding growing evidence that the potential for employee ownership to enhance worker motivation and commitment to the firm may be greatly enhanced if ownership is complemented by worker participation. In fact, in some cases, ownership without participation may lead to negative effects, as evidenced by occasional strikes at a few majority employee-owned companies. It appears that when workers are made owners, they often acquire expectations that they will be treated with more dignity and that their input in decisions will be requested and respected. When these expectations are disappointed, workers may react even more strongly against management than they would if they had never come to share in ownership. Unlike managers and private investors, workers are unaccustomed to thinking in terms of separation between ownership and control. If they are told the company is theirs, they naturally assume that they should have some say in how their property is managed.

There are a number of other important contributions ownership can make, however, besides improved company performance and greater job satisfaction:

1. Employee ownership makes possible greater flexibility in adjusting wages and work time to changing market conditions. When all workers are co-owners, it becomes much easier to reduce the hours without reducing the workforce, thus maintaining overall employment.

2. Employee ownership makes "concession bargaining" more equitable. In fact, when workers get stock for wage reductions, as they have at Chrysler, Pan Am, and several other firms, they are really making a "tradeoff," not a "concession." Concessions are made when something is given up and nothing is given back in return; tradeoffs involve an exchange. Workers should be more inclined to accept financial sacrifices when they get stock in return. They recognize that, if their company goes bankrupt, their stock will be worthless, but, if they help their company make a comeback, they stand to gain back some or all (if not more) of what they sacrificed. Furthermore, this kind of bargaining is likely to bring with it greater worker participation in management.

3. Employee ownership also contributes to job retention because worker owners can accept a lower return on capital than private investors. For example, when Bates Fabrics Company became employee owned, the treasurer said he expected the new company to have enough money from bank loans to modernize its equipment and still make 7 percent on invested capital. No private investor simply interested in a high and secure return on capital would have been attracted by a 7 percent return (U.S. Congress 1979). For workers, the potential dividends were insignificant compared with keeping their jobs.

The same logic applies to the decision of management to continue manufacturing in the United States or to open a subsidiary abroad. Suppose studies indicate that a U.S. plant can only be expected to make 5 percent on invested capital whereas a comparable plant in Taiwan or elsewhere promises to yield 20 percent. For a privately owned corporation, this comparison calls for a decision to close the U.S. plant; for an employee-owned company, the logic is quite different.

4. Employee ownership is also gaining importance as a means of protecting a company from corporate raiders. In 1978, in a much publicized case, employees of Continental Airlines formed an ESOP in an attempt to prevent Texas International from taking over their company. The employees agreed to trade major wage cuts for bank loans to enable the ESOP to purchase 51 percent of Continental's stock. After a long legal struggle, the Continental employees failed, but they did not launch their ESOP until Texas International had already acquired almost 49 percent of the stock. Had the ESOP been started sooner, employees might well have bought the company ("Continental Workers Fly as They Buy" 1981). In a major case now in progress, Dan River, Inc., a 100-year-old textile firm employing 12,000 people, is establishing an ESOP and bringing suit to block a takeover attempt. In this case, the ESOP is being set up at management's initiative (NCEO June 1983).

To be sure, in academic circles the effects of mergers and takeovers on the economy are controversial. At the very least, however, it is often clear the corporate raiders are not really interested in managing companies so much as collecting them, often for tax or cash management purposes. Thus, it is often in the interest of workers, managers, and the community to be able to block such takeovers.

5. Employee ownership can also be important in keeping small businesses in operation. Many profitable small firms cease to exist when entreprenuer-owners approach retirement and have no heirs interested in the business. In such a situation, the owner or owners can sometimes get their money out by selling to a larger corporation. In many cases, however, this is either not possible or the owners do not want to see their company owned by another firm. In these cases, an ESOP provides a mechanism whereby employees can acquire the firm through the pre-tax earnings of the corporation, rather than their own after-tax savings. The owners get tax breaks as well (though not tax breaks as beneficial as when selling to large companies for an exchange of stock). This device is certainly preferable to the usual other alternative—liquidating the firm to provide cash for retirement or estate taxes.

6. Finally, employee ownership offers an intangible but important value in terms of our democratic ideology: it contributes to a more equitable distribution of wealth. In companies that are just marginally profitable, employees would make small but significant gains. In companies that are highly profitable, the financial rewards could be broadly shared among the labor force.

Moreover, employee-owners are, all other things being equal, more likely to pursue a course of long-term investment strategies, strategies that can maintain their jobs, as opposed to the short-term profit-maximizing strategies preferred by most non-employee shareholders, particularly large institutions.

III. The Future of Employee Ownership

Is employee ownership simply a passing fad or is it a broad social movement that is bound to become increasingly important? We believe that employee ownership has a growing appeal as a means of solving labor-management conflicts, improving productivity and the quality of working life, saving jobs, maintaining successful small businesses, and protecting firms from corporate raiders. We also believe it can be an integral part of an effort to revitalize our democratic system.

There is a growing network of people actively involved in employee ownership, including students and professors capable of providing technical assistance and research, non-profit organizations, professional consultants, government institutions, and a variety of other groups. It is reasonable to argue that all of this comprises the necessary elements for a possible "take-off" of this relatively new idea.

Employee ownership is also now widely accepted by the American population. In 1975, Peter Hart found that Americans would prefer to work in an employee-owned company by a 66–25 percent margin (see NCEO 1982).

The major obstacle to continued growth now seems to be inertia and a lack of understanding. Unions, for instance, often perceive employee ownership primarily as a device for saving failing firms. They also incorrectly perceive that unions will not continue in employee-owned companies. In fact, these firms are more unionized than conventional firms. Even in employee-controlled companies, unions continue to play a traditional role, bargaining over wages and management, settling grievances, working with management to set up participation programs, etc. Moreover, they take on the added role of organizing employees to vote their stock. Business leaders, on the other hand, often are simply unaware of employee ownership. Those that are familiar with the concept often fear providing workers with participation rights, even though, in practice, managers at democratic companies are virtually unanimous in reporting that their democratic structure is good for business and for themselves. While it would be naive to argue that if people just understood the idea better they would embrace it eagerly, it is also true that understanding is a necessary first step. Beyond this, a great deal of inertial commitment to old ways would have to be overcome.

The role of government becomes more clear in this context, for both at the federal and state levels, there is much government can do to encourage people to consider ownership and participation.

IV. Policy Options for the Federal Government

People who find the arguments just presented persuasive often wonder how the federal government can take effective action to create a more participatory economy. There is now an almost automatic assumption that major social changes, such as broad employee ownership and participation, require equally major federal initiatives. In this case however, the federal government is probably not the crucial lynchpin of the kind of economic revolution we hope to see. The fate of employee ownership and participation is probably more in the hands of business and union leaders, entrepreneurs, and employees themselves. If these people become persuaded that employee ownership and participation are in their own economic and social self-interest, then these ideas will spread quickly. If they do not, there is probably little the government can do to convince them otherwise.

There is, however, a gap between the practical reality that employee ownership and participation may be in the self-interest of many diverse people and the actual perception of these benefits by the crucial private interests in society. The federal government's role should be to help bridge this gap by making people more aware of what their options are, by encouraging people to overcome their inertia and experiment with these concepts, by sponsoring research to learn how these ideas can work best, and by providing limited financial assistance in those situations where the market is not yet ready to supply all the capital needed. The government can also be effective by creating structures that will enable people who are not regularly employed with opportunities to participate in economic growth. A mechanism for doing that is laid out at the end of this section. While the policies described here are modest compared to many other government efforts, we should not assume that their results will be similarly modest. As in many other areas, seemingly small government initiatives can have major impacts on the processes of social change. Doubters, for instance, need look no further than the "maximum feasible participation" clause of the original anti-poverty laws or the environmental impact statement requirement of the National Environmental Policy Act.

A. Declaring a National Policy in Support of Employee Ownership and Participation

One of the first steps that could be taken is simply to declare a national policy of supporting employee ownership and participation, perhaps as an amendment to the Full Employment Act. Such a policy would direct each agency of the federal government to report annually on what it had done to carry out this policy. Agencies that support research on work and the economy, for instance, might fund research on these issues; agencies that regulate stock ownership might review their regulations to make sure they do not unintentionally raise barriers; agencies that hold conferences and workshops for business and labor groups could include these subjects in their agendas; agencies that make loans and loan guarantees could make them available for employee ownership. Clearly, the list can extend to a very wide variety of activities. Equally clearly, the effectiveness of the law would primarily depend on the interest of its congressional supporters in overseeing its implementation. Vague policy statements such as these are, in fact, notorious for accomplishing very little.

In this case however, there is reason to believe that even a very general policy such as this could have significant impact. First, the very act of passing it would provide legitimacy and publicity to the concepts, and both are needed. Second, there are inevitably activists in government who would like their agencies to do one thing or another, and who can use policy statements such as this to justify their efforts. Third, there is at least the possibility that some agencies would take the policy statement seriously and actually do something. Finally, there are a number of specific cases where a law such as this would make a difference. Employees of Conrail, for instance, want to buy it from the government (see NCEO 1982). While there is much to recommend this plan, current DOT officials are, reportedly, skeptical about the very notion of employee ownership. A national policy could be just the remedy to this situation. Federal employees have not had much in the way of "quality of worklife" or "participation in management" programs. While a few agencies have experimented with these concepts very successfully, most would rather stick with the old hierarchies. Employee groups interested in changing this pattern might find a national policy very helpful.

B. Creating a Technical Assistance and Promotion Capacity within the Federal Government

The next step might be to authorize a specific federal agency to provide technical assistance and promotional services for participation and ownership efforts. One program, the Labor-Management Cooperation Act, already authorizes the Federal Mediation and Conciliation Service (FMCS) to provide grants to area labor-management committees and joint union-management cooperation programs in individual companies (see NCEO 1982 for this and all other state and federal laws referred to). Although the program is very underfunded ($500,000 in fiscal 1982), it has been able to fund a number of innovative efforts that might not otherwise have been started.

Since this act has already been passed, the most logical approach to creating a broader technical assistance and promotion program would be to expand it. There are several ways in which this could be done. First, the program should have a larger (but still modest) amount of funds, perhaps $5,000,000 to fund research, innovative labor-management cooperation efforts, and outreach programs. The reasons these funds are needed are twofold. First, a number of labor-management efforts, especially labor-management committees and academic research, are intended to benefit a broad constituency. Many of the members of this constituency will benefit from these efforts, even if they do not directly participate in or pay for them (e.g., other firms in a community who benefit from better labor-management relations). As a result, it is difficult to fund such programs privately. Second, and more significant, the most innovative efforts are, by definition, experimental and uncertain. Businesses and unions are generally very reluctant to pay for such high-risk endeavors. By providing small amounts of funding for the costs of these programs, the government can help determine what approaches are most successful, and then publicize these to others. Federal funds, in other words, would be providing the basis for experimentation.

In addition to providing grants for cooperative efforts aimed at increasing worker participation and ownership, the FMCS could, itself, develop outreach and technical assistance expertise. The development of publications, the convening of regional conferences, and the ability of a resource center could all significantly help facilitate the process of creating a more participatory economy. One of the major impediments to change, after all, is uncertainty. By providing a central source of objective information and experimentation, this uncertainty could be lessened.

C. Providing Tax Incentives for Employee Ownership and Participation

As previously noted, under the leadership of Russell Long Congress has already provided employee stock ownership plans with significant tax incentives. These tax incentives are designed to get people interested in employee ownership, in the hopes that once they try the idea, they will become committed to it. Apparently, this approach has had at least some success, since, by a large margin, ESOP company executives report that "creating an employee benefit plan" and "increasing employee motivation" were much more significant reasons for setting up their ESOPs than getting tax benefits (see NCEO 1982). The potential to make employees owners and get these motivational benefits, however, has always existed. The creation of the special incentives for ESOPs, it would appear, was the necessary "sweetener" that moved people to act. Research and experience shows, however, that for most companies the tax benefits are only that—a "sweetener."

Effective as these benefits have been, two other incentives for employee ownership plans could be very useful. The first would be to allow owners of small businesses who sell their stock to employees to defer taxes on their gains if they reinvest the stock in another small business. Currently, if a small business owner sells his or her company to a larger company, and receives stock in that company in exchange, the owner does not have to pay capital gains tax on the sale until the stock is sold. This means that there is an incentive for small business owners to sell to large firms, rather than keeping their company independent. By enacting the deferral provision suggested here (technically called a "rollover"), this perverse incentive for conglomeration could be partially offset, while at the same time encouraging employee ownership. A 1980 Treasury revenue estimate for the cost of this provision was less than $25 million a year (see NCEO 1982).

A second minor change would be to allow companies to deduct any dividends they pay to employee-owners. Passing through dividends is an effective way to make ownership more real to employees, but since under current law both the company and the employee must pay taxes on these dividends, there is a disincentive to do it. Again, the cost of such a provision would be small.

It is more difficult to stimulate participation programs through tax incentives. Congress might provide tax credits for the cost of installing participation plans, but it does not seem likely that this would be a major incentive. The cost of setting up a plan has not been identified as a major barrier in the literature on participation (see NCEO 1982). Government support for participation plans should focus on other areas.

D. Employee Ownership as a Takeover Defense

One of the most controversial issues of an employee ownership plan is as a defense against hostile takeovers. For instance, as cited earlier, employees at Continental Airlines proposed to buy 51 percent of the company to thwart a takeover bid. Continental's management agreed with the idea, but the New York Stock Exchange and the California Comptroller insisted that it be put to a vote of the shareholders. Convinced that Continental's shareholders would oppose the dilution in equity the plan would require, Continental did not put the ESOP to a vote and was bought by Texas International.

Given the persistent quality of hostile takeovers, and the lack of defenses faced by most publicly traded companies faced with a well-financed aggressor, it would seem that any device that could effectively be used to prevent takeovers would gain wide popularity. If that device were an ESOP, then in short order a substantial number of major companies might become employee owned.

ESOPs have not been used for this purpose very often. The major reason is that an ESOP is supposed to operate for the exclusive benefit of the participants. The Internal Revenue Service and the Securities and Exchange Commission would generally define that interest in terms of the value of the stock. An ESOP trustee who voted the ESOP shares in opposition to a takeover, even when offered a higher than market price for them, would be violating his or her fiduciary responsibilities.

There is some merit in this approach, although there is the potential that the management of a company may set up and fund an ESOP solely to fend off a takeover, even though the employees might be better off if the company were bought out. Moreover, management might set up the ESOP in a way that they exercised effective control over it, making the employees little more than pawns in someone else's chess game.

On the other hand, in many cases, such as Continental's, employees may be very strongly opposed to a takeover, or at least might be very happy to use a takeover threat as an opportunity to gain substantial or majority ownership in their company. If the company already has an ESOP and wants to use it to oppose a takeover, employees might well prefer to keep the company independent and lose the increase in their stock value, rather than gain a windfall from the sale of their stock but become a part of some conglomerate.

It would seem that a very sensible approach to this situation would be to declare that if employees, by secret ballot supervised by the National Labor Relations Board, were to vote with management in setting up an ESOP or using an existing ESOP to block a takeover, then the ESOP trustees' actions in not tendering the ESOP's shares to the aggressor would, per se, not be a violation of fiduciary responsibility. To further protect employees, Congress could require that any ESOP used in a takeover defense must, if it does not already do so, pass through voting rights on all shares held in the trust to the employees.

Such a law would both encourage employee ownership and discourage conglomeration. By making a relatively small change in our anti-trust laws, we could, in a few years, create a significant employee ownership sector in the economy.

E. Supporting Employee Buyouts

As we have noted, employee buyouts of companies that might otherwise close are a relatively minor part of the employee ownership movement. Nonetheless, they do involve a large number of employees (over 50,000 so far), and they often, out of necessity, are laboratories for some of the most dramatic and innovative restructurings of the workplace. Most of these buyouts have been privately financed, but a number of them have required some government assistance (see NCEO 1982). All the government supported projects (thirteen so far) have succeeded. By making loans or loan guarantees in these cases (or occasionally grants to communities which then lend the money to the employee group), the government has avoided the enormous costs that would otherwise result from a plant shutdown.

Assuming the kind of cautious evaluation of buyout applications that has marked past practice, it would seem only prudent for the government to continue to support employee buyouts. Such a policy not only promotes employee ownership, but saves the government money. Instead of having hundreds or thousands of unemployed workers, there is a tax-paying corporation, and tax-paying workers. The major federal agency that has supported these buyouts is the Economic Development Administration. Unfortunately, the EDA has been targeted for abolition by the Reagan administration. Congress has only barely kept the agency alive.

H.R. 10, the National Development Investment Act, would reauthorize the EDA and provide, for the first time, specific statutory authority for it to support employee ownership. Some of the language doing that draws on an earlier bill, the Voluntary Jobs Preservation and Community Stabilization Act (introduced by Congressmen Lundine, Kostmayer, and McHugh in 1979). At the very least, Congress should pass H.R. 10, if not the original Lundine bill. Congress should also exercise oversight on the Small Business Employee Ownership Act (PL 96-302), which gives the Small Business Administration the authority to make loan guarantees of up to $500,000 to support employee ownership. Existing business development programs at the Department of Housing and Urban Development (the Urban Development Action Grant Program) and Farmers' Home Administration (the Business and Industrial Loan Program) should, as they have in the past, continue to consider employee buyouts an eligible activity.

F. Supporting Research on Employee Ownership and Participation

Employee ownership and participation are significant social inventions. For them to work efficiently, it is vital that practitioners know how successful other efforts in these areas have been.

In the early stages of the development of these concepts, the federal government did fund considerable research along these lines. Under the current administration, however, "social research" has been virtually eliminated. This is a shortsighted policy. We are no more likely to make effective use of human resources without good research than we are likely to make effective use of physical capital or technology without good research. Social research can have substantial payoffs in terms of productivity, societal well-being, and overall economic performance. Funding research on employee ownership and participation is as essential to its success as any other element of government policy.

G. Industrial Policy and Employee Ownership and Participation

The need to create a specific industrial policy is the subject of considerable debate. It is not our purpose here to address whether we should have one or not, but we do believe it imperative that any industrial policy be rooted in broadened ownership and participation.

If, for instance, the government creates some sort of new Reconstruction Finance Corporation (RFC), and the RFC bails out a troubled firm, it is likely that employees, management, the government, the banks, and several other parties – save one – will be called on to make sacrifices. That one group, of course, is the shareholders. For them, the bailout is an unmitigated and unearned blessing. Chrysler's shareholders held stock worth $6 per share at the time of their company's bailout. Now it is worth five times that. A very good way for the shareholders to share in the sacrifice would be to dilute their equity to share ownership with employees. This would, we believe, give the company an added edge on its competitors, while at the same time using the bailout as an opportunity to create a more equitable economy. It would also make sense for the RFC to require that the company and the employees get together to set up a meaningful and far-reaching participation program. Given all the evidence that participation has a beneficial impact on productivity, and given the relatively low cost of setting up a participation program, any other course would be a negligent violation of the RFC's fiduciary responsibility to the taxpayers.

Industrial policy might take another turn, however, by seeking to promote certain kinds of businesses or business activities, rather than saving failing firms. Here too, ownership and participation are essential. The idea of such an industrial policy would be to provide special incentives or favorable environments for certain kinds of firms. These carrots should only be available to those firms who are willing to make their employees substantial partners. Again, it just makes sense to do so, for companies following this approach are more likely to be more productive. And greater productivity, after all, is what industrial policy is all about. Since we know these approaches work, why not use them?

More basically, however, industrial policy, of whatever stripe, threatens to be profoundly anti-democratic. At best, it places control over basic economic decisions in the hands of a small group of people. Most advocates of industrial policy would not hold these people directly accountable to elected officials (they fear that these officials would simply make sure policy follows its present course), but even those who do must admit that anything like real popular control is not very likely. By insisting that any industrial policy promote broadened employee ownership and participation, we would be assuring that a considerable measure of democracy would be introduced to our currently least-democratic sector—the economy.

H. Broadened Ownership for Low-Income People

So far, our suggestions have all focused on people who are employed, and even then primarily among those employed in relatively stable and often well-paying jobs. There is a large sector of the population, however, that has not been able to participate in the economy this successfully. For the millions of low-income Americans, many of whom are not or cannot be employed in a company likely to be engaged in ownership and participation programs, other means need to be devised to enable them to participate more fully in the economy.

Traditionally, policymakers have pursued three paths to encourage development in low-income areas. The first provides a variety of direct income or services subsidies—food stamps, housing, AFDC, etc. As important as these programs are, they have done little to provide people with more than the barest essentials. Moreover, they have not been able to address the basic causes of poverty. In response to this, conservatives, and some liberals, have promoted economic development schemes, such as enterprise zones or model cities, which seek to lure businesses to low-income areas. Unfortunately, even when these programs "succeed," they often do little more than provide dead-end, low-income jobs only marginally better than welfare. Local residents, moreover, have little control over how their area is developed.

A third alternative, community-based economic development, has received some support, particularly in the 1960s, as an alternative to these two paths. In this approach, local community organizations, often community development corporations, are provided with private or government support to improve housing, develop businesses, and engage in other economic development activities. Although these efforts have often been successful, they have been very limited in scale and, by design, have not provided ownership benefits to neighborhood people. Community development groups, in fact, focus much of their efforts on attracting outside entrepreneurs. While the community-based development approach has the benefit of community control and local involvement, it does not, as currently practiced, have the ability to involve more than a relatively small number of low-income people in development efforts.

Ideally, an economic development program would combine the three elements these different approaches have incorporated: it would provide people with additional income, it would help stimulate business development, and it would be locally controlled. This may seem to be an impossible agenda, but it is not. In fact, the framework for a successful program along these lines already exists.

In 1978, Congress created the "GSOC" (General Stock Ownership Corporation). GSOCs are corporations established by states and owned equally by all state residents. The corporations issue one share of voting stock to each permanent resident. Ninety percent of the corporation's earnings must be returned to the owners (and the returned portion is non-taxable to the corporation). The corporation can engage in any kind of business development, including real estate. The law envisioned that GSOCs would be run by states with a substantial amount of their own business activity.

GSOCs have never been used, however. Only Alaska, for which they were specifically intended, had enough of its own business activity to make the administrative plans worth the benefits. Alaska debated the idea, but took another approach for dividing its oil revenues.

A much better use of the GSOC concept has been proposed by Senator Gary Hart (D-Co) and Congressman Parren Mitchell (D-Md). They have suggested in a draft enterprise zone bill that low-income areas be authorized to set up their own GSOCs. Each resident would be issued a share of non-transferable stock in the corporation and would vote for its board of directors. In all likelihood, the corporation would be organized by an existing community group. The corporation would engage in a variety of economic development activities, such as real estate development, housing rehabilitation, business investment and development, etc. It would qualify for government community development grants and loans, could receive condemned city property, would be eligible for tax-deductible private contributions, and could, on its own, seek loans and other capital from private sources. It would be required to return 50 percent of its profits to its shareholders. Shareholders could sell their shares back to the GSOC (but not to anyone else) after five years. The issuance of shares could be handled in a variety of ways (census data, for instance, could be made available for this specific purpose, or registration at local banks could be provided).

GSOCs would have a variety of tax advantages, but would be tax-paying corporations. They would be governed by a community-elected board and could command substantial economic resources. As profit-making entities, they would have a clear interest in developing the kind of sustainable business activities that enterprise zones or model cities envisioned, but as locally based organizations, they would have an equally clear interest in assuring that local people, not outside investors and speculators, would benefit from this effort.

Making GSOCs available to all neighborhoods meeting certain economic criteria would require only minor changes in the existing law. No additional government funding would be required, and no new bureaucracy would need to be created. The idea should appeal to conservatives (it is free enterprise) and liberals alike. In fact, enterprise zone advocate Stuart Butler of the Heritage Foundation, as well as several others, has already endorsed the concept. This small change in the law, however, could have a major impact on how economic development occurs—and for whom.

V. Policy Options for States

Over the last ten years, most of the incentives for employee ownership and participation programs have come from the federal government. States, however, have an equally important role to play. Most states have actively provided businesses with a variety of financial, management, and technical resources. Many of these resources could be effectively used to promote employee ownership and participation programs.

The state role, however, should not just be a smaller version of the federal effort. State tax incentives for employee ownership programs, for instance, are not likely to be very effective since, as a number of studies have shown, the state tax burden is too small for most businesses to have a significant impact on behavior. Most states are also not in a position to provide the kind of multi-million dollar financing for employee buyouts that the federal government occasionally has. Few states have bureau-cracies large enough to create separate programs, as the federal Labor Department has, in labor-management cooperation. States do have a num-ber of unique capacities, however. In particular, states can capitalize on the close contact many of their agencies have with individual businesses and labor organizations to provide publicity, information, outreach, and refer-rals on ownership and participation programs. At least some states can also provide financing and/or expertise for technical assistance to area labor-management committees, employee buyout feasibility studies, and ex-perimental participation programs. States can fund private or university projects, or conduct them in-house in their own agencies. State legislation can encourage adequate plant closing pre-notification, while state financing programs can be directed towards employee ownership efforts in ongoing firms, new enterprises, and employee buyouts. On a more ambitious level, states could set up a private organization to help finance, advise, and facili-tate the creation of a network of employee-owned and controlled businesses.

The state interest in pursuing these policies is much the same as the federal government's: increasing productivity, encouraging a broader owner-ship of wealth, improving labor-management relations, and, where appro-priate, preventing plant shutdowns. Perhaps more importantly, however, it seems likely that the federal role in promoting and subsidizing social in-novation generally will continue to decline. As states are given more and more responsibility to "promote the common good," concepts such as employee ownership and participation should become increasingly attractive. They provide a means by which states can simultaneously encourage business development and social equity—not a common combination in most state commercial efforts. Best of all, this can be done at a very modest cost.

A. Declaring a State Employee Ownership and Participation Policy

California, Delaware, and Maryland have already declared it the policy of the state to promote broadened ownership. Other states can follow this lead, or, even better, extend it to add worker participation as well. Creating such a policy makes all the other steps that might follow considerably easier. Since it has no cost, it can be relatively easy to pass, especially given the broad political appeal the concepts have already demonstrated.

In itself, a policy of this nature can be very effective. Delaware and Maryland, for instance, directed each state agency to report annually on what it has done to promote employee ownership. Some agencies can (and have in these states) take steps to provide information resources, as described in the next section. Other agencies can provide preferential financing for employee ownership, while still others can, as California directed its comptroller to do with respect to securities laws, change regulations that (usually inadvertently) discourage broadened ownership. A broad promotional policy may even be possible without specific legislation. Pennsylvania governor Richard Thornburg, for example, made promoting employee ownership part of his "advanced technology" program for the state and directed a quasi-public agency, the Pennsylvania MILRITE Council, to help publicize the idea and provide technical assistance to those interested in pursuing it.

The success of these policies, of course, depends on the interest of the agencies involved and the willingness of state legislators to put pressure on agency officials to enforce them. Given their ambiguity, it is also difficult to have a consistent, effective set of programs that will survive from one set of legislators and administrators to the next. For these reasons, more thoroughly elaborated legislation is also desirable.

B. A State Role in Promotion and Education

One of the questions most commonly asked about employee ownership and participation is "If it is such a good idea, why isn't it used more widely?" After all, proponents of the concept argue that employee ownership already is a tax-favored method of raising capital, providing employee benefits, and facilitating business continuity. Both ownership and participation in management, moreover, appear to have potentially dramatic effects on productivity. As we argue in the federal policy section, a large part of the explanation is a combination of inertia and a lack of awareness. Many union and business leaders have little or no familiarity with these relatively new concepts. Those who do are often reluctant to proceed precisely because the concept is a new one. As with most new ideas, even when people agree with them, it takes a great deal of encouragement and reinforcement to get things started.

The federal education and promotion policy outlined earlier can help to address these problems, but the federal government is not in a good position to work on a regular and ongoing basis with local businesses and unions. States, by contrast, do this all the time, through several outlets. Moreover, the fifty states and their respective business and labor agencies can reach many times more people than can one federal agency.

Most states, for instance, have small business development programs. Many of these are university based and, in some cases, are directly linked to the Small Business Administration's Small Business Development Center Program. Others are run directly out of a state department of commerce or economic development. These programs provide a variety of services: they publish pamphlets, hold workshops, make referrals, give hands-on management advice, suggest sources of financing, etc. A few of these programs have made an effort to learn about employee ownership and participation, but the vast majority have done little in this respect. Clearly, these programs could provide a great deal of information and outreach. Working with the growing number of professional consultants in this field, most of whom, for advertising purposes, would be only too happy to volunteer time to speak at workshops, develop brochures, or provide other information services, these small business programs could leverage a great deal of informational resources. There is no reason, for instance, why one of these offices could not hold a workshop in every major city in a state.

States can also distribute information directly to businesses. Delaware and California, for instance, have printed and widely distributed a brief brochure explaining how ESOPs work. The brochures, in themselves, are not likely to motivate many people, but they provide another reminder that the concept is available. As part of a larger promotional program, they can be a key element in reinforcing the propensity to act.

States also work directly with many larger businesses, often providing job training, financial placement services, site location assistance, etc. This more intensive assistance could also have an employee ownership and participation component. State business advisors could provide information, set up meetings with other executives who have employee ownership plans, or hire an employee ownership specialist to confer with the executives of the corporation.

Finally, states work with communities. Perhaps one of the most effective steps here would be to make communities more aware of their options, such as setting up area labor-management committees, or, in plant closing situations, community response teams. As in all of these outreach efforts, the ideas are often good enough to sell themselves.

C. State Financing Options

An increasing number of states have taken an aggressive role in providing financing for large and small businesses. Many of these programs would be appropriate to facilitate employee ownership and participation.

Virtually every state, for instance, has a large array of bonding programs. The most common, industrial revenue bonds, can provide up to $10 million in financing, generally to buy land or fixed capital for new or expanding firms. An issuing authority sells a bond issue, then uses the proceeds either to lend the money to the business or to develop property and lease it. Since the bonds are exempt from federal and sometimes state taxes, interest rates are significantly lower. (The federal tax exemption for interest on industrial revenue bonds is scheduled to end in 1986.)

Other states make direct or guaranteed loans to businesses, usually small businesses. The loans are generally financed out of general revenues, although sometimes they are based on bond issues. Some loan programs provide for interest subsidies. States often also charter business development corporations (BIDCOs) or local development corporations, both of which are primarily funded by private investors, often banks. The special state chartering allows banks to take equity positions, something they cannot otherwise do, or invest in higher risk enterprises than they normally could.

Finally, several states have created venture capital funds. These funds provide equity financing for new firms, usually relying on a combination of government and private monies. States have been particularly interested in using the funds to encourage high-growth, technology-based firms. Equity financing is particularly advantageous in these situations, since the new firms often require a long start-up period before they generate enough revenue to repay investors. Conventional debt-financing (loans, for instance) requires firms to start repaying too soon, before their new product can be expected to generate sufficient income. From the investor's standpoint, these new firms are high-risk, but provide a chance for extraordinary returns. Investors have a problem, however, in that they can usually only liquidate their investment (get cash for stocks) if the company sells out to another firm, goes public (sells its stock to the public), or buys back the stock out of after-tax earnings. Any of these routes requires an unusual level of profitability or growth. Firms with ESOPs, however, can use their plans to buy out the investor in pre-tax dollars, using techniques described earlier in this paper. At the same time, by offering employees a share of the company's growth, an ESOP can help the firm attract highly qualified employees at all levels, even though the company may not be able to pay high wages. State venture capital concerns, therefore, should encourage clients to consider this option. One, the Alaska Renewable Resources Corporation, actually requires companies to set up an ESOP.

States might also help finance technical assistance projects. Area labor-management committees, such as the one in Jamestown, New York, for instance, have demonstrated an important capacity to bring business, labor, and public officials together to work out innovative voluntary solutions to local economic problems. The federal Labor-Management Cooperation Act, described earlier, already provides some funding for these efforts, but that program, at best, can only assist a small number of projects. Since these projects are providing a service that benefits the entire community (including those not represented on the committee), they are classically the kinds of projects that are difficult to fund on a private basis. Moreover, getting these committees off the ground often requires an outside "push" to make people aware of the concept, to hire trained facilitators, and to get the process started. State business development programs would be ideally situated to help finance and encourage these efforts.

Technical assistance can also be critically important in plant closing situations. States can help evaluate, for instance, whether an employee buyout is practical. It is often the case in these situations that employees, facing imminent unemployment, are reluctant or unable to put up the money to finance a feasibility study. If a feasibility study indicates the company can be saved, however, the chances of obtaining private financing for a buyout are increasingly positive. A minimal state investment, therefore, may be able to avoid a very large drain on state unemployment and welfare services. If a buyout is not feasible, states might help fund community response teams to help locate and create training and employment opportunities and facilitate the difficult adjustment process. Michigan and Illinois have already created a technical assistance capacity for buyouts, and the State Department of Labor in New Jersey recommended that that state do the same. Legislation along these lines appears likely to pass.

Finally, states can provide specific financing for buyouts (in addition to or in place of making other state business financing programs available for employee ownership generally). New York, Illinois, and Michigan, for instance, have provided bonding authority for appropriate state agencies to raise funds to lend for these purposes. The loans would be limited in amount, would require private participation, and would be at least somewhat below market rates. These amounts are not likely, in themselves, to finance a major portion of a buyout, but since the state can take a subordinated position on them, they can make it much easier for employees to locate the additional financing that is required. Most state efforts such as these, then, can have very significant leveraging ability.

D. *Plant Closing Notification Legislation*

People interested in employee ownership and participation at the management level often see plant closings as the major opportunity to reform the workplace. As we have argued, there is actually a much greater opportunity to implement these changes in a new and ongoing business, and that, in fact, is where most of them are occurring. Nonetheless, employee buyouts of companies that might otherwise close are an important area for state legislation. We have already discussed technical assistance and financing options for buyouts, but none of this will have much value if employees do not learn of an impending shutdown until shortly before it occurs. Employee buyouts typically take 6–18 months to complete, so notification must be early. Once a company has closed, customers and markets are very quickly lost to competitors, making a buyout increasingly difficult. Moreover, many employees will find new jobs or leave the area. Early notice, therefore, is virtually a necessity.

Recognizing this, many people have argued that plant closing prenotification requirements should be on the agenda of employee ownership advocates. Two states—Maine and Wisconsin—already have 60-day prenotification laws, although neither law has been forcefully implemented. Efforts for similar legislation in other states have had little success, although a great deal of time and money have gone into them. Companies have effectively argued that pre-notification is impractical in many cases (once notice is given, they contend, customers would stop ordering, employee morale would deteriorate, working capital loans would cease, suppliers would be hesitant to deliver products, etc.) and impossible in others (where efforts to save the company go to the last minute). Moreover, they contend that pre-notification requirements discourage businesses from moving to a state.

Regardless of the merits of these contentions, it does not seem that pre-notification laws represent an effective use of limited advocacy resources. A more promising approach might be to give companies a set of plant closing options. Companies, for instance, might be required to provide a fixed amount of severance pay when they closed. If they provided less than six weeks' notice, they would be responsible for 100 percent of this amount. For every additional week of notice up to one year, the percentage would be reduced, ultimately to zero. Alternatively, all companies over a certain size could be required to set up a plant closing fund into which they would contribute 1 percent of payroll for ten years. The fund would be invested much as a pension fund. If a company did close, the full amount in the fund would be released to the company if one year's notice were provided, with declining percentages as the notification period declined. The unreleased money could be used as equity for employees to help buy the company, as a retraining fund, or as severance pay. If a company did not close at the end of the ten year period, it could start using the accumulated and future interest over and above that needed to keep up with inflation. States would preferably designate amounts put into the fund as deductible from state corporate taxes, or, more generously, as eligible for a tax credit. Either option described here would provide meaningful incentive for pre-notification, without the problems of a simple requirement. As a result, their political prospects would be much improved.

E. Creating a Cooperative Business Center

States seeking a more ambitious alternative might consider setting up a specific organization to promote, finance, and support employee-owned and controlled companies. Modelled after the very successful Mondragon cooperatives in Spain (see Blasi, Mehrline, and Whyte 1982), the organization would have several components:

1. A BIDCO: The state would provide initial capitalization and operating authority for an employee ownership business development corporation. The BIDCO would, as all BIDCOs can, seek additional private funding from banks, companies, and private investors. It could take both debt and equity positions in client companies. The BIDCO would only invest, however, in companies who were (or who had a specific timetable to become) majority employee owned and controlled.

2. A technical assistance capacity: BIDCO clients would be eligible for technical assistance on a fee basis. Services could include loan placement, legal advice, referrals, and management assistance. These services would be coordinated through the BIDCO, which would be provided with a small state grant to cover start-up costs.

3. Shared facilities: Finally, the BIDCO might offer shared facilities — space, computer time, mail and reception services, etc. — for new entrepreneurial firms. Similar entrepreneurial centers have started in many places, but this one would be limited to employee-owned and controlled firms. Again, states might subsidize start-up costs.

For several million dollars, states could then establish the seeds of what could become a self-perpetuating system, similar to Mondragon, of employee-owned and controlled firms.

F. Conclusion

All of the policies suggested here are modest, yet each could have far-reaching benefits. States that vigorously pursue any one of them might well find that they "get the ball rolling" and that the private sector will follow from there. Given the low cost, low risk, high potential benefit of these policies, it seems that the opportunity for state (as well as federal) action is significant.

Notes

1. The authors wish to thank and acknowledge the "Democracy Project" under whose auspices this article was written.
2. There is also a special kind of ESOP called a "PAYSOP" which provides a tax credit to small companies, but the amount of ownership transferred from these plans is too small really to be considered "employee ownership." For more information on ESOPs and other plans, see *Employee Ownership: A Handbook* (NCEO 1982).

References

Blasi, Joseph, Perry Mehrline, and William F. Whyte. "Environmental Influences on the Growth of Worker Ownership." Unpublished mimeograph, 1982.

Conte, Michael, and Arnold Tannenbaum. "Employee Ownership." Survey Research Center, University of Michigan, 1980.

"Continental Workers Fly as They Buy." *Los Angeles Times*, June 24, 1981.

Long, Russell. "Employee Ownership: A Political History." Paper presented at the Conference on Employee Participation, Ownership and Management, April 17, 1982. Available from Senator Long's office, or the Project for Kibbutz Studies, Harvard University.

Marsh, Thomas, and Dale McAllister. "ESOP Tables." *Journal of Corporation Law* (Spring 1981).

Mason, Ron. *Participatory and Workplace Democracy*. Carbondale: Southern Illinois University Press, 1982.

Mill, John Stuart. *Principles of Political Economy*. Downsview, Toronto: University of Toronto Press, 1965.

National Center for Employee Ownership (NCEO). *Employee Ownership: A Handbook*. Arlington, VA, 1982.

_____."Characteristics of Majority Employee Owned Firms." *Employee Ownership* (NCEO's Newsletter). March 1983.

_____.*Employee Ownership*. June 1983.

New York Stock Exchange. "People and Productivity." Office of Economic Research, 1982.

Philadelphia Association for Cooperative Enterprise. *PACE News* (Newsletter of the Association). Summer 1982.

Rosen, Corey. "Making Employee Ownership Work." *National Productivity Review* (Winter 1982–83): 13–21.

Simmons, John, and Bill Mares. *Working Together*. New York: Alfred Knopf, 1983.

Sokoloff, Gail. "The Creation of an Employee Owned Firm: A Case Study of Hyatt-Clark Industries." In *Case Studies of Worker Ownership in the U.S.* Norwood, PA: Norwood Editions, forthcoming, 1984. (Currently available at Harvard University's Project for Kibbutz Studies).

U.S. Congress. House Small Business Committee. Hearings on Conglomerate Mergers: Testimony of Raymond St. Pierre, 1979.

_____.Joint Economic Committee. *Broadening the Ownership of New Capital: ESOPs of Other Alternatives*. Washington: U.S. Government Printing Office, June 17, 1976.

Whyte, William F., et al. *Worker Participation and Ownership*. Ithaca, NY: New York State School of Industrial and Labor Relations Press, 1983.

10

Towards a Democratic Alternative: Neo-Liberals vs. Economic Democrats

MARTIN CARNOY and
DEREK SHEARER[1]

Reaganomics as an alternative to exhausted New Deal liberalism has public appeal because it promises simple solutions: The more we can get government—especially taxes—out of the economy, the better things will be. Reaganomics is also backed by American business, which has not enjoyed such a profit-oriented administration since the 1920s. But the blatantly pro-business, pro-high-income policies of supply-side economics have an important drawback: by taking away hard-won entitlements and shifting national production to profits and the rich, the policies create serious resistance among the vast majority of voters.

Apparently set adrift by the disintegration of New Deal accords, Democrats have been slow to develop or embrace sensible alternatives for actual and potential victims of supply-side policies. One widely discussed solution to the present crisis comes from neo-liberal economist Lester Thurow and financier Felix Rohatyn. That solution calls for the creation of a Reconstruction Finance Corporation that would use tax monies to fund America's reindustrialization. In other words, the RFC would be a kind of national bank in the business of promoting capital investment in U.S. industry.

There is not total agreement among neo-liberals about what kind of industry would be supported by the RFC. Thurow thinks that unprofitable, "sunset" industries should be allowed to die and "sunrise" industries like high-tech computer firms should be promoted. Rohatyn feels that RFC should save America's sunset heavy industry base by renovating its machinery and equipment (robotizing the automobile industry, for example), even

167

though such industries may have difficulty competing in international markets. Nevertheless, a national public financial institution investing directly in American business—like the Japanese government invests in Japanese business—is central to the neo-liberal approach. Who will run the RFC is less clear, but it seems likely that financiers and corporate managers are the kind of people Thurow and Rohatyn have in mind, perhaps with a few labor leaders included for show.[2]

Thurow's brand of neo-liberal economics includes many of our views: He believes that full employment is the only real answer to poverty and the welfare spending problem. He argues for a more equal income distribution for Americans, more like that of the white and male 40 percent of the labor force. He wants fairer taxation rather than higher tax rates. He agrees that government is not only here to stay, but that it can play an active and creative role in making America a better place for everyone to work and live. He believes that Americans' innovativeness is a source for continued economic renewal and that high technology and increased education and research can provide solutions to productivity and production.

However, with all this agreement there is also profound disagreement. We are firmly convinced that Thurow and other neo-liberals make crucial errors at several levels.

They place all their confidence in the very same big business community that contributed and is continuing to contribute so actively to the present crisis. Indeed, they share with Reaganomics the erroneous assumptions of private business' social conscience and managerial efficiency. They focus so heavily on the emergence of high-tech industry that they ignore the tremendous concentration of profits in oil/gas companies and the financial sector. The structure of the economy has changed drastically and with it control of investments. How will neo-liberals deal with these new concentrations of private capital, if at all?

The neo-liberals' fondness for a high-tech future ignores a number of less than pleasant realities about the electronics industry. The employment structure of microchip production is highly segmented between high-paying good jobs for engineers or trained specialists and jobs for the chip producers and circuit assemblers. Production and assembly work in what has been dubbed "Silicon Valley"—the home of hundreds of computer firms in California's Santa Clara Valley—is carried out almost entirely by women and minorities, increasingly by women immigrants from Korea, Thailand, the Philippines, and Vietnam. The work is low-paying, non-union labor, frequently being done under arduous and hazardous conditions—for example, the acids and solvents used in the production of microchips pose a number of health hazards (See Howard 1981).

Economists Barry Bluestone and Ben Harrison, in their study of unemployed manufacturing workers in the Northeast, *The Deindustrialization of*

America (1982), found that a middle-aged machinist who loses his job in basic industry almost never finds a job with high tech firms. In Oregon, high-tech industries coming into the Willamette Valley hired newly arrived workers from out-of-state and local women but did not pick up the unemployed from the wood and timber industry. The growth of high tech computer industry will not provide jobs for the unionized blue-collar workers who lose jobs as plants in heavy industry continue to shut down. Where will the jobs for these skilled workers come from?

Another social effect of making computer high tech into *the* growth industry of the future is that the increased use of computers and robotics will, in many other sectors of the economy, actually cause greater unemployment. It might make sense to introduce robots into a new auto plant or to computerize office services to increase productivity, but both will certainly put workers out on the street. Little thought is given by the neo-liberals to the management of this transition.

There is also the sticky problem of *already* world-wide overcapacity in the microchip industry. Every country cannot be a winner in the world high-tech sweepstakes. To rely mainly on computers to win back international economic strength is to gamble the nation's future on a single horse.

Neo-liberals view high tech as a breeding ground for entrepreneurs—a hotbed of opportunities for small businesses to appear, grow, create jobs, and prosper. While it is true that many successful computer fims have been started in garages or spare rooms by a few engineers or software geniuses, the staying power of these new firms is often weak. For example, take Bowmar Instrument Corporation—the firm that produced one of the first hand-held calculators, the Bowmar Brain, in the early 1970s. Large corporations soon produced cheaper copies, undersold Bowmar, and it went out of business. As the technology matures, large corporations with tremendous capital resources and marketing/advertising capabilities come to dominate industries.

Finally, much of the other high-tech production being touted as the growth engine of the future—particularly bio-engineering and robotics—is heavily capital intensive and will generate relatively few jobs. Bio-engineering plants, for example, are similar to breweries in that the processing of the organic product is highly mechanized and computer-controlled.[3]

The neo-liberal solution also counts heavily on wage accords that make and supposedly keep American industry competitive in world markets. Yet, these wage accords seem primarily to promote higher profits. What does labor get in return? A full-employment policy? Legislation to promote union organizing? More control over the work process? Equal representation on boards of directors? Open books? Participation in investment decisions? Neo-liberals do not discuss these crucial matters.

Neo-liberals stress the need to compete in world markets. They support "free trade" and deplore union attempts to save jobs through protective legislation. The problem with simply being pro-world trade without considering the power of multinational corporations is that such a narrow perspective takes the increasing world-wide division of labor as given. The working conditions of "cheap labor" in many Third World countries raise questions about how human beings should be treated. Some neo-liberals argue that the shift of low-wage manufacturing to these countries will help them develop economically, but all too frequently economic growth occurs with little sustained economic development for the mass of the population. Puerto Rico is just one case in point. In the 1950s and 1960s, many American firms located manufacturing plants on the island, attracted by low wages and special tax breaks. In the 1970s, however, industry left the island for areas of even cheaper labor. Unemployment in Puerto Rico soared. Seventy percent of the population remains below the poverty line; 60 percent are on food stamps. The firms took their profits and invested elsewhere. For a time there was economic growth, but not balanced, indigenous economic development.

And what about national self-sufficiency in basic industry like steel and automobiles? Should the United States shut down its steel and auto plants and rely on Brazil or Taiwan or Japan for these products? What is the optimal way of producing steel if we think it should continue to be produced? How much are we willing to pay to have a national auto industry? What has to happen to wages in these industries if they are to keep producing without large deficits? Who should manage them? These are matters for national debate, but neo-liberals tend to downplay such questions by focussing so heavily on high tech and free trade.

Finally, the neo-liberals are fundamentally elitist. They believe that in this technology-oriented world, "experts" should make decisions for the mass of non-experts. It is no accident that Gary Hart—an admitted product of the JFK era—should embrace the neo-liberal technocracy. The early 1960s were the zenith of belief in technical solutions to social problems, including solving guerrilla wars in Vietnam and poverty in Watts and Detroit. The point is that "experts" like those economists who thought they could fine-tune the American economy and the bankers who now sit on the Federal Reserve Board (and those who would undoubtedly run the neo-liberal RFC) ultimately make *political* decisions that benefit some at the expense of others. For Thurow, this is the very reason to have experts rather than representatives of constituencies like labor or consumers on the RFC board. But experts have a way of making serious errors because of their distance from the political and economic consequences of their acts. Most people support democracy because in a democracy the people who decide are those who must live with the results of their decisions. Rather than moving toward less democratic solutions for the sake of increased capital accumulation, we must find ways to reach full employment, more effective investment policies, higher productivity, a better environment, and income security through *greater* democratic participation, not less.

I. Democracy and Economics: The Crucial Link

What both Reaganomics and the neo-liberals propose has the great appeal of leaving to others the responsibility over our lives. The conservative philosophy—based on Adam Smith's "invisible hand"—tells us straightforwardly and simply that if each of us pursues individual goals and tries to maximize income, the total benefits to the *whole society* are maximized. No one has to be concerned with the collective welfare because it is mysteriously taken care of by all of us doing the best we can individually. In fact, any interference by a collective institution like government can only reduce the chances of achieving that maximum collective welfare. How convenient. The only public function we as individuals have to be concerned about is to elect governments that will consistently insure private enterprise and minimum government interference in our economic and social lives. Other than that, we should concentrate—as individuals—on succeeding economically (or not succeeding, if that's our thing).

Unfortunately, the leap of faith that allowed Adam Smith and later generations of utilitarians and conservatives to invoke "laissez-faire" never had any empirical or even theoretical basis: there is absolutely no evidence that individuals pursuing their own greedy ambitions produce maximum collective good (see Hirschman 1977; Colletti 1972). On the contrary, we have seen under laissez-faire the development of huge fortunes, the concentration of industry, and the influence of giant, unaccountable corporations on allegedly "laissez-faire" government. And what might Adam Smith say about a conservative administration's huge expansion of military expenditures in the name of defense (one of the "legitimate" functions of a laissez-faire government)? And what about the "invisible hand" of nuclear armaments destruction enough to end all economic systems? Must not the public be ever vigilant and participative to ensure that the collective good is maximized?

Neo-liberals reject Adam Smith's philosophy. The collective good can only be assured and improved on through government intervention in what is a corporate system dominated by large, non-competitive institutions. But neo-liberals—like conservatives—also let the public off the hook. Elect us, they say, and we shall turn over the economy and government to experts who know the ropes. Experts will solve our economic and social problems, problems too complex to be left either to the marketplace or public participation. Again, the proposal is appealing politically. The public often wants to avoid getting involved—wants to avoid the anxiety and tediousness of political participation. Reflected in an apparently deeply ingrained American political cynicism (54 percent voter turnouts in national elections), "leave it to us" has a continuing appeal for a public steeped in individualism.

Economic democracy's emphasis on greater and wider participation, therefore, goes against the grain of recent American political history. For us, neither the Big Daddy of the "invisible hand" nor of government "expertise" will work in the public interest. Democracy means *increasing* responsibility for the collective good by each and every citizen rather than giving that responsibility away. Democracy is participation and struggle, not something that was signed into being at a constitutional convention two hundred years ago and then signed away to others.

The reform policies that we propose here are necessarily short-term, although they indicate a long-term direction for the economy. They speak most immediately to the next five to ten years. They are not revolutionary; they will not lead to a perfect society. But they can bring about a substantially more decent and democratic form of a mixed economy. Whether this is labeled a more humane capitalism or a step toward democratic socialism, we leave to theorists. We are interested in what will work to promote balanced economic growth, greater equity, and, above all, more democracy.

While taking a pragmatic view of the economy, we are not technocrats. We do not believe that simply having better managers at the heads of the major corporations or smarter economists in Washington is the answer to the nation's economic problems. Unlike some neo-liberal politicians, we do not naively endorse reliance on high-tech or export-oriented industries as a magic solution. Science has certainly produced many miracles in the last century, but it has not and cannot solve the world's social problems. The social advances that have been made are the result of greater participation in governing science and the development of its use.

The reform policies that we advocate are *inseparable* from the democratic means of carrying them out. Raising wages and productivity, creating new enterprises, rebuilding inner cities—these and other vital economic tasks can only be carried out with the fullest cooperation and participation of a majority of citizens who are allowed and encouraged to take part—as citizens, workers, and consumers—in economic decision making. This is, in simple form, the idea of economic democracy. If short-run sacrifices such as wage restraint or cuts in social benefits are required of some Americans to revive the economy—and they may well be necessary—then the sacrifices should be shared, and the decisions about the nature of the sacrifices and trade-offs should be made as democratically as possible and include those affected by the results of the decision-making process. Closing a large plant in a community, for example, affects the workers at the plant and the community's small businesses, its schools and other services, and, in some cases, its very existence. The citizens of the community should therefore be represented in a company's decision to shut down or move.

Our analysis leads inescapably to the conclusion that, ineffective as it may be presently, the public sector has fulfilled the democratic mandate much more successfully than the corporations could ever hope or want to. While we believe in democratizing private corporations, it would be naive to count on such a reform as the sole basis of economic democracy. Historically, it has been government that has recognized the demands of working Americans for collective bargaining representation and the demands of minorities and women for upward mobility. It has been government that has protected Americans' health and safety on the job and the right to guaranteed health care off the job. Wherever the issue of economic and social security and equality has arisen, we have turned to the public sector, exercising our democratic prerogatives to attain these goals. Our task, then, is to make our existing public institutions more democratic, to create new, democratic public institutions where necessary, and to use those institutions to make the private sector more responsive to public needs. The private sector can and probably should continue to play an important role in production, but if economic democracy is to be achieved, corporations' autonomy in investment and social decisions must be severely reduced at the same time that efforts are made to democratize them.

Economic democracy can produce steady, equitable growth without inflation and with far less unemployment. While monetarists have associated inflation solely with expansion of the money supply, and thus with government over-intervention, we have argued that much of the seventies' inflation was due to attempts by large corporations to recover so-called normal profits and by labor reaction to falling real wage rates. American business abandoned investment policies that raise worker productivity, opting instead for speculating in real estate and for wage-reducing moves to "better business climates." A program for growth that returns to investing in workers and adds increased participation could raise productivity sharply and increase employment with increased real wages and without inflation. And a more concerted attack on the structural components of inflation through fuel conservation and rationalization of the health care system, food production, and housing, would also help move us toward full employment and equity without rapid price increases.

The winning of these new reform policies will require a mass-based, democratic movement which supports political leaders who believe in economic democracy. The movement and its leaders must be willing to confront the established, corporate-supported, economic reasoning that has led us into our present impasse. They must be willing to move beyond many of the traditional views of the relation between government and economy. We discuss the possibilities for such a movement later, but before doing that, we address the movement's need for a clearly spelled out and relatively simple set of new national economic policies that it can advocate, and outline how to make our present public institutions more democratic.

II. Elements of a National Economic Policy

Greater Public Investment Jobs and Balanced Growth

The road to economic recovery should be led by increased investment in non-military goods and services. The case for cutting back ever higher military spending has been made persuasively by other experts (see particularly Boston Study Group 1979), and we will not repeat it here. What we argue for is a well-planned expansion of the public sector in non-military areas. The goal is not only jobs per se, but the production of socially desirable goods and services to meet unmet needs, and the shift from jobs that are primarily filled by already highly demanded and high-wage, skilled white male workers to more jobs for minorities and women, especially high-unemployed, low-wage minorities and women. These goals point to fuller employment and the economic/social mobility of the least incorporated groups in the labor force, as well as improving the quality of American life.

Government cuts in social public spending in the name of halting inflation are consistent with private sector investment shifts from productivity-increasing to wage-reducing investment (see Carnoy, Shearer, and Rumberger 1983, ch. 4). Rather than investing in higher worker productivity, private firms have concentrated their spending on lowering costs, particularly labor costs, even if this also means lower productivity. Cost-effectiveness and profitability in the short term now dominate corporate thinking. Influenced by·this trend, government, particularly under the Reagan administration, has reduced human services without taking account of the productivity effects of those reductions, especially in the long term. The maintenance and renewal of our urban centers, the expansion of public education and health care, and the maintenance and development of transportation systems, are all crucial to the quality of life, people's well-being, and labor's productivity. Beyond these obvious needs, we should be thinking about ways to improve American life in the coming decades, including new ways of looking at health care, the use of increased leisure time in more active and self-educational ways (rather than simply increasing television viewing), and the relationship between the educational system and the workplace.

The case for decreasing the role of government in the economy is based on the relative inefficiency of public spending. We not only question the validity of that idea, but argue that when "employment efficiency" and "equality efficiency" are included in social performance criteria, government has done much better than private enterprise. Private enterprise is either unwilling or unable to achieve full employment at wages that are socially acceptable to the American people. Government has provided jobs and social mobility to minorities, women, and the growing percentage of college graduates in the labor force. It is inconceivable that America can significantly reduce unemployment and equalize opportunity for minorities and women (thus reducing poverty) without increased public investment and public intervention. In addition, production of goods and services for improving the quality of American life rather than jeopardizing it through an arms race requires a shift in federal spending from military to non-military purposes.

The process of identifying the kinds of non-military spending most needed can be democratized by asking city councils and local planning commissions to draw up an inventory of unmet public infrastructure needs. The Congress, each year, would establish a National Capital Budget to identify public infrastructure investments and to allocate public funds to decentralized grants programs in cities and states. A new vehicle might be created—a National Development Bank—to provide federal front-end financing for major regional and local economic development projects. (There are a number of legislative proposals for such a bank now in Congress.)

Democratization of Investment

The economy needs more than just greater public investment and greater accountability for that investment to workers and consumers. The private investment process itself must be democratized. Investment decisions by large banks and insurance companies and by the managers of large pension funds have played a significant role in creating the current economic crisis. The large banks have rushed to finance mergers and real estate speculations and to lend billions overseas. The largest insurance companies have financed suburban malls and high-rise office buildings and helped to dehumanize America's urban landscape, force reliance on the private automobile, and isolate minorities in the inner city. Manufacturers have moved operations away from the Northeast and Midwest to the union-free South and Southwest, destroying communities and forcing labor to follow capital to areas of "better business climate." Large-scale investment decisions need to include the perspective of a longer-run Public Balance Sheet. It is not simply a question of an investment's profitability, but also of the social costs of different investments—costs that are usually borne by the taxpayer. A decision not to modernize a plant and instead to invest abroad or to purchase a company in another industry or to move to a low-wage, non-unionized area in the United States has effects on workers and communities that private investment bodies ignore.

In many European countries, the largest banks and insurance companies are publicly owned. We believe that the federal government must take stock ownership in and give direct investment guidance to some major banks and insurance companies. During the Franklin National Bank crisis in the late 1970s, Congressman Henry Reuss proposed that instead of bailing out the troubled bank, the government should purchase it and run it as a model of how a bank ought to operate. Working through an investment holding company similar to Canada's Canadian Development Corporation, the federal government should purchase a controlling interest in at least three major banks and three major insurance companies, and place representatives of the government, labor, and small business on the boards of these financial institutions.

The operation of these institutions would obviously not change overnight, and they would not be required to invest in unprofitable schemes requiring subsidies; that would be the responsibility of other programs. They would, however, be required to take account of the nation's need for a balanced economic growth that creates jobs at home and does not destroy either the environment or the nation's cities. Such banks and insurance companies would invest in public-private partnerships that assume a longer time horizon and are willing to broaden their concept of profitability to include social costs of production. (The National Council for Urban Economic Development, for example, has compiled a number of case studies of successful coordinated public-private economic development projects in American cities.)

Pension funds are another major source of investment. Pension funds collectively own over 25 percent of the stock on the New York and American stock exchanges. During the 1970s, pension funds accounted for half of all new common stock purchases. Efforts are now underway in the labor movement to exercise greater employee control over pension fund investments. The AFL-CIO recently commissioned two studies on pension fund operations, and in 1980, the Executive Board of the AFL-CIO called for pension fund investments to increase employment through reindustrialization, to advance socially desirable spending, such as on housing, and to increase the ability of workers to exercise stockholder rights. Unions are now working for at least joint administration of their pension funds—a right that is already exercised by unions in most European countries—and for establishment of a labor data exchange on corporate performance, anti-union activities, and investment in undemocratic countries such as South Africa.

One serious argument against controls on credit and investment is that the largest corporations will ignore or get around such controls by tapping the free-floating and largely unregulated international money market and by exporting even more capital abroad. In recognition of this likelihood, we propose direct government involvement in investment decisions through public ownership of some financial institutions. It is also certain that export controls on capital will be needed. The major European countries and Japan already have such controls, and the United States should also have them, with stiff penalties for major violations.

Credit Allocation

Credit should be expanded, in a targeted fashion, for housing, small business, and urban revitalization projects. In the past, the Federal Reserve, particularly under Chairman Arthur Burns, used the system to bail out such large corporations as W. T. Grants, Pan Am, and Chrysler. The system under current chairman Paul Volcker has made no effort to stem the tide of corporate mergers. Intervention is therefore selective and questionable in its public interest.

The reforms that we propose are hardly unprecedented. Central banks in most industrialized countries designate sectors of the economy that are to receive greater availability of credit, and, in some cases, at below-market rates of interest. In some instances, this is done to aid particular industries and offset the uneven operation of private credit markets. For example, the Riksbank in Sweden targets credit for housing and export-oriented growth industries. Japan's Central Bank (Nihon Ginko) has indirectly financed Japan's economic growth through loans to commercial banks that were reloaned to expanding industries. In France, the central bank carries out credit policies in line with national economic development plans drawn up by a national planning agency. All of these banks engage in direct credit creation using quantity restraints on credit, limitations on borrowing from the central bank, and direct limits on commercial bank credit. They also directly allocate credit at subsidized rates for special purposes targeted by national development plans.

Similar credit allocation plans have been endorsed by Congressman Henry Reuss, an expert in banking and urban development, and by the late Wright Patman. The goal of these reforms is to reduce, de facto, allocation of credit to the largest corporations and richest individuals who least need it, while other sectors are credit starved. Furthermore, credit allocation assures that funds are available for productive economic enterprises and socially needed products and services.

Industrial Policy

Ira Magaziner and Robert Reich amply demonstrate in their study, *Minding America's Business* (1982), that the United States has the worst possible industrial policy. Inefficient, dying industries are protected with a variety of subsidies; large corporations are showered with unneeded tax breaks and subsidies; the consequences of corporate disinvestment in America for workers and communities are left untreated—disinvestment's social costs fall to the public; opportunities for new economic growth, particularly in the export market, are not encouraged; and public spending is not consciously used to stimulate new industries nor to create needed jobs.

A rational, fair, and democratic industrial policy would have the following elements:

1. Plant Closing Legislation and Worker Retraining. As is common practice in Europe, corporations should be required by law to provide advance notice of major plant closings. Advance notice allows communities and workers time to plan for alternative sources of employment. Corporations should also be required to contribute to a government-administered worker retraining fund that would underwrite local efforts to retrain displaced employees for new jobs (see Choate 1982).

2. Worker Ownership and Participation in Management. Worker purchase of branch plants is an alternative to plant shutdowns, but it is an approach that needs to be taken with care. There is danger that workers will be pressured into buying losers—firms that stand no real chance of making it economically—and that departing corporations will be let off the hook under the guise of promoting economic democracy. Each situation must be evaluated on its merits. Where feasible, the government should support efforts at worker ownership. This support should include government funding for market studies and government assistance in management after conversion to worker ownership.

3. Government Purchasing and Production as Stimulant. U.S. government purchase of computers and airplanes in the 1950s provided the market demand that allowed American manufacturers to develop a low-cost, high-quality product. In both cases, American firms—stimulated by government purchases—went on to dominate world markets in these products for decades. The government should also provide R & D grants for new technology through a Department of Technology. These might be in the form of matching funds or joint ventures via a government investment firm. The department should pay particular attention to firms producing products for potential export.

4. Policy Coordination and Economic Data. Nobel Prize economist Wassily Leontief points out that the United States relies too much for its economic policies on abstract theories and wishful thinking (supply-side

economics, for example) and not enough on the actual facts of economic operations. Some data-gathering is necessary to develop a rational industrial policy. One agency of the government—either the Council of Economic Advisors or a section of the Commerce Department—must build up its capability as a national planning agency similar to France's Plan Commission or Japan's Ministry of International Trade and Industry (MITI). This planning body would bring together all of the existing government programs that affect industry, analyze them, and spell out a more rational industrial policy for the administration and for Congress. The agency would also increase data collection on the economy using input-output tables. As Leontief (1982, 33) notes, "Creating and maintaining a comprehensive supply of data would permit a drastic reduction in the amount of guesswork and idle theorizing that goes into our policymaking now."

5. Wage Policy and Collective Bargaining. Will increased participation in corporate policy (including open books), alter the collective bargaining process? For some industries, like autos and steel, where mismanagement and rapid wage increases in the 1960s and early 1970s have put the industry on the brink of extinction at the hands of foreign competitors, wage givebacks and high unemployment are already the order of the day. Wage restraint (although not necessarily givebacks) may and probably should continue even under a more effective management in which workers and consumers participate: it is likely that the steel industry, for example, can only be competitive domestically if wages are restrained and productivity increased, at least in the short run. Steel, auto, and some other groups of workers did much better wage-wise in the 1970s than labor as a whole (*U.S. News and World Report*, March 31, 1981). It is possible that, with a different social contract, such unions would voluntarily allow wages to equalize with those of less well-paid labor by holding down wage demands. Right now these workers and even those who have not done as well are forced into taking wage reductions only through fear of unemployment— with little recourse. The corporations can still close plants if they, not the union, deem them unprofitable. But under an economic democracy model labor will get something in return for wage restraint: a national full-employment policy, participation in deciding investment and management directives for the industry and economy, and legislation that would make it easier for unions to organize in non-unionized regions and industries. And rather than practically unenforceable agreements regarding lower prices if profits rise, as in the UAW-General Motors contract, labor will have access to the books and some direct control over pricing policy. Further, plants will not be able to close by management's directive alone.

Increasing employment with rising real wages and rising labor productivity are still the essential elements of a growth economy. Unless the United States intends to live off the export sector—with all the implications that has for depending on other countries' growth and wage policies—demand for U.S. output will continue to come largely from U.S. workers. The decisions about how rapidly the economy should grow and how that growth should be distributed are also part of a democratic wage policy, but the fundamental facts of demand-pull growth mean that real wages and full employment are unavoidably important components of any industrial rehabilitations.

Environmental and Worker Protection

The arguments against government regulation of unsafe products, protection of the environment, and concern for worker health and safety are largely specious. This short-run, fast-buck mentality ignores the long-run needs of a healthy society. The attack on regulation is often used to blackmail workers or communities into risking their health or physical environment in return for jobs or taxes.

Staff researchers at Environmentals for Full Employment, in their study, "Jobs and Environment," conclude that hundreds of thousands of jobs can be created through environmental protection. A 1981 study done for the President's Council on Environmental Quality predicted a net gain of more than 500,000 jobs by 1987 as a result of pollution controls alone (Kazis and Grossman 1982, 177).

Economic activity is supposed to increase our standard of living. The economy exists for people, rather than vice-versa. Public investment in environmental protection produces jobs and balanced economic growth. Both Japan and West Germany have tough environmental protection laws *and* highly productive economies. A study by Ruth Ruttenberg found that tough consumer and environmental protection laws actually encourage industrial innovations as firms compete to improve products and production processes (Ruttenberg 1981).

Democratic Tax Reform

The current tax code with the supply-side additions virtually eliminates the corporate income tax. While the 1982 tax bill somewhat revised the huge 1981 corporate tax cuts, the trend of declining corporate contributions to the overall tax burden will continue. The 1981 cuts further shifted the federal tax burden to the working and middle class. Since many states and counties collect an important part of their revenues from sales taxes, local taxes tend to be regressive rather than progressive. The tax code contains numerous incentives for unproductive activity, including speculation in real estate and other commodities, and encourages corporate mergers. The tax investment credits do little to stimulate new, productive, job-creating activities. Instead, they are gifts to the largest, most capital-intensive corporations, many of whom have chosen to disinvest in American communities and are being rewarded for the move. The tax system is failing in its original purpose of simultaneously raising revenue and equalizing the economic condition of America's rich and poor.

The latest fad in tax "reforms" is the idea of a flat rate tax (i.e., a tax rate that is a fixed percentage of income) with no deductions. This proposal is premised on the belief that the rich will (always) escape from paying taxes under a progressive system, so why not junk whatever semblance of progressivity (an ability to pay criterion) remaining in the federal tax system? Variants of the flat-tax that keep some progressivity and limited deductions such as those for homeownership have been introduced by moderate Democrats (for example, Senator Bill Bradley, D-New Jersey, and Representative Richard Gephardt, D-Missouri) who propose a flat 14 percent for most taxpayers, with a maximum rate of 28 percent)

Some neo-liberals like Senator Gary Hart and economist Lester Thurow advocate taxing consumption rather than income. This would supposedly provide more savings for productive investment since only consumption, not savings, would be taxed. But because low-income earners consume a greater percentage of income than higher earners, such a tax would have to be much more progressive than an income tax in order to avoid hitting the poor and middle class harder than the rich. Thurow also proposes to eliminate corporate taxes altogether and, apparently, either tax the increased personal consumption spending stock and bond holders would undertake as they became wealthier, or tax the annual increases or decreases in the value of their stocks and bonds as income.

Associates of Ralph Nader have developed a simplified, reformed tax system which has been drafted into the Tax Justice Act (Brandon, Rowe, and Stanton 1976, 193). It embodies a simplified code with lower but still progressive rates. Among the many loopholes the Tax Justice Act would close are: the oil depletion allowance and other tax breaks for industry; accelerated depreciation provisions for business machinery and real estate; foreign investment loopholes; the tax-exempt status of state and municipal bonds; the investment tax credit; tax-loss farming; and inheritance tax avoidance schemes.

The purpose of a tax system in a democratic society is to raise revenues needed for public purposes in as fair a manner as possible with as little socio-economic distortion as possible. Obviously such an ideal is difficult to achieve; however, it should not be abandoned as a goal. Whether taxes are on income or consumption, the progressive nature of taxation is crucial to this goal, and so is the elimination of deductions or subsidies.

Tax preferences cost the Treasury billions of dollars every year, dollars that are made up by higher tax rates for wage earners. The argument of the tax reformers is that loopholes—"tax expenditures," Harvard professor Stanley Surrey has labeled them—should not be used to make economic policy. If the government wants to encourage a particular set of activities (for example, home ownership or new investment), it should allocate grants or subsidies to the private sector as part of a regular budgetary process, not covertly as part of the tax system. Alternatively, the government itself could invest directly in such activities through development banks or by subsidizing community corporations. In both cases, appropriations and programs would be subject to normal congressional scrutiny, and the tax system would levy an equitable burden on all.

The argument for maintaining progressivity while closing loopholes is that it is both fair and just. Those who benefit more from the economic system and who have a greater ability to pay without cutting into their necessities such as food and shelter, should contribute relatively more than those who benefit less. Or, put another way: since the society values the extra food that a working mother can buy for her children more than the executive's extra drink at the country club, that woman's income should be taxed at a lower rate than the much higher income of the executive.

Energy

The next administration should adopt an overall energy policy that gradually moves the economy away from reliance on fossil fuels (coal, oil, and natural gas) and, at the same time, begins to take control of energy policy away from the large, private energy corporations.

At home, conservation in residential and commercial use should have first priority. Other advanced economies do a far better job at energy-efficient production. West German industry, for example, uses 38 percent less energy per unit of output than American industry, and Sweden 40 percent less than the United States for each dollar of GNP. Using existing methods and technology, the United States could save between 20 and 30 percent of energy used in manufacturing. A national residential energy conservation program could provide home energy audits and low-interest energy conservation loans to home and apartment owners (Schneider 1978).

But gasoline consumption also has to be reduced. To its credit, the Carter conservation effort made the United States the first industrial country to reduce its absolute fuel consumption. This helped cut U.S. petroleum imports. During the 1980 presidential campaign, both Edward Kennedy and John Anderson pushed for further reductions either through rationing or placing an additional 50-cent tax on gas at the pump. Such measures would go far in changing fuel consumption habits. Gas prices might initially rise by the full amount of a tax, but reduced consumption would eventually bring down the price. In any case, the effect of reducing consumption would be exactly what it has been until now—significantly reduced imports, downward pressure on the wholesale petroleum price, and decreasing prices for industrial uses of petroleum—hence downward pressure on the prices of industrial and agricultural goods.

New federal agencies are needed to shift control of energy policy into public hands. First the government should create a Federal Oil Purchasing Agency that would control the importation of all foreign oil. The agency would buy oil on a nation-to-nation basis and would wield greater strength in foreign markets than individual companies. Once the agency has purchased oil, it would sell it to various customers in the United States.

More than 50 percent of America's domestic fuel lies on federal land, most of it unexploited. Reagan's Secretary of the Interior, James Watt, attempted to auction off these natural resources at bargain basement prices with little regard for the environment. This public resource should, alternatively, be developed by a public body—a Federal Oil and Gas Corporation—as proposed by Senators Kennedy, Mondale, and others in 1973. The corporation would be mandated to develop oil and gas resources on such federal land. It would be similar to the public energy companies that exist in most European countries. In addition to developing public energy resources in a responsible way, the corporation would give the government direct and dependable data on the drilling, pumping, refining, and marketing of oil and gas.

Social Policy: Welfare and Health

Numerous studies document the relationship between the state of the economy and such social problems as crime, welfare, and health.[4] Again, it is ironic that the Reagan administration can mouth pro-family rhetoric but carry out economic policies that destroy families' health and drive people to criminal acts or onto welfare rolls. The administration's attack on the existing welfare system—food stamps, aid to families with dependent children, general assistance, supplemental security income, and Medicaid—is premised on the Social Darwinist view that welfare traps the poor in a permanent condition of poverty and dependence.

There is little evidence to support this position. In fact, Notre Dame economist Richard D. Coe, who analyzed the experience of 5,000 families receiving welfare between 1969 and 1978, found that although the percentage of welfare recipients was a steady 10 percent of the population, 25 percent of all American households had received some welfare assistance during the decade. Over half were on welfare for no more than one or two years. Coe found that only 7.7 percent of all recipients were dependent on welfare for their basic support in eight or more years of the decade (Coe 1982).

So, the existing welfare system—even with its flaws and limitations (and miniscule percentage of "cheaters")—is a real benefit to the working poor. It is part of the overall social wage that has come under attack by Reagan and his corporate allies. The attack on welfare, as Pivan and Cloward point out in *The New Class War* (1982), is part of the attempt by business to discipline labor and bend it to business's purposes.

The current panoply of welfare programs should be replaced by a decent, guaranteed family income and the opportunity for everyone who can work to get a job. National spending on health could be reduced through a combination of national health insurance delivered through consumer-controlled, employment-oriented health maintenance organizations at the community level, cost-control measures, and greater emphasis on preventive medicine.

America in the World Economy

The United States still has the largest, most productive economy, the strongest military force, and the greatest cultural influence in the world. While we are still number one and will be for many years to come, we are no longer an imperial power that can dominate the world economy and dictate terms to the industrial countries and Third World nations. The Reagan administration's yearning for empire is hopelessly nostalgic and out of touch with reality. Worse, its policies do not deal adequately with the deteriorating competitive position of U.S. industries. Administration militarism and monetarism have alienated our European allies and threatened millions in the developing countries.

Most proposed solutions to the present economic crisis concentrate on making the United States more competitive with Japanese imports. Should the United States pursue a free-trade or a "fair-trade" (quotas and tariffs to match Japanese import restrictions) policy on imported goods? We think that the democratization and public planning of America's business would go far toward increasing its competitiveness in world markets. The United States could achieve fuller employment, less costly transitions to produce those goods in which we are competitive, and a more rational, long-term investment policy in physical and human capital—investment that would keep us at the forefront of developing new products that meet our own and the world population's real needs.

The issue of free versus fair trade in the context of a full-employment, democratization policy cannot be decided just in terms of imports and exports. Many imports do not come from Japan but from U.S.-based transnational firms producing abroad and exporting to the U.S. market. What kind of stance should U.S. policy take toward these "runaway shops"? What goods do we want to produce domestically regardless of our competitiveness in world markets? Should the United States have a domestic steel industry even if it requires protection? Right now, if we wanted to revitalize rail transport by building high-speed intercity train systems, we would have to import passenger railroad cars, since no U.S. producer makes them. Should we produce passenger rail cars ourselves? These are just some of the questions regarding free-trade policies, and the choice of free versus fair trade hinges as much on what kind of economy we would like to have as on what goods we can produce cheaply.

Even as the United States revitalizes domestic production to meet real domestic needs and full employment, our international economic policy has to help stimulate other countries' economic development. Any democratic alternative must simultaneously recognize the dominant U.S. position in the world economy and at the same time promote increased economic participation by lower income countries and presently excluded groups in those countries. Just as democracy should be extended within our own society through greater economic and political participation, so American economic power should be used to promote similar trends in other countries.

Our present foreign policy is precisely the opposite: the Reagan administration supports dictatorships as long as they are favorable to American foreign investment and are staunchly anti-Communist. Often, by supporting such dictatorships and trying to undermine genuinely populist (but leftist) governments in other Third World countries, the United States pushes those governments to much less populist, more dictatorial positions. When, for example, the Nicaraguan or Angolan government has to face economic pressures and U.S.-financed military operations on and within its borders, the government itself becomes more militaristic and less populist.

These policies are based on the myth that all Left-populist governments are Soviet stooges and therefore must be opposed as part of the geopolitical struggle against Soviet hegemony. Nothing could be farther from the truth. In fact, if the United States stood for and supported popular social change, almost all Third World countries would much rather turn to us for technical assistance and trade than to the Soviets. We have the products and technology that—adapted to their conditions by them—are much more relevant and up-to-date than those made in the Eastern bloc.

But this mythology is not just plucked out of thin air. It does serve to support the "business climate" that American corporations prefer to have for their investments, the same business climate that they are looking for within the United States—non-unionized, unpoliticized labor; governments that will do anything necessary to bring investments into their coun-

try or county, low taxes, and no regulation. The largest U.S. corporations—
oil/gas, manufacturing, financial, heavy construction, mineral extraction—
dictate our foreign economic policies in the Third World and even Europe.
And they push for the support of governments and policies in the Third
World that would be totally unacceptable to voters if they existed in the
United States. Imagine the National Guard shooting striking miners in
West Virginia. But that is exactly what some of the Reagan administra-
tion's favorite governments do (South Africa; Chile).

The first axiom of an alternative international economic policy should
therefore be to promote *participative development policies* around the world.
Although such policies may not produce the appearance of luxury goods
in the stores of Third World capitals, they will assure that the fruits of
development will reach the large majority rather than a small minority.
This corresponds precisely to the kinds of changes we are calling for within
the United States. Those countries that do engage in such development
policies should receive our economic and technological support, in accord
with the way they define their needs.

The main way that dollars and technology now get from us to the Third
World is through U.S. transnational corporations. And while these corporations would like to pretend that they are independent of the U.S.
government, they in fact depend in all kinds of ways on U.S. government
bilateral and multilateral pressures (even military intervention) for the
business climate in which they invest. A crucial element in international
economic policy therefore is our government policy toward U.S. transnationals. Since they do many things well, the real issue is the conditions in
which they have to operate and whether they choose to invest under less
favorable conditions. The first issue depends in part on U.S. foreign policy:
if the U.S. government makes clear that it will not intervene to support
U.S. companies' commercial interests in those countries with dictatorial,
repressive governments of both Right and Left (essentially Carter's human
rights policy), transnationals operating there are forewarned that they do
so at their own risk. The second issue can only be influenced if transnationals have public and worker participation in their investment decision
making. If our suggested domestic reforms are implemented, investment
decisions of large corporations will, in fact, be subject to public and worker
influence, and their foreign investments would be part of an overall social
investment strategy. This strategy should include U.S. political-economic
objectives in a world system, not just island America.

Government monetary and fiscal policies should also be changed to promote a different set of worldwide growth strategies. The Reagan administration firmly believes that returning to market capitalism in the United
States, Third World, and Europe will promote more rapid growth na-
tionally and internationally if inflation is first cured through deflationary

monetary policies. This strategy has had an incredible negative impact world-wide. Rather than the present "Beggar-thy-Neighbor" deflationary policies, the next administration should launch a "Better-thy-Neighbor" international development program that concentrates on increased productivity, fuller employment, the production of useful, needed products instead of military hardware, appropriate technology transfers to Third World countries, and the conservation of non-renewable resources.

As part of this strategy, the activities of American-owned transnational banks will have to be more closely regulated. In search of greater profits, these banks have extended billions in loans to some "newly-industrializing" Third World countries, such as Mexico, Brazil, and South Korea, while turning away from other, poorer countries. What is needed is a targeted, global, U.S.-led Marshall Plan that channels development funds through a multinational development authority—in concert with other industrial countries. Economic development in the Third World can provide markets for U.S. and other industrial-country products, but these development projects must be carefully designed, not left to unregulated transnational banks to finance by themselves.[5]

The second part of an international macroeconomic policy would be to cut energy consumption in the United States, putting increased downward pressure on petroleum prices. While this would lower oil company profits and some countries' rates of growth, it would make expansion of most of the world's agricultural and industrial production less expensive, especially in terms of foreign exchange.

Finally, an alternative international economic policy will have to deal with U.S. agricultural exports and the role they play in world food policy. It is likely that in the next ten years there will be massive food shortages in many countries. Since the United States is the world's largest food and fertilizer producer, it is essential that some U.S.-led coordinated efforts be started to develop a food production and distribution policy on a world scale.

The Nixon administration's emphasis on promoting farm product exports has been continued by all administrations that followed. But this orientation is exactly the opposite of what we should do to lower inflation and solve world food problems. Instead we should be looking down the road a few years to the time when we cannot meet world demand for food without huge increases in farm and food prices. We are now very close to the limit of our productive capacity, and if food supplies are not increased in the United States, then the only place they can be increased is in those regions that now underutilize their production potential—mainly in the Third World.

The United States traditionally has not seriously supported agricultural development in the Third World because U.S. farmers do not want competition in world markets. Nevertheless, every dollar invested in developing Third World agriculture has a potential pay-off much greater than the same dollar invested in the United States. Promoting the revitalization of agricultural development in these nations would serve the immediate interests of consumers in the United States whose food costs will otherwise rise. More important, if U.S. policy continues to insist that the United States can feed the world, and if we do not take steps immediately to increase food production where food is being consumed, we will contribute to the impoverishment of Third World countries and to a potentially disastrous Malthusian crisis (see Collins and Lappe 1977).

As in the case of oil, a rational long-term U.S. agricultural policy in a world economy will be opposed by powerful vested domestic interests. Even with conservation and Third World agricultural development, however, U.S. oil producers and farmers will survive and should do well. The upward pressure on oil and grain prices will continue in the long term. The United States will also remain a food exporter. The more relevant issue is whether we in an economically democratic United States can implement reasonable fuel conservation programs that will increase the economic viability of Third World countries. Ultimately, this would both increase the demand for a host of other U.S. goods, increase world trade, and help make the world a better, healthier place to live.

Notes

1. This paper is based on chapter 7 of Carnoy, Shearer, and Rumberger 1983.
2. The original RFC was run by big businessmen and used public funds to subsidize America's largest corporations throughout the 1930s and 1940s. For an excellent discussion of the RFC experience and corporate influence over public agencies, see McQuaid 1982.
3. For the challenge posed by increasing mechanization see the special issue of *Scientific American* (September 1982) on the mechanization of work.
4. See, for example, the comprehensive study by Brenner 1976. Brenner found that a 1.4 percent increase in unemployment costs society nearly $7 billion in lost income due to illness, mortality, and added prison and mental health spending.
5. On the expansion of transnational bank activities in the Third World and its dangers to international economic stability, see Sampson 1981.

References

Bluestone, Barry, and Ben Harrison. *The Deindustrialization of America: Plant Closings, Community Abandonment, and the Dismantling of Basic Industries.* New York: Basic Books, 1982.

Boston Study Group. *The Price of Defense: A New Strategy for Military Spending.* New York: Times Books, 1979.

Brandon, Robert, Jonathan Rowe, and Thomas H. Stanton. *Tax Policies.* New York: Pantheon, 1976.

Brenner, Harvey. "Estimating the Social Costs of National Economic Policy: Implications for Mental and Physical Health, and Criminal Agression." U.S. Congress. Joint Economic Committee. Washington: U.S. Government Printing Office, October 26, 1976.

Carnoy, Martin, Derek Shearer, and Russell Rumberger. *A New Social Contract.* New York: Harper & Row, 1983.

Choate, Pat. *Retooling the American Workforce.* Washington: Northeast-Midwest Institute, July 1982.

Coe, Richard D. "Welfare Dependency: Fact or Myth?" *Challenge* 25 (September/October 1982): 43–49.

Colletti, Luico. *From Rosseau to Lenin: Studies in Ideology and Society.* New York: Monthly Review Press, 1972.

Collins, Joseph, and Frances Moore Lappe. *Food First: Beyond the Myth of Scarcity.* Boston: Houghton-Mifflin, 1977.

Hirschman, Albert O. *The Passions and the Interests: Political Arguments for Capitalism Before its Triumph.* Princeton, N.J.: Princeton University Press, 1977.

Howard, Robert. "Second Class in Silicon Valley." *Working Papers* 8 (September/October 1981): 20-31.

Kazis, Richard, and Richard Grossman. *Fear at Work: Job Blackmail, Labor and Environment.* New York: Pilgrim Press, 1982.

Leontief, Wassily. "What Hope for the Economy." *New York Review of Books* 29 (August 12, 1982): 31-34.

Magaziner, Ira C., and Robert B. Reich. *Minding America's Business: The Decline and Rise of the American Economy.* New York: Harcourt Brace Jovanovich, 1982.

McQuaid, Kim. *Big Business and Presidential Power from FDR to Reagan.* New York: Morrow, 1982.

Piven, Frances Fox, and Richard A. Cloward. *The New Class War: Reagan's Attack on the Welfare State and its Consequences.* New York: Pantheon Books, 1982.

Ruttenberg, Ruth. "Regulation is the Mother of Invention." *Working Papers* 8 (May/June 1981): 42-47.

Sampson, Anthony. *The Money Lenders.* London: Hodder and Stoughton, 1981.

Schneider, Steven A. "Common Sense About Energy." *Working Papers* 6 (January/February 1978): 30–42; (March/April 1978): 49–58.